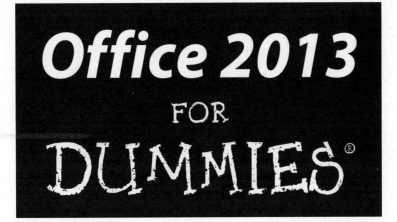

Office 2013

FOR

DUMMIES®

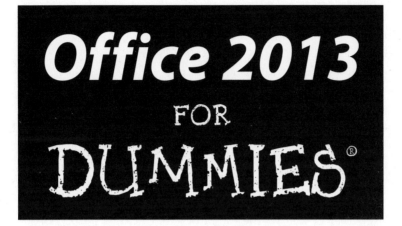

Office 2013 FOR DUMMIES®

by Wallace Wang

WILEY

John Wiley & Sons, Inc.

Office 2013 For Dummies®

Published by
John Wiley & Sons, Inc.
111 River Street
Hoboken, NJ 07030-5774

www.wiley.com

For general information on our other products and services, please contact our Customer Care Department within the U.S. at 877-762-2974, outside the U.S. at 317-572-3993, or fax 317-572-4002.

For technical support, please visit www.wiley.com/techsupport.

Wiley publishes in a variety of print and electronic formats and by print-on-demand. Some material included with standard print versions of this book may not be included in e-books or in print-on-demand. If this book refers to media such as a CD or DVD that is not included in the version you purchased, you may download this material at http://booksupport.wiley.com. For more information about Wiley products, visit www.wiley.com.

Library of Congress Control Number: 2012956422

ISBN 978-1-118-49715-9 (pbk); ISBN 978-1-118-49714-2 (ebk); ISBN 978-1-118-62022-9 (ebk); ISBN 978-1-118-62028-1 (ebk)

Manufactured in the United States of America

10 9 8 7 6 5 4 3 2 1

WILEY

About the Author

The author, **Wallace Wang,** currently exists as a carbon-based life form, consuming precious natural resources for his own survival at the expense of the rest of the planet. Despite his dislike of unnecessary complexity, the author actually enjoys what computers can do, even if they tend to fail spectacularly in everyday use at the worst possible time (details, details . . .). Besides writing computer books, the author also enjoys studying movies and performing stand-up comedy just to do something creative that involves human beings as opposed to machines. In addition, the author also refers to himself in the third person in imitation of professional athletes and other personages who like pretending that they're more important than they really are.

Dedication

This book is dedicated to all those people forced to use Microsoft Office because everyone else uses it so they have to use it too. To all those people searching for mental relief from the collective insanity that results from standards imposed upon the unwilling, this book and its instructions are dedicated to making your life easier and more bearable so you can actually use your computer for a change.

Author's Acknowledgments

I'd like to thank all the friendly people who helped put this book together, especially Pat O'Brien. Additional thanks go to my radio co-hosts (Wes Sample, Dane Henderson, Sherri Diaz, and Joe Shattuck) at My107.9FM in beautifully isolated Alpine, California where we host a weekly radio show called "Notes From the Underground." Thanks also go to Johannes Gutenberg for inventing the printing press, which is currently being defeated by armies of people dismissing the invention of mass printing by refusing to read any books at all.

Publisher's Acknowledgments

We're proud of this book; please send us your comments at http://dummies.custhelp.com. For other comments, please contact our Customer Care Department within the U.S. at 877-762-2974, outside the U.S. at 317-572-3993, or fax 317-572-4002.

Some of the people who helped bring this book to market include the following:

Acquisitions, Editorial, and Vertical Websites

Project Editor: Pat O'Brien

Acquisitions Editor: Bob Woerner

Senior Copy Editor: Barry Childs-Helton

Technical Editor: Vince McCune

Editorial Manager: Kevin Kirschner

Editorial Assistant: Annie Sullivan

Sr. Editorial Assistant: Cherie Case

Cover Photo: © iStockphoto.com / Cary Westfall

Cartoons: Rich Tennant (www.the5thwave.com)

Composition Services

Project Coordinator: Kristie Rees

Layout and Graphics: Carl Byers, Jennifer Creasey

Proofreaders: Lindsay Amones, Toni Settle

Indexer: Sharon Shock

Publishing and Editorial for Technology Dummies

Richard Swadley, Vice President and Executive Group Publisher

Andy Cummings, Vice President and Publisher

Mary Bednarek, Executive Acquisitions Director

Mary C. Corder, Editorial Director

Publishing for Consumer Dummies

Kathleen Nebenhaus, Vice President and Executive Publisher

Composition Services

Debbie Stailey, Director of Composition Services

Contents at a Glance

Table of Contents

Introduction

Welcome to the most popular office productivity software in the world. If you're already familiar with Microsoft Office 2007 or Microsoft Office 2010, you'll find that the new Microsoft Office 2013 is familiar enough to use right away with minimal training, but comes jam-packed with additional features to make Office even more useful than ever before. If you've been using a much older version of Office (such as Office 2003 or earlier), you'll find Office 2013 to be a radical leap forward in both features and its new user interface.

Like most software, the real challenge is figuring out where to find the commands you need to do something useful. While this book won't turn you into a Microsoft Office 2013 expert overnight, it will give you just enough information so you can feel confident using the new Office 2013 and get something done quickly and easily without tearing your hair out and losing your mind in the process.

In this book, you find out how to master the "Ribbon" user interface along with discovering the dozens of new features that Microsoft added to your favorite program in Office 2013. More importantly, you find a host of shortcuts and tips to help you work faster and more efficiently than ever before. Whether you rely on Word, Excel, PowerPoint, Access, or Outlook, you're sure to glean something new from this book to help you master Office 2013 on your own computer.

Who Should Buy This Book

This book is targeted toward three distinct groups. First, there are the people already familiar with Microsoft Office 2007 or Office 2010 who want to catch up with the new features of Office 2013. For these people, this book can serve as a handy reference for finding out how to use the latest features.

Second, there are people upgrading from an older version of Microsoft Office, such as Office 2003 or Office XP. For these people, this book can serve as a gentle guide to help you make a less-painful transition from traditional pull-down menus to the new "Ribbon" user interface.

Finally, there may be people who may have rarely (if ever) used any version of Microsoft Office at all. For those people, this book can serve as a guide through word processing (Microsoft Word), number calculations (Microsoft Excel), presentations (Microsoft PowerPoint), database management (Microsoft Access), and managing your personal resources such as time, appointments, and e-mail (Microsoft Outlook).

No matter how much (or how little) you may know about Microsoft Office, this book can show you how to use the most common and most useful features of Office 2013 so you can start being productive right away.

How This Book Is Organized

To help you find what you need, this book is organized into parts where each part covers a different program in Office 2010.

Part I: Getting Started with Microsoft Office 2013

To use Microsoft Office 2013, you need to know how to find the commands you need. This part of the book focuses on showing you how to use the Ribbon user interface that appears in all Office 2013 programs. By the time you finish this part of the book, you'll feel comfortable using any program in Office 2013.

Part II: Working with Word

Word processing is the most popular use for Office 2013, so this part of the book explains the basics of using Word. Not only will you find out how to create and save different types of documents, but you'll also master different ways to alter text, such as using color, changing fonts, adding headers and footers, checking spelling and grammar, and printing your written masterpiece so it looks perfect.

Part III: Playing the Numbers with Excel

If you need to manipulate numbers, you need Microsoft Excel. This part of the book explains the three basic parts of any spreadsheet, how to format data, how to create formulas, and how to create different types of charts to help you visualize what your spreadsheet numbers really mean. Not only will you discover how to calculate and "crunch" numbers, but you'll also find how to analyze the results and turn them into eye-catching charts to help you understand trends that may be buried within your data. If you want to find out how to use Microsoft Excel to create, format, and display spreadsheets, this is the part of the book for you.

Part IV: Making Presentations with PowerPoint

Throw away your overhead transparencies and clumsy whiteboard and pads of paper. If you need to give a presentation to a large group, you need to know how to create colorful and visually interesting presentations with PowerPoint instead. With PowerPoint, you can organize a presentation into slides that can display text, pictures, animation, and even video. By mastering PowerPoint, you can create presentations that grab an audience's attention and emphasize the points you want to make while holding their interest at the same time.

Part V: Getting Organized with Outlook

Almost nobody feels that they have enough time to stay organized, so this part of the book explains why and how to use Microsoft Outlook. With Outlook, you can read, sort, and write e-mail, keep track of appointments, store names and addresses of your most important contacts, and even organize your daily to-do tasks. By using Outlook to manage your busy schedule, you can turn your computer into a personal assistant to make you more productive than ever before.

Part VI: Storing Stuff in Access

If you need to store large amounts of information, such as tracking inventories, organizing customer orders, or storing names and addresses of prospective customers, you may need to use a database program like Microsoft Access. In this part of the book, you see how to use Access to store, retrieve, sort, and print your data in different ways. With Access able to slice and dice your information, you can better analyze your data to understand how your business really works.

Part VII: The Part of Tens

Almost every program offers multiple ways of accomplishing the same task, and Office 2013 is no exception. After you get familiar with using Office, take a peek in this part of the book to read about different types of shortcuts you can use to work with Office even faster than before. By the time you get to this part of the book, you'll be much more comfortable using Office 2013 so you can feel comfortable exploring and experimenting with different features on your own.

How to Use This Book

Although you can just flip through this book to find the features you need, browse through Part I for a quick refresher (or introduction) to the Office 2013 user interface Ribbon. After you understand the basics of using this new Ribbon user interface, you'll be able to master any Office 2013 program in no time.

Conventions

To get the most from this book, you need to understand the following conventions:

- The *mouse pointer* usually appears as an arrow and serves multiple purposes. First, you use the mouse pointer to select data (text, numbers, e-mail messages, and so on) to change. Second, you use the mouse pointer to tell Office 2013 which commands you want to use to change the data you selected. Finally, the appearance of the mouse pointer can reveal the options available to you at that moment.

- *Clicking* means moving the mouse pointer over something on the screen (such as a menu command or a button), pressing the left mouse button once, and then letting go. Clicking tells the computer, "See what I'm pointing at? That's what I want to choose right now."

- *Double-clicking* means pointing at something with the mouse pointer and clicking the left mouse button twice in rapid succession.

- *Dragging* means holding down the left mouse button while moving the mouse. Dragging typically moves something from one onscreen location to another, such as moving a word from the top of a paragraph to the bottom.

- *Right-clicking* means moving the mouse pointer over something and clicking the right mouse button once. Right-clicking typically displays a shortcut menu of additional options.

In addition to understanding these terms to describe different mouse actions, you also need to understand different keystroke conventions too. When you see an instruction that reads Ctrl+P, that means to hold down the Ctrl key, press the P key, and then let go of both the Ctrl and P key at the same time.

Finally, most computer mice offer a scroll wheel that lets you roll it up or down, or press on it. This scroll wheel works to scroll windows up or down, whether you're using Office 2013 or nearly any other type of program as well. In Office 2013, the scroll wheel doesn't serve any unique purpose, but it can be a handy tool for rapidly scrolling through windows in any Office 2013 program.

Icons Used in This Book

Icons highlight important or useful information.

This icon highlights information that can save you time or make it easier for you to do something.

This icon emphasizes information that can be helpful, although not crucial, when using Office 2013.

Watch out! This icon highlights something that can hurt or wipe out important data. Read this information before making a mistake that you may not be able to recover from again.

This icon highlights interesting technical information that you can safely ignore but may answer some questions about why Office 2013 works a certain way.

Getting Started

The best way to master anything is to jump right in and start fiddling with different commands just to see what they do and how they work. In case you're afraid of breaking your computer or wiping out important data, play around with Office 2013 on a "dummy" document filled with useless information you can afford to lose (like your boss's income tax returns — kidding!).

Here's your first tip. Any time you do something in Office 2013, you can undo or take back your last command by pressing Ctrl+Z. (Just hold down the Ctrl key, press the Z key, and release both keys at the same time.) There, now that you know about the powerful Undo command, you should have a surging sense of invulnerability when using Office 2013, knowing that at any time you make a mistake, you can turn back time by pressing Ctrl+Z to undo your last command.

If you get nothing else from this book, always remember that the Ctrl+Z command can save you from yourself. See? Mastering Office 2013 is going to be easier than you think.

Part I

getting started
with
Office
2013

In this part . . .

- ✔ Starting an Office 2013 program
- ✔ Using the pop-up toolbar
- ✔ Modifying pictures
- ✔ Opening and browsing the Help window
- ✔ Visit `www.dummies.com` for great Dummies content online.

Chapter 1

Introducing Microsoft Office 2013

Microsoft Office 2013 consists of five core programs: Word, Excel, PowerPoint, Access, and Outlook, where each program specializes in manipulating different data. Word manipulates text; Excel manipulates numbers; PowerPoint manipulates text and pictures to create a slide show; Access manipulates organized, repetitive data such as inventories; and Outlook manipulates personal information such as e-mail addresses and phone numbers.

Although each Office 2013 program stores and manipulates different types of data, they all work in similar ways. First, you have to enter data into an Office 2013 program by typing on the keyboard or loading data from an existing file. Second, you have to tell Office 2013 how to manipulate your data, such as underlining, sorting, arranging it on the screen, or deleting it. Third, you have to save your data as a file.

To help you understand this three-step process of entering, manipulating, and saving data, all Office 2013 programs offer similar commands so you can quickly jump from Word to PowerPoint to Excel without having to learn entirely new commands for each program. Even better, Office 2013 organizes commands in tabs to make finding the command you need faster and easier than ever before.

If you're already familiar with computers and previous editions of Microsoft Office, you may want to browse through this chapter just to get acquainted with the appearance and organization of Office 2013. If you've never used a computer before or just don't feel comfortable using Microsoft Office, read this chapter first.

Starting an Office 2013 Program

Microsoft Office 2013 runs on both Windows 7 and Windows 8.

To start Office 2013 on Windows 7, you can go through the Start menu. To start Office 2013 on Windows 8, you must click the Office 2013 tile that represents the program you want to run.

To load Office 2013 in Windows 7, follow these steps:

1. **Click the Start button on the Windows taskbar.**

   A pop-up menu appears.

2. **Choose All Programs.**

   Another pop-up menu appears.

3. **Choose Microsoft Office.**

   A list of programs appears on the Start menu.

4. **Choose the Office 2013 program you want to use, such as Microsoft Word 2013 or Microsoft PowerPoint 2013.**

   Your chosen program appears on the screen. At this point, you can open an existing file.

To load Office 2013 in Windows 8, follow these steps:

1. **Open the Windows 8 tiles by either pressing the Windows key on your keyboard or moving the mouse pointer to the bottom-left corner of the screen and clicking when the Start preview window appears.**

   The Windows 8 tile interface appears.

2. **Scroll sideways until you see the Office 2013 tiles that represent the program you want to start as shown in Figure 1-1.**

Figure 1-1:
The tile interface of Windows 8 displays the Office 2013 programs as individual tiles.

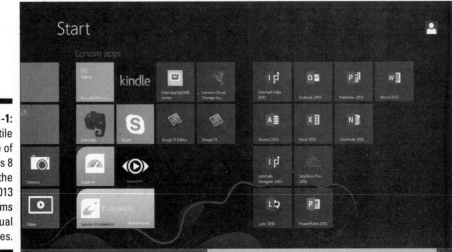

3. **Click the tile that represents the Office 2013 program you want to run, such as Microsoft Word 2013 or Microsoft PowerPoint 2013.**

   Your chosen program appears on the screen. At this point, you can open an existing file.

Introducing the Microsoft Office Ribbon

In older Windows programs, such as Microsoft Office 2003, the program displayed pull-down menus at the top of the screen. To find a command, you had to click a pull-down menu and then search for a command buried in the menu. Since this can get tedious and confusing, later versions of Microsoft Office introduced a Ribbon interface.

The basic idea behind this Ribbon interface is to store commonly used commands under separate tabs. Clicking each tab displays icons that represent related commands. Now you can see groups of related commands at a glance.

Although every Office 2013 program displays different tabs, the three most common tabs are the File tab, the Home tab, and the Insert tab.

The File tab lets you open, save, and print your files. In addition, the File tab also lets you exit out of the program and customize an Office 2013 program as shown in Figure 1-2.

Figure 1-2: The types of commands available through the File tab.

The Home tab displays icons that represent the most common commands for that particular Office 2013 program, such as formatting commands (as shown in Figure 1-3).

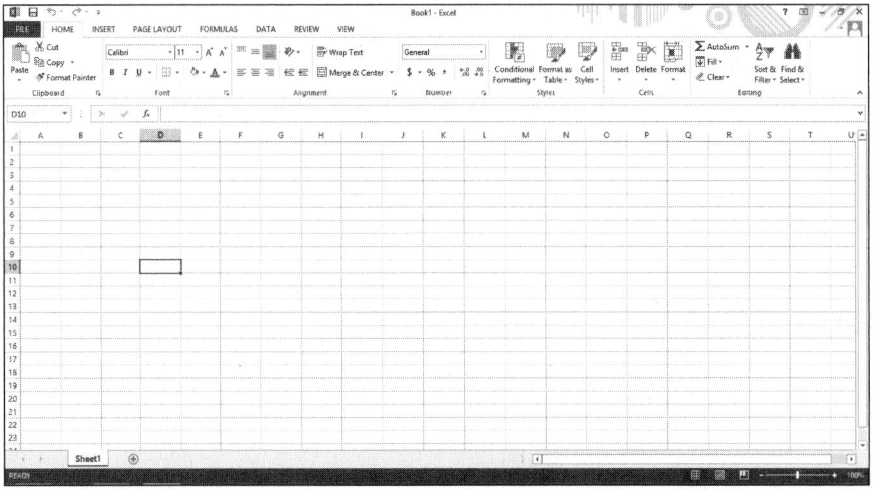

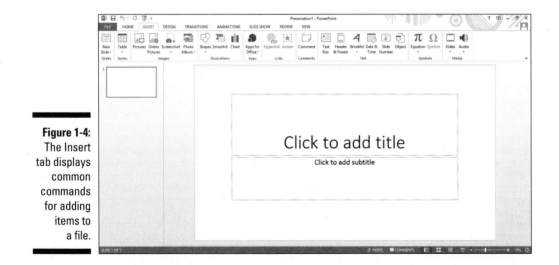

Figure 1-3:
The Home tab displays common formatting commands.

The Insert tab displays icons that represent common commands for adding items to a file such as pictures and tables, as shown in Figure 1-4.

Figure 1-4:
The Insert tab displays common commands for adding items to a file.

In addition to the File, Home, and Insert tabs, every Office 2013 program also includes tabs that contain commands specific to that particular program. For example, Excel contains a Formulas tab that contains commands for creating a formula in a spreadsheet while PowerPoint contains a Transitions tab for adding transitions to your presentation slideshows.

The File tab

The various commands available on the File tab include

- **Info:** Protects your file from changes, inspects a file for compatibility issues with older programs, and manages different versions of your file. The Info command also lets you view the details of your file such as the file's size and the date you created it, as shown in Figure 1-5.

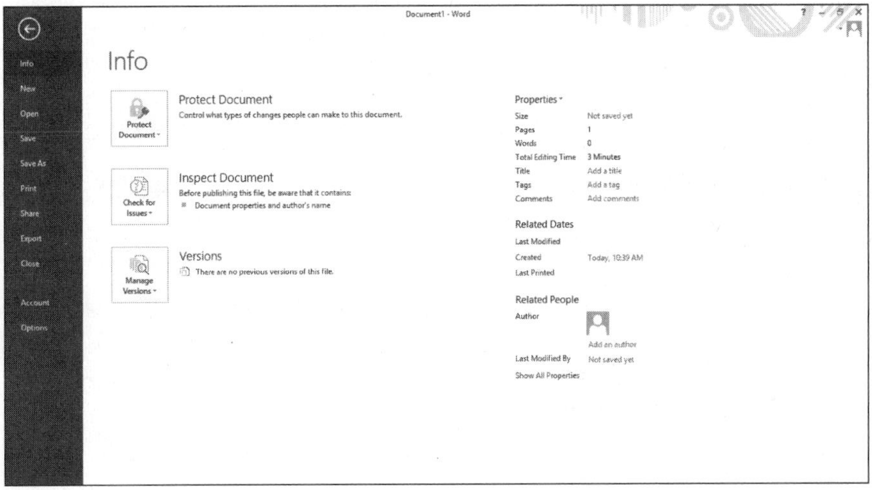

Figure 1-5: The Info command on the File tab lets you protect or inspect a file.

- **New:** Creates a new file.

- **Open:** Loads an existing file.

- **Save:** Saves your file. If you haven't named your file yet, the Save command is equivalent to the Save As command.

- **Save As:** Save the current file under a new name and/or in a different location such as a different folder or computer.

- **Print:** Prints the current file.

- **Share:** Sends a file as an e-mail attachment or posts it online.

- **Export:** Saves the current file in a different file format.

- **Close:** Closes an open file but keeps the Office 2013 program running.

- **Account:** Displays information about your SkyDrive account.

SkyDrive is Microsoft's cloud computing service that lets you store files online so you can access them from other types of devices such as a smart phone, a tablet, or another computer.

  ✔ **Options:** Displays various options for customizing the way each Office 2013 program behaves.

  ✔ **Exit:** Closes any open files and exits the Office 2013 program.

In Word, a file is called a *document.* In Excel, a file is called a *workbook.* In PowerPoint, a file is called a *presentation.* In Access, a file is called a *database.*

Creating a new file

Each time you create a new file, you have the option of choosing different types of templates that are already formatted and designed for specific purposes, such as a calendar, newsletter, sales report, or corporate slide-show presentation, as shown in Figure 1-6.

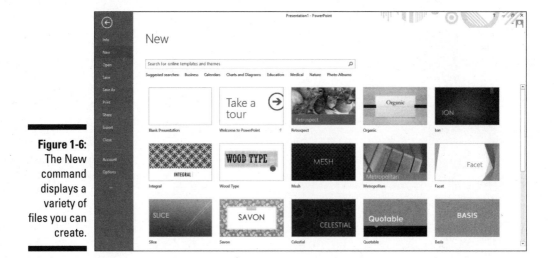

Figure 1-6: The New command displays a variety of files you can create.

To create a new file, follow these steps:

  1. **Click the File tab.**

  2. **Click New.**

     A list of templates appears (see Figure 1-6).

  3. **Double-click the template you want to use.**

     Office 2013 creates a new file based on your chosen template. For some templates, you may need access to the Internet to download the templates from Microsoft's website.

Opening an existing file

When you load an Office 2013 program, you may want to edit a file that you created and modified earlier. To open an existing file, you need to tell Office 2013 the location and name of the file you want to open.

The four options for finding an existing file include

- **Recent Documents/Workbooks/Presentations:** Displays a list of files you recently opened.
- **Someone's SkyDrive:** Displays a list of files stored on another person's SkyDrive account. (You may need to get permission from that other person to access certain files.)
- **Computer:** Lets you browse through the folders stored on your computer to find a file.
- **Add a place:** Lets you define a new location for storing files in the cloud such as your SkyDrive account.

To open a file, follow these steps:

1. **Click the File tab.**

2. **Click Open.**

   An Open pane appears, as shown in Figure 1-7.

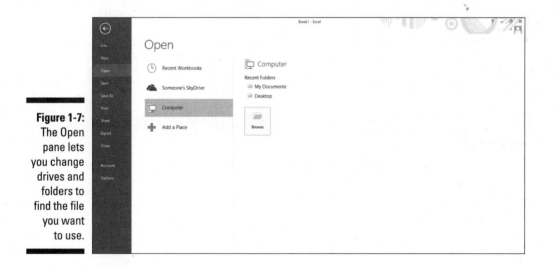

Figure 1-7:
The Open pane lets you change drives and folders to find the file you want to use.

3. **Choose an option such as Recent Documents or Computer.**

   You may need to click the Browse button to access different folders.

4. Click the file you want to open.

Your chosen file appears.

If you deleted or moved a file, Office 2013 may still list that filename under the Recent category even if that file no longer exists or has been moved.

Saving files

Saving a file stores all your data on a hard drive or other storage device (such as a USB flash drive). You can also save your files to a SkyDrive account so you can access that file anywhere you have Internet access. The first time you save a file, you need to specify three items:

- ✔ The location in which to store your file
- ✔ The name of your file
- ✔ The format in which to save your file

The location can be any folder on your hard drive or in your SkyDrive account. It's a good idea to store similar files in a folder with a descriptive name, such as *Tax Evasion Information for 2015* or *Extortion Letters to Grandma.* If you save your files to your computer, Office 2013 stores all your files in the Documents folder unless you specify otherwise.

You can give a file any name you want, but it's also a good idea to give your file a descriptive name, such as *Latest Resume to Escape My Dead-End Job* or *Global Trade Presentation for World Domination Meeting on October 29, 2014.*

The format of your file defines how Office 2013 stores your data. The default file format is simply called Word Document, Excel Workbook, PowerPoint Presentation, or Access Database. Anyone using Office 2013, 2010, or Office 2007 can open these files.

For a quick way to save a file, click the Save icon that appears above the File tab or press Ctrl+S.

Saving a file in other file formats

If you need to share files with people using older versions of Microsoft Office or other word processors, spreadsheets, or database programs, you need to save your files in a different file format. To share files with people using older versions of Microsoft Office, you need to save your files in a format known as *97-2003,* such as *Word 97-2003 Document* or *PowerPoint 97-2003 Presentation.*

This special 97-2003 file format saves Office 2013 files so that previous versions of Microsoft Office 97/2000/XP/2003 can open and edit your files.

When you save files in the 97-2003 format, Microsoft Office 2013 saves your files with a three-letter file extension, like .doc or .xls. When you save files in the Office 2013 format, Microsoft Office 2013 saves your files with a four- or five-letter file extension, such as .docx or .pptx, as shown in Table 1-1.

Table 1-1	File Extension Names Used by Different Versions of Microsoft Office	
Program	*Microsoft Office 2013 File Extension*	*Microsoft Office 97-2003 File Extension*
Microsoft Word	.docx	.doc
Microsoft Excel	.xlsx	.xls
Microsoft PowerPoint	.pptx	.ppt
Microsoft Access	.accdb	.mdb

To save your Office 2013 files in the 97-2003 format, follow these steps:

1. **Click the File tab.**

2. **Click Export.**

    The middle pane displays different options.

3. **Click Change File Type.**

    A list of different formats appears, as shown in Figure 1-8.

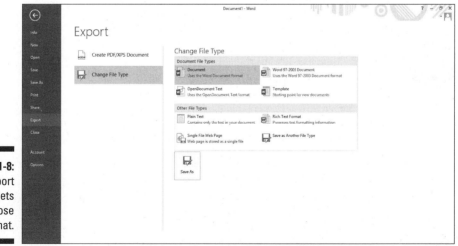

Figure 1-8:
The Export pane lets you choose a file format.

4. **Click the 97-2003 format option, such as Word 97-2003 Document or Excel 97-2003 Workbook.**

5. **Click the Save As button near the bottom of the screen.**

The Save As dialog box appears.

If you want to share your file with different types of programs, you may need to choose a different file format, such as Rich Text Format or Text.

6. **(Optional) Click in the File Name text box and type a descriptive name for your file.**

7. **Click Save.**

Closing a file

When you're done editing a file, you need to close it. Closing a file simply removes the file from your screen but keeps your Office 2013 program running so you can edit or open another file. If you haven't saved your file, closing a file will prompt you to save your changes.

To close a file, follow these steps:

1. **Click the File tab.**

2. **Click Close.**

If you haven't saved your file, a dialog box appears asking whether you want to save your changes.

For a faster way to choose the Close command, press Ctrl+F4.

3. **Click Save to save your changes, Don't Save to discard any changes, or Cancel to keep your file open.**

If you click either Save or Don't Save, Office 2013 closes your file.

Using the Ribbon

The Ribbon interface displays tabs that contain groups of related commands. For example, the Page Layout tab displays only those commands related to designing a page, and the Insert tab displays only those commands related to inserting items into a file, such as a page break or a picture.

Using the Ribbon is a two-step process. First, you must click the tab that contains the command you want. Second, you click the actual command.

Tabs act exactly like traditional pull-down menus. Whereas a pull-down menu simply displays a list of commands, tabs display a list of icons that represent different commands.

Deciphering Ribbon icons

Each Ribbon tab displays commands as buttons or icons, organized into groups. There are four types of icons displayed on the Ribbon:

- **One-click icons:** These icons do something with a single click.
- **Menu icons:** These icons display a pull-down menu of options you can choose.
- **Split-menu icons:** These icons consist of two halves. The left or top half lets you choose a command like a one-click icon, and the right or bottom half displays a downward-pointing arrow, which displays additional options.
- **Combo boxes:** These display a text box where you can type a value in or click a downward-pointing arrow to choose from a menu of options.

Using one-click icons

If you're in too much of a hurry to double-click, Office 2013 offers you two types of one-click icons (as shown in Figure 1-9).

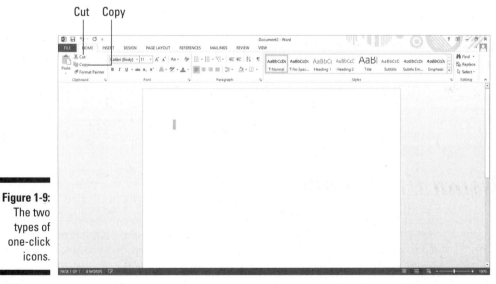

Figure 1-9:
The two types of one-click icons.

The most common one-click icons are the Cut and Copy commands, which appear on the Home tab of every Office 2013 program.

Using menu icons

A one-click icon represents a single command. However, there isn't enough room on the Ribbon to display every possible command as a single icon. As a result, menu icons display a pull-down menu that stores multiple options within a single icon, as shown in Figure 1-10.

Additional options

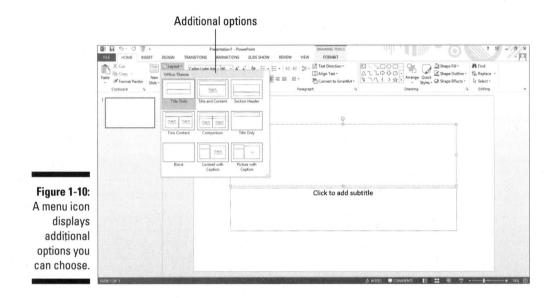

Figure 1-10:
A menu icon displays additional options you can choose.

Selecting an option in the pull-down menu immediately manipulates your selected data.

Using split-menu icons

Split-menu icons give you two choices:

- ✔ If you click the top or left half of a split-menu icon, you choose a default value. For example, the left half of the Font Color icon lets you choose the currently displayed color.

- ✔ If you click the bottom or right half of a split-menu icon, a pull-down menu appears, letting you choose a new default option, as shown in Figure 1-11.

The Paste and Font Color icons, found on the Home tab of Word, Excel, and PowerPoint, are typical split-menu icons.

You can identify split-menu icons because only half of the icon appears highlighted when you move the mouse pointer over that half.

Split menu

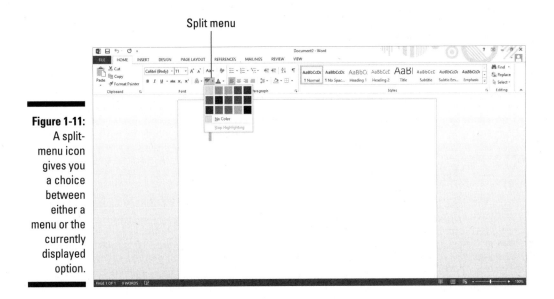

Figure 1-11:
A split-menu icon gives you a choice between either a menu or the currently displayed option.

Using combo boxes

A combo box gives you two ways to choose an option:

- ✔ Type directly into the combo box.
- ✔ Click the downward-pointing arrow to display a list of options, as shown in Figure 1-12.

Combo box

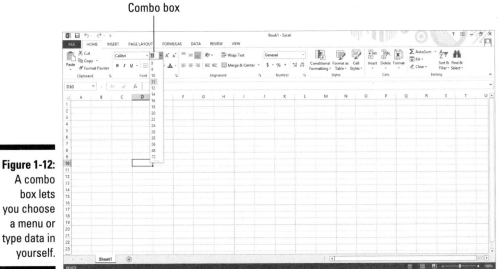

Figure 1-12:
A combo box lets you choose a menu or type data in yourself.

The Font and Font Size combo boxes, found on the Home tab of Word, Excel and PowerPoint, are typical combo boxes:

- ✔ If you click the left side of the Font Size combo box, you can type your own value in for a font size.
- ✔ If you click the downward-pointing arrow on the right side of the Font Size combo box, you can choose a value from a pull-down menu.

Identifying Ribbon icons

While some icons include descriptive text (such as Format Painter or Paste), most icons simply look like cryptic symbols from an alien language. To get additional help deciphering icons on the Ribbon, just point the mouse pointer over an icon, and a short explanation appears, called a ScreenTip, as shown in Figure 1-13.

ScreenTips provide the following information:

- ✔ The official name of the command (which is Format Painter in Figure 1-13)
- ✔ The equivalent keystroke shortcut you can use to run the command (which is Ctrl+Shift+C in the figure)
- ✔ A short explanation of what the command does

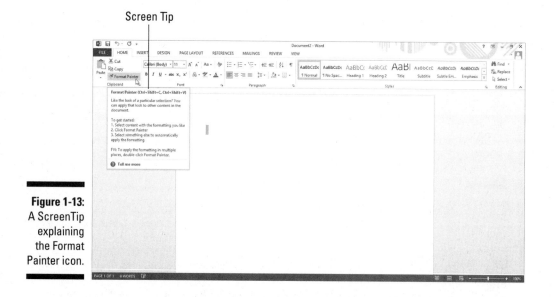

Figure 1-13: A ScreenTip explaining the Format Painter icon.

To view the ScreenTip for any icon on the Ribbon, move the mouse pointer over that icon and wait a few seconds for the ScreenTip to appear.

Shortcut keystrokes let you choose a command from the keyboard without the hassle of clicking a tab and then clicking the icon buried inside that tab. Most shortcut keystrokes consist of two or three keys, such as Ctrl+P or Ctrl+Shift+C.

Displaying dialog boxes

On each tab, the Ribbon displays related commands in a group. For example, the Home tab groups the Cut, Copy, and Paste commands within the Clipboard group and the text alignment and line-spacing commands within the Paragraph group.

Although you can choose the most commonly used commands directly from the Ribbon, Word often contains dozens of additional commands that don't appear on the Ribbon. To access these more obscure commands, you need to open a dialog box.

In the bottom-right corner of a group of icons on the Ribbon, you'll see the Show Dialog Box icon, which looks like an arrow pointing diagonally downward, as shown in Figure 1-14.

Dialog box

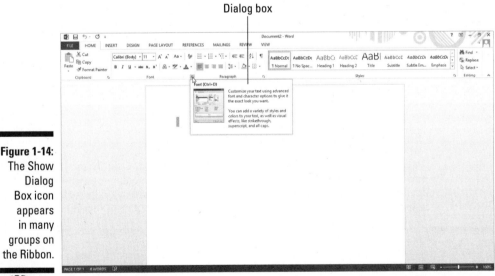

Figure 1-14:
The Show
Dialog
Box icon
appears
in many
groups on
the Ribbon.

Not every group of icons on the Ribbon displays the Show Dialog Box icon.

To open a dialog box that contains additional options, follow these steps:

1. **Click a tab on the Ribbon, such as the Home or Page Layout tab.**

2. **Click the Show Dialog Box icon in the bottom-right corner of a group such as the Font or Paragraph group found on the Home tab.**

   Office 2013 displays a dialog box, as shown in Figure 1-15.

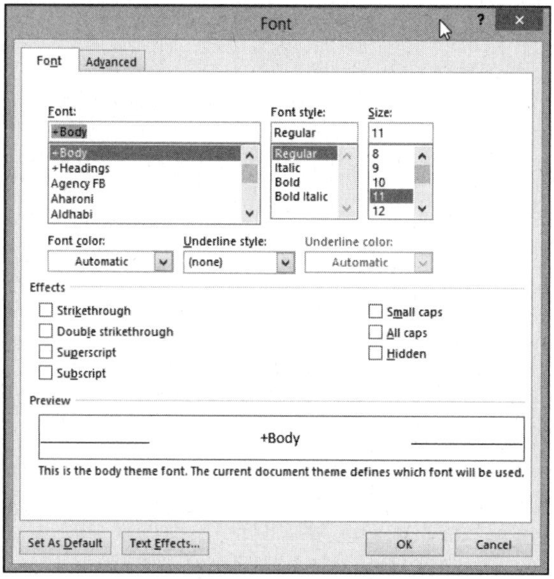

Figure 1-15: Clicking the Show Dialog Box icon displays a dialog box.

3. **Choose any options in the dialog box, and then click OK or Cancel when you're done.**

Minimizing the Ribbon

Some people like the Ribbon displaying various icons at all times, but others find that it makes the screen appear too cluttered. In case you want to tuck the Ribbon out of sight (or display a Ribbon that is already tucked out of sight) so icons only appear when you click a tab, choose one of the following methods:

✔ Double-click the current tab.

✔ Press Ctrl+F1.

✔ Click the Full Screen Mode icon that appears on the far right next to the Help (Question Mark) icon.

When you choose either of the first two methods, the Ribbon displays its tabs but hides any icons that normally appear underneath. When you click the Full Screen Mode icon, a menu appears (as shown in Figure 1-16) and gives you three options:

✔ **Auto-hide Ribbon:** Completely hides the Ribbon including tabs and icons.

✔ **Show Tabs:** Displays the Ribbon tabs but hides the icons on each tab.

✔ **Show Tabs and Commands:** Displays the Ribbon tabs and icons on each tab.

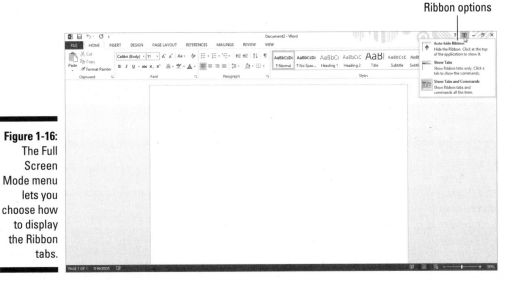

Ribbon options

Figure 1-16:
The Full
Screen
Mode menu
lets you
choose how
to display
the Ribbon
tabs.

Using the Quick Access Toolbar

The Quick Access toolbar appears in the upper-left corner of the screen, directly above the File and Home tabs. The Quick Access toolbar displays icons that represent commonly used commands such as Save and Undo, as shown in Figure 1-17.

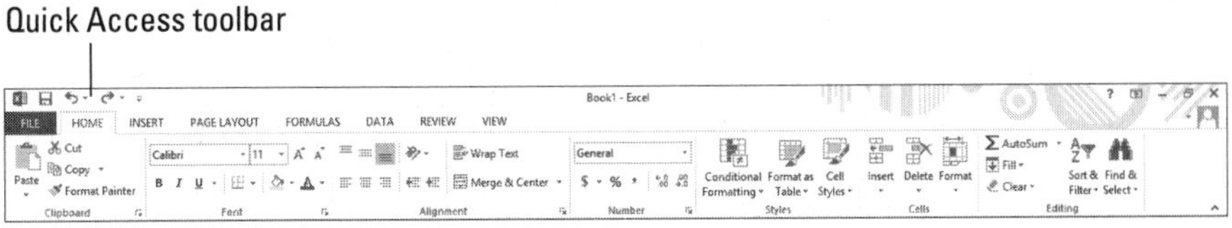

Figure 1-17:
The Quick
Access tool-
bar provides
one-click
access to
the most
commonly
used
commands.

Quick Access toolbar

Using the Quick Access icons

If you click the Save icon in the Quick Access toolbar, Office 2013 saves your current file. If you're saving a new file, a dialog box pops up, asking you to choose a name for your file.

The Undo icon is unique in that it offers two ways to use it. First, you can click the Undo icon to undo the last action you chose. Second, you can click the downward-pointing arrow that appears to the right of the Undo icon to display a list of one or more of your previous actions, as shown in Figure 1-18.

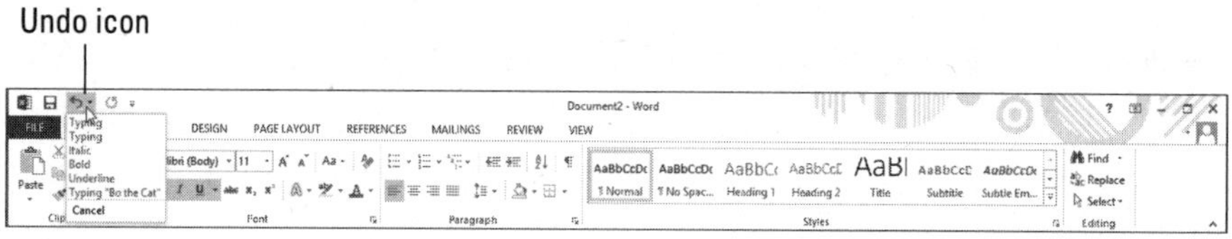

Figure 1-18:
The Undo icon displays a list of actions you can undo.

Undo icon

The most recent action you chose appears at the top of this list, the second most recent action appears second, and so on. To undo multiple commands, follow these steps:

1. **Click the downward-pointing arrow that appears to the right of the Undo icon in the Quick Access toolbar.**

2. **Move the mouse pointer to highlight one or more actions you want to undo.**

3. **Click the left mouse button.**

   Office 2013 undoes all the multiple actions you selected.

Adding icons

The Quick Access toolbar is designed to put your most commonly used commands (such as the Save and Undo commands) where you can find them quickly. To add other icons to the Quick Access toolbar, follow these steps:

1. **Click the Customize Quick Access Toolbar arrow.**

   A pull-down menu appears, as shown in Figure 1-19.

Quick Access toolbar

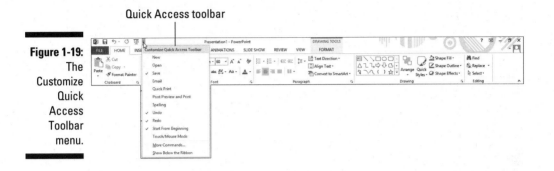

2. **Click a command that you want to add to the Quick Access toolbar such as Open or Quick Print.**

   A check mark appears next to each command that currently appears on the Quick Access toolbar. If you want to add more commands that aren't displayed on the Quick Access toolbar menu, continue with the rest of Steps 3 through 7.

3. **Click More Commands.**

   An Options window appears, as shown in Figure 1-20. The panel on the right shows all the current icons on the Quick Access toolbar. The panel on the left shows all the other icons you can add.

4. **Click in the Choose commands from list box and choose a title, such as Home Tab or Insert Tab.**

   The left panel displays a list of icons and commands.

5. **Click an icon and then click the Add button.**

6. **(Optional) Repeat Steps 4 and 5 for each icon you want to add to the Quick Access toolbar.**

7. **Click OK.**

   Your chosen icon (or icons) now appears on the Quick Access toolbar.

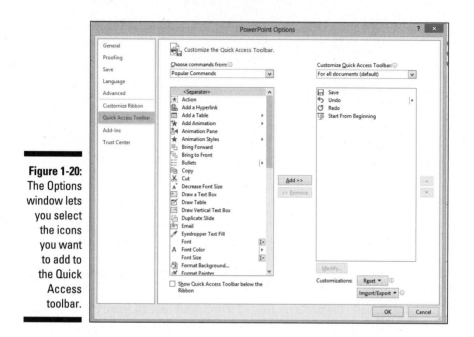

Figure 1-20:
The Options
window lets
you select
the icons
you want
to add to
the Quick
Access
toolbar.

Removing icons

You can remove icons from the Quick Access toolbar at any time. To remove an icon, follow these steps:

1. **Right-click an icon on the Quick Access toolbar.**

   A pull-down menu appears.

2. **Click Remove from Quick Access Toolbar.**

   Office 2013 removes your selected icon from the Quick Access toolbar.

Moving the Quick Access toolbar

The Quick Access toolbar can appear in one of two places:

- ✔ Above the Ribbon (its default location)
- ✔ Below the Ribbon

To move the Quick Access toolbar, follow these steps:

1. **Click the Customize Quick Access Toolbar arrow.**

   A pull-down menu appears.

2. **Choose Show Below/Above the Ribbon.**

   If the Quick Access toolbar currently appears *over* the Ribbon, you'll see the Show Below the Ribbon command.

   If the Quick Access toolbar appears *under* the Ribbon, you'll see the Show Above the Ribbon command.

Customizing an Office 2013 Program

If you don't like the default settings of your favorite Office 2013 program, you can modify them. Some common ways to modify an Office 2013 program include

 ✔ Changing the file format and location to save files

 ✔ Customizing the icons that appear on the Ribbon

Changing the file format and default location

Every Office 2013 program is designed to share files easily with anyone who uses Office 2013, 2010, or 2007. However, if you need to share files with people who use earlier versions of Office or other programs altogether, you may need to save your files in a different format.

To choose a default file format that each Office 2013 program will use every time you choose the Save command, follow these steps:

1. **Load an Office 2013 program.**

2. **Click the File tab.**

3. **Click the Options button in the left pane.**

   An Options dialog box appears.

4. Click Save.

The Options dialog box displays multiple options for defining a default file format and file location, as shown in Figure 1-21.

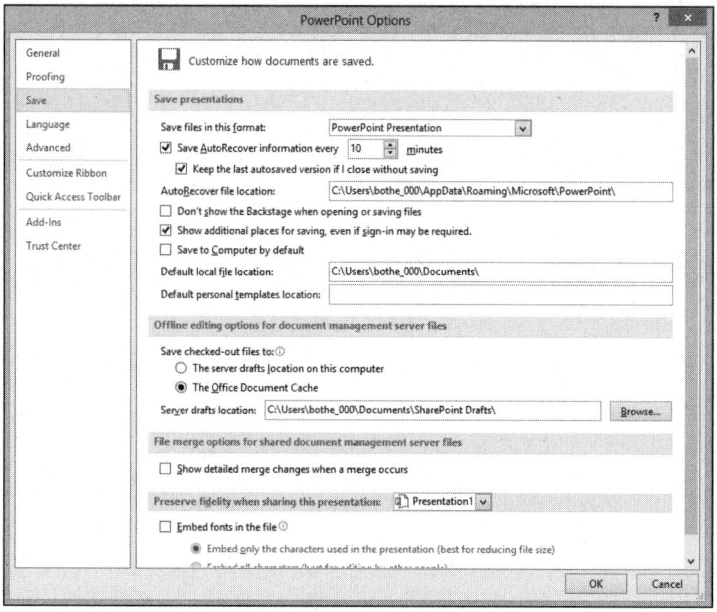

Figure 1-21:
The Options dialog box lets you choose a default file format and location.

5. Choose a different file format and location.

6. Click OK when you're done choosing different options.

Customizing the Ribbon icons

If you don't use certain Ribbon icons, you can remove them and replace them with icons that represent the commands you do use most often. To customize the Ribbon icons, follow these steps:

1. Load an Office 2013 program.

2. Click the File tab.

3. Click the Options button in the left pane.

An Options dialog box appears.

4. Click Customize Ribbon.

The Options dialog box displays multiple options for you to customize, as shown in Figure 1-22.

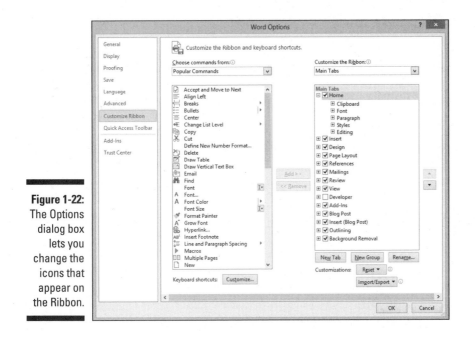

Figure 1-22:
The Options
dialog box
lets you
change the
icons that
appear on
the Ribbon.

5. **Click different icons and click the Add or Remove buttons.**

6. **Click OK when you're done choosing different options.**

Exiting Office 2013

No matter how much you may love using Office 2013, eventually there will come a time when you need to exit an Office 2013 program and do something else with your life. To exit from any Office 2013 program, choose one of the following:

✔ Click the Close box in the upper-right corner of the Office 2013 window.

✔ Click the program icon in the upper-left corner and when a menu appears, click Close.

✔ Press Alt+F4.

If you try to close an Office 2013 program before saving your file, a dialog box pops up to give you a chance to save your file. If you don't save your file before exiting, you'll lose any changes you made to that file.

Chapter 2

Selecting and Editing Data

- -

- -

*A*lthough you create a file only once, you can edit it many times. *Editing* can add, rearrange, or delete data, such as text, numbers, or pictures. All Office 2013 programs work in similar ways to edit data, so whether you use Word, Excel, PowerPoint, or Access, you'll know the right commands to edit data, no matter which program you may be using.

Whenever you edit a file, save your file periodically by clicking the Save icon in the Quick Access toolbar, pressing Ctrl+S, or clicking the File tab and choosing Save. That way if your computer crashes or the power goes out, you won't lose all the editing changes you made.

Adding Data by Pointing

When you enter data into a file, your data appears wherever the cursor appears on the screen. The cursor appears as a blinking vertical bar, which basically says, "Anything you type now will appear right here!"

Because the cursor won't always magically appear exactly where you want to type data, you must move the cursor by using either the mouse or the keyboard. To move the cursor by using the mouse, follow these steps:

1. **Move the mouse pointer where you want to move the cursor.**

2. **Click the left mouse button.**

   The cursor appears where you click the mouse pointer.

To move the cursor by using the keyboard, you can use one of many cursor movement keys:

- ✔ **The (up/down/left/right) arrow keys**
- ✔ **The Home/End keys**
- ✔ **The Page Up/Page Down keys**

Use the up/down/right/left arrow keys when you want to move the cursor a small distance, such as up one line or right to the next cell in an Excel spreadsheet.

To move the cursor faster, hold down the Ctrl key and then press the arrow keys. If you hold down the Ctrl key, the up-arrow key moves the cursor up one paragraph, the down-arrow key moves the cursor down one paragraph, the left-arrow key moves the cursor left one word, and the right-arrow key moves the cursor right one word.

Pressing the Home key moves the cursor to the beginning of a sentence (or a row in a spreadsheet), and pressing the End key moves the cursor to the end of a sentence (or a row in a spreadsheet).

Pressing the Page Up/Page Down keys moves the cursor up or down one screen at a time.

Using any of the cursor-movement keys puts the cursor in a new location. Wherever the cursor appears will be where you can enter new data. Table 2-1 lists ways to move the cursor in each Office 2013 program.

Table 2-1	Moving the Cursor in Office 2013 Programs			
Keystroke	*Word*	*Excel*	*PowerPoint*	*Access*
Home	Beginning of the line	Column A of the current row that the cursor appears in; (Ctrl+Home moves to cell A1)	Displays first slide; beginning of the line (when text box is selected)	First field of the current record
End	End of the line	NA; (Ctrl+End moves to last cell)	Displays last slide; end of the line (when text box is selected)	Add New Field of current record

Keystroke	Word	Excel	PowerPoint	Access
Page Up	Half a page up	Up 23 rows	Displays preceding slide	Up 25 records
Page Down	Half a page down	Down 23 rows	Displays next slide	Down 25 records
Up/Down arrow	Up/down one line	Up/down one row	Next/ previous slide; up/ down one line (when text box is selected)	Up/down one record
Left/Right arrow	Left/right one char- acter	Left/right one column	Next/pre- ceding slide; left/right one char- acter (when text box is selected)	Left/right one field

Selecting Data

To modify data, you must tell Office 2013 what you want to change by selecting it. Then choose a command that changes your data, such as underlining
text or deleting a picture.

To select anything in Office 2013, you can use either the mouse or the keyboard. Generally the mouse is faster — but getting used to coordinating the
motion of the mouse with the movement of the mouse pointer onscreen takes
some time. The keyboard is slower but much simpler to use.

Selecting data with the mouse

The mouse provides two ways to select data. The first way involves pointing
and dragging the mouse:

1. **Point the mouse pointer at the beginning or end of the data you want
   to select.**

2. **Hold down the left mouse button and drag (move) the mouse pointer
   over the data to select it.**

When you *drag* the mouse, hold down the left mouse button. If you don't hold down the left mouse button as you move the mouse, you won't select any data when you move the mouse pointer across the screen.

You can also select data by clicking the mouse. To select a picture, such as a chart in Microsoft Excel or a photograph added to a Microsoft Word document, just click the picture to select it. Office 2013 displays rectangles, called *handles,* around the border of any selected picture, as shown in Figure 2-1.

Handle

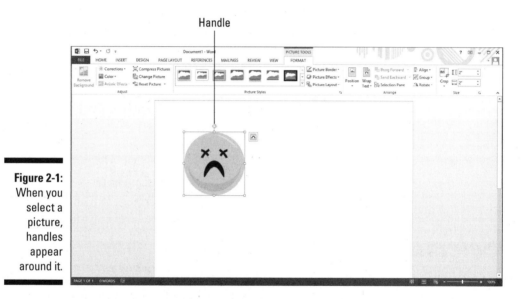

Figure 2-1:
When you select a picture, handles appear around it.

To select text with the mouse, you can click the mouse in one of three ways:

- **Single-click:** Moves the cursor
- **Double-click:** Selects the word that you click
- **Triple-click:** Selects the entire paragraph that contains the word you click

Office 2013 defines a *paragraph* as any chunk of text that begins on a separate line and ends with a Return character (¶), created by pressing the Enter key.

Selecting data with the keyboard

To select data with the keyboard, you need to use the following keys:

- **The cursor movement keys (up/down/left/right arrow keys, Home/End keys, or Page Up/Page Down keys)**
- **The Shift key**

To select all the data in a file, press Ctrl+A.

The cursor movement keys simply move the cursor. When moving the cursor, you can also hold down the Shift key to tell Office 2013 what to select. To select data, follow these steps:

1. **Move the cursor to the beginning or end of the data you want to select.**

2. **Hold down the Shift key. (Keep it pressed down.)**

3. **Move the cursor by using any of the cursor movement keys, such as the up-arrow key or the End key.**

4. **Release the Shift key.**

Instead of dragging the mouse to select data, you may find it easier to place the cursor by using the mouse and then hold down the Shift key while pressing a cursor movement.

Selecting multiple chunks of data with the mouse and keyboard

For greater flexibility in selecting data, you can use both the mouse and the keyboard to select multiple chunks of data that are not located next to each other. To select two or more chunks of data, follow these steps:

1. **Select a picture or chunk of text, using either the keyboard or the mouse.**

2. **Hold down the Ctrl key.**

3. **Select another picture or chunk of text, using either the keyboard or the mouse.**

4. **Repeat Step 3 for each additional item you want to select.**

5. **Release the Ctrl key when you're done selecting data.**

Editing Text with the Pop-up Toolbar

As soon as you select text with the mouse, Office 2013 displays a pop-up toolbar that displays the most commonly used commands (displayed as icons). The closer you move the mouse toward this pop-up toolbar, the darker and sharper the toolbar appears, as shown in Figure 2-2. The farther you move away from the toolbar, the fainter it appears.

Pop-up toolbar

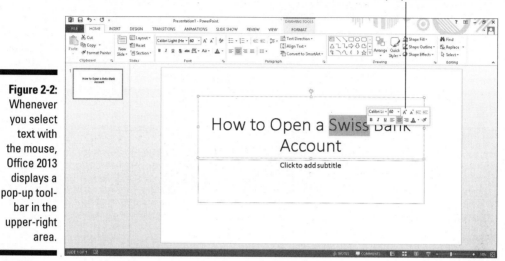

Figure 2-2:
Whenever
you select
text with
the mouse,
Office 2013
displays a
pop-up tool-
bar in the
upper-right
area.

The pop-up toolbar appears only if you select text by using the mouse. If you select text by using the keyboard, this pop-up toolbar will not appear.

To use this pop-up toolbar, follow these steps:

1. **Select data by using the mouse.**

   Selecting data with the keyboard will *not* display the pop-up toolbar.

2. **Move the mouse pointer to the area to the upper right of the selected data.**

   The pop-up toolbar appears.

   The closer you move the mouse to the toolbar, the more visible the tool-bar will appear.

3. **Click a command (icon) on the pop-up toolbar.**

Deleting Data

The simplest way to edit a file is to delete your existing data. If you just need to delete a single character, you can use one of two keys:

- **Backspace:** Deletes the character immediately to the left of the cursor
- **Delete:** Deletes the character immediately to the right of the cursor

If you need to delete large chunks of text, follow these steps:

1. **Select the data you want to delete, using either the keyboard or the mouse. (See the earlier section, "Selecting Data.")**

2. **Press the Delete (or Backspace) key.**

   Office 2013 wipes away your data.

Cutting and Pasting (Moving) Data

Moving data in Office 2013 requires a two-step process: cut and paste. When you *cut* data, you delete it but save a copy in a special area of the computer's memory known as the *Clipboard.* When you *paste* data to a new location, you copy the data off the Clipboard and paste it into your file.

To move data, follow these steps:

1. **Select the data you want to move, using the keyboard or mouse as explained in the earlier section, "Selecting Data."**

2. **Choose one of the following:**

   • Click the Cut icon (on the Home tab).

   • Right-click the mouse; when the pop-up menu appears, choose Cut.

   • Press Ctrl+X.

3. **Move the cursor to a new location.**

4. **Choose one of the following:**

   • Click the Paste icon (on the Home tab).

   • Right-click the mouse; when the pop-up menu appears, choose Paste.

   • Press Ctrl+V.

If you select data in Step 3, you can replace that selected data with the pasted data you selected in Step 1.

Copying and Pasting Data

Unlike the Cut command, the Copy command leaves your selected data in its original location but places a second copy of that data somewhere else. To copy and paste data, follow these steps:

1. **Select the data you want to copy, using the keyboard or mouse, as explained in the earlier section, "Selecting Data."**

2. **Choose one of the following:**

    • Click the Copy icon (on the Home tab).

    • Right-click the mouse; when the pop-up menu appears, choose Copy.

    • Press Ctrl+C.

3. **Move the cursor to a new location.**

4. **Choose one of the following:**

    • Click the Paste icon.

    • Right-click the mouse; when the pop-up menu appears, choose Paste.

    • Press Ctrl+V.

Using Paste Options

Cutting, copying, and pasting text from one location to another is easy. However, a problem can occur when you paste formatted text from one location to another. When you paste formatted text, you have several choices, depending on the Office 2013 program you're using. Three common choices include:

✔ Paste the text with the original formatting of the copied or cut text.

✔ Merge the pasted data with the formatting of the current text.

✔ Paste the text but strip away the formatting.

Each Office 2013 program displays slightly different options for Paste Options.

To use the Paste Options feature, follow these steps:

1. **Select text.**

    You can select text by either dragging the mouse over text or holding down the Shift key and pressing an arrow key.

2. **Click the Home tab and click the Cut or Copy icon.**

   If you select the Cut icon, your selected text disappears.

3. **Move the cursor to where you want to paste your cut or copied text.**

4. **Click the Home tab, and then click the downward-pointing arrow at the bottom of the Paste icon.**

   The Paste Options menu appears, displaying the different ways you can paste, as shown in Figure 2-3.

Paste Options menu

Figure 2-3:
The Paste Options menu appears when you click the bottom half of the Paste icon.

5. **Move the mouse pointer over each Paste Options icon to see how your pasted text will look in the file.**

   Each time you move the mouse pointer over a different Paste Options icon, the appearance of the pasted text will change.

6. **Click the Paste Options icon that you want to use.**

If you right-click in Step 3, a pop-up menu appears with the Paste Options displayed, as shown in Figure 2-4.

Paste Options

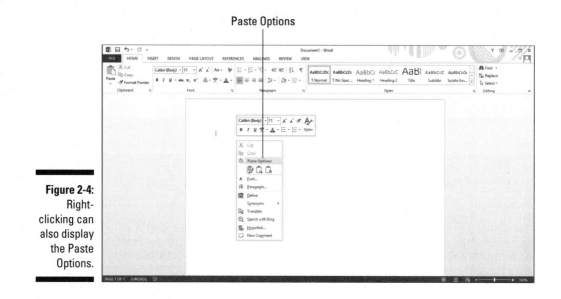

Figure 2-4:
Right-
clicking can
also display
the Paste
Options.

Dragging with the Mouse to Cut, Copy, and Paste

The mouse can also cut/copy and paste data. To move data with the mouse, follow these steps:

1. **Select the data you want to move by using the methods described in the earlier section, "Selecting Data."**

2. **Move the mouse pointer over the highlighted data.**

3. **Hold down the left mouse button and drag (move) the mouse.**

   The mouse pointer displays an arrow and a box while the cursor turns into a dotted vertical line.

   Alternatively, to copy data, hold down the Ctrl key while holding down the left mouse button and dragging (moving) the mouse. The mouse pointer displays an arrow and a box with a plus sign while the cursor turns into a dotted vertical line.

4. **Move the dotted vertical line cursor where you want to place the data you selected in Step 1.**

5. **Release the left mouse button.**

   Your data appears in its new location.

Undo and Redo

To protect you from mistakes, Office 2013 offers a special Undo command, which essentially tells the computer, "Remember that last command I just gave? Pretend I never chose it."

You can use the Undo command any time you edit data and want to reverse your changes. The two ways to choose the Undo command are

✔ **Click the Undo icon on the Quick Access toolbar.**

✔ **Press Ctrl+Z.**

Sometimes you may make many changes to your file and suddenly realize that the last five or ten changes you made messed up your data by mistake. To undo multiple commands, follow these steps:

1. **Click the downward-pointing arrow that appears to the right of the Undo icon.**

   A list of your previously chosen commands appears.

2. **Move the mouse pointer to highlight all the commands that you want to undo, as shown in Figure 2-5.**

3. **Click the left mouse button.**

   Office 2013 undoes your chosen commands.

The Redo command lets you reapply the last command you chose to undo. To choose the Redo command, press Ctrl+Y.

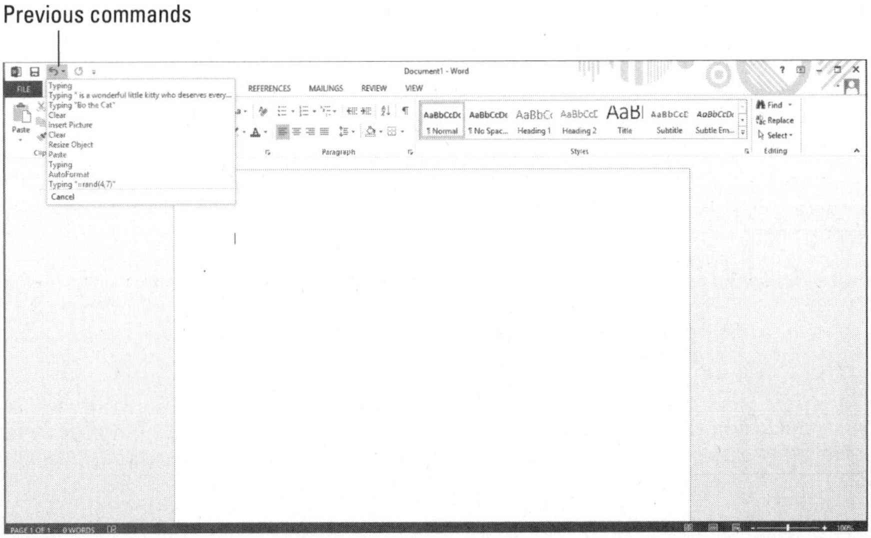

Previous commands

Figure 2-5:
The downward-pointing arrow to the right of the Undo icon lets you view a list of your last commands.

Each time you choose the Redo command, you reverse the effect of the last Undo command. For example, if you use the Undo command four times, you can choose the Redo command only up to four times.

Sharing Data with Other Office 2013 Programs

Cutting, copying, and pasting data may be handy within the same file, but Office 2013 also gives you the ability to cut, copy, and paste data between different programs, as when you copy a chart from Excel and paste it into a PowerPoint presentation.

Using the Office Clipboard

When you cut or copy any data, Windows stores it in a special part of memory called the *Clipboard.* This Windows Clipboard can only hold one item at a time, so Office 2013 comes with its own Clipboard called the *Office Clipboard,* which can store up to 24 items.

Whereas the Windows Clipboard works with any Windows program (such as Microsoft Paint or Internet Explorer), the Office Clipboard works only with Office 2013 programs (such as Word, Excel, PowerPoint, Access, and Outlook). To store data on the Office Clipboard, you just need to use the Cut or Copy command, and Office 2013 automatically stores your data on the Office Clipboard.

The two big advantages of the Office Clipboard are

- ✔ **You can store up to 24 items.**

    The Windows Clipboard can store only one item.

- ✔ **You can select what you want to paste from the Clipboard.**

    The Windows Clipboard lets you paste only the last item cut or copied.

Viewing and pasting items off the Office Clipboard

After you use the Cut or Copy command at least once, your data gets stored on the Office Clipboard. You can then view the Office Clipboard and choose which data you want to paste from the Clipboard into your file.

To view the Office Clipboard and paste items from it, follow these steps:

1. **Move the cursor to the spot where you want to paste an item from the Office Clipboard.**

2. **Click the Home tab.**

3. **Click the Show Dialog Box icon in the bottom-right corner of the Clipboard group.**

   The Office Clipboard pane appears on the left side of the screen, as shown in Figure 2-6. The Office Clipboard also displays an icon that shows you the program where the data came from, such as Word or PowerPoint.

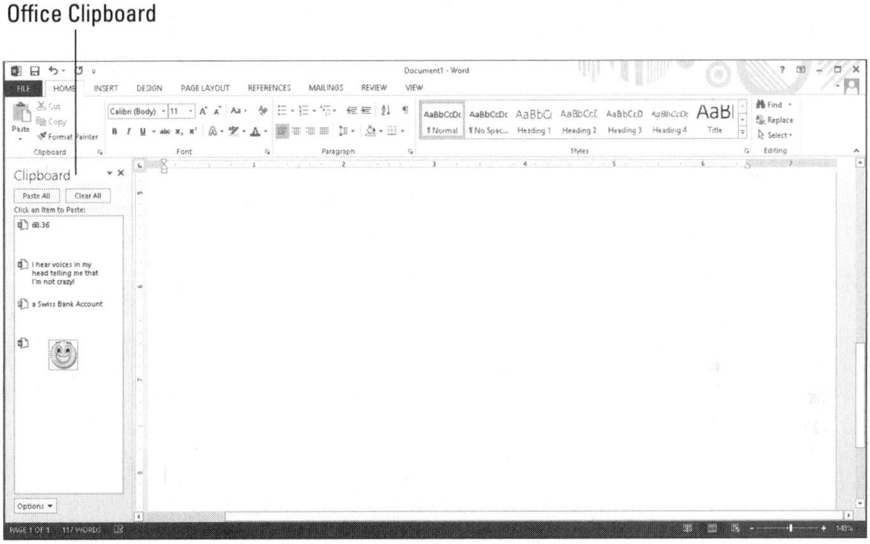

Office Clipboard

Figure 2-6:
The Office Clipboard pane lets you view the current contents of the Office Clipboard.

4. **Click the item you want to paste.**

   Office 2013 pastes your chosen item into the file where you moved the cursor in Step 1.

5. **Click the Close box of the Office Clipboard window to tuck it out of sight.**

If you click the Paste All button, you can paste every item on the Office Clipboard into your file.

Deleting items from the Office Clipboard

You can add up to 24 items to the Office Clipboard. The moment you add a 25th item, Office 2013 deletes the oldest item from the Office Clipboard to make room for the new cut or copied item.

You can also manually delete items from the Office Clipboard, by following these steps:

1. **Click the Home tab.**

2. **Click the Show Dialog Box icon in the bottom-right corner of the Clipboard group.**

   The Office Clipboard appears.

3. **Move the mouse pointer over an item on the Office Clipboard.**

   A downward-pointing arrow appears to the right.

4. **Click the downward-pointing arrow to the right of an item.**

   A pop-up menu appears, as shown in Figure 2-7.

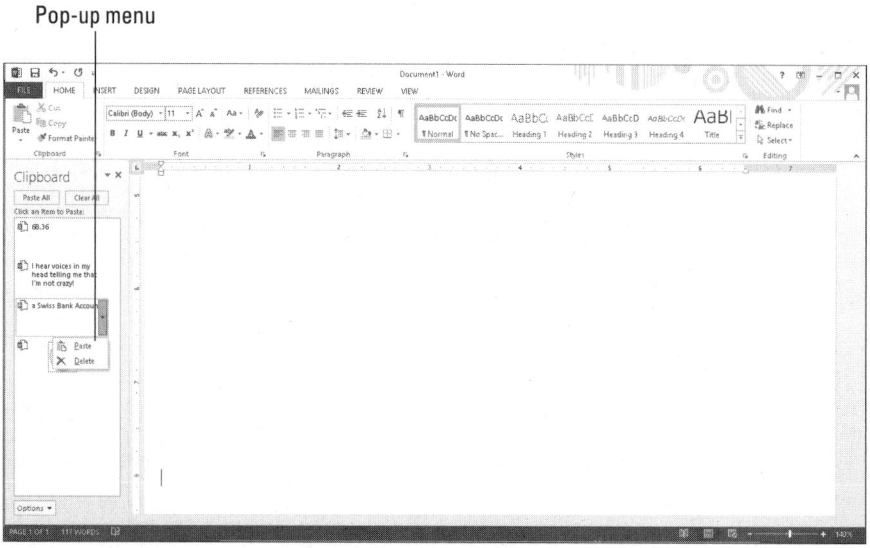

Pop-up menu

Figure 2-7:
To remove
an item from
the Office
Clipboard,
click the
downward-
pointing
arrow and
click Delete.

5. **Click Delete.**

   Office 2013 deletes your chosen item.

6. **Click the Close box to tuck the Office Clipboard out of sight.**

If you click the Clear All button, you can delete every item currently stored on the Office Clipboard.

Make sure that you really want to delete an item from the Office Clipboard before you do so, because after you delete it, you can't retrieve it.

Chapter 3

Modifying Pictures

*O*ne way to spice up your Word documents, Excel spreadsheets, or PowerPoint presentations is to add photographs that you've captured through a digital camera. Adding photographs is simple enough, but Office 2013 also includes different ways to manipulate your picture by using special visual effects.

One common problem with photographs is that they may appear too light or too dark. In the past, the only way to correct these types of problems was to edit the picture in a photo-editing program like Adobe Photoshop. Because not many people have Photoshop or know how to use it, Office 2013 now contains simple photo-editing tools that anyone can use to correct minor flaws.

After you've corrected any flaws, Office 2013 also lets you turn your photographs into art by adding frames, tilting the picture sideways, or adding a visual effect that makes the picture look more like a painting.

With Office 2013, you can add photographs, correct them, and modify them to give all your Word, Excel, or PowerPoint files that extra bit of color and showmanship.

Adding (and Deleting) Pictures

To add a picture to a file, follow these steps:

1. **Click the Insert tab.**
2. **Click the Picture icon.**

   The Insert Picture dialog box appears.

3. **Select the picture file you want to insert.**

   You may need to select a different folder or drive that contains the picture you want to insert.

4. **Click the Insert button.**

   - In Word, your picture appears wherever the cursor appears.
   - In Excel, the upper-left corner of your picture appears in the cell where the cursor appears.
   - In PowerPoint, your picture appears in the center of the currently displayed slide.

To delete a picture in a file, follow these steps:

1. **Select the picture that you want to delete.**

   Handles appear around your selected picture.

2. **Press the Delete or Backspace key.**

Manipulating Pictures

After you add a picture to a file, it may not be in the correct position or be the right size. As a result, you may want to move, resize, or rotate it.

Moving a picture

To move a picture, follow these steps:

1. **Select the picture that you want to move.**

   Handles appear around your selected picture, as shown in Figure 3-1.

Handle

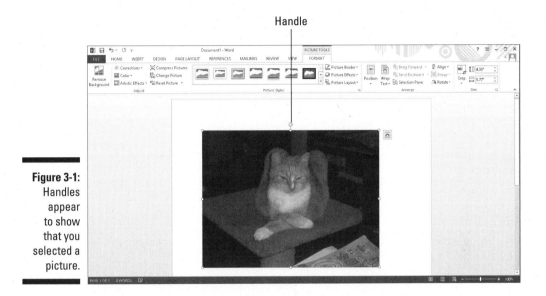

Figure 3-1:
Handles
appear
to show
that you
selected a
picture.

2. **Move the picture, using one of the following methods:**

    • Move the mouse pointer over the picture and drag the mouse.

    • Press the up/down or left/right arrow keys.

Resizing a picture

To resize a picture, follow these steps:

1. **Select the picture that you want to move.**

    Handles appear around your selected picture.

2. **Move the mouse pointer over a handle and drag the mouse.**

If you drag a corner handle, you can change the height and width of a picture at the same time.

If you click the Format tab, you can type a precise width and height for your picture in the Height and Width text box displayed in the Size group.

Rotating a picture

To create an interesting effect, you may want to rotate a picture in a file. To rotate a picture, follow these steps:

1. **Select the picture that you want to rotate.**

   Handles appear around your selected picture. Note that the *rotate handle* appears to be sticking up from the top of the picture, as shown in Figure 3-2.

Rotate handle

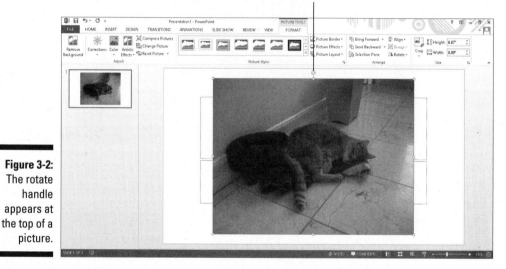

Figure 3-2: The rotate handle appears at the top of a picture.

2. **Move the mouse pointer over the rotate handle and drag the mouse.**

   The mouse pointer turns into a circular arrow icon when you move it over the rotate handle.

Enhancing Pictures

Sometimes a picture may look almost perfect, but still need some minor corrections. Other times a picture may look plain, but by adding some visual effects, you can turn a plain picture into a work of art.

To help you make your pictures look prettier and more visually engaging, Office 2013 lets you choose different effects, colors, frames, and styles.

Choosing visual effects

Office 2013 offers several different ways to alter a picture's visual appearance:

- ✔ **Corrections:** Sharpens or softens a picture, or adjusts the brightness or contrast.
- ✔ **Color:** Adjusts the tone or saturation of a picture's color, or lets you change the color of a picture altogether.
- ✔ **Artistic Effects:** Makes a picture appear as different styles, such as a mosaic or watercolor painting.
- ✔ **Picture Effects:** Lets you add visual effects to a picture, such as shadows, glows, or rotation.

To choose a visual effect for a picture, follow these steps:

1. **Click the picture that you want to modify.**

   The Format tab appears on the Ribbon.

2. **Click the Corrections icon.**

   When you click the Corrections icon, a menu of correction options appears, as shown in Figure 3-3.

3. **Select a Corrections option from the menu.**

Corrections options

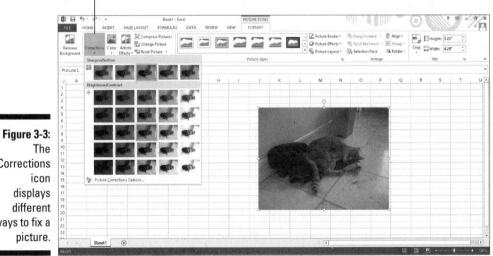

Figure 3-3:
The
Corrections
icon
displays
different
ways to fix a
picture.

4. **Click the Color icon.**

   A menu of color options appears, as shown in Figure 3-4.

Color options

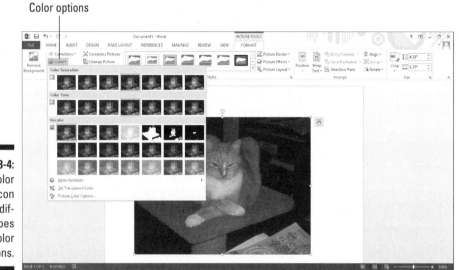

Figure 3-4:
The Color icon displays different types of color options.

5. **Select a Color option from the menu.**

6. **Click the Artistic Effects icon.**

   A menu of visual effects options appears, as shown in Figure 3-5.

Artistic Effects

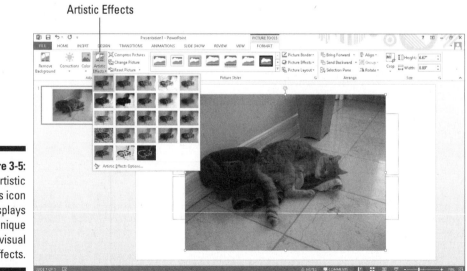

Figure 3-5:
The Artistic Effects icon displays unique visual effects.

7. **Select an Artistic Effects option from the menu.**

8. **Click the Picture Effects icon.**

   A menu of color options appears. You may need to click a submenu to display additional options, as shown in Figure 3-6.

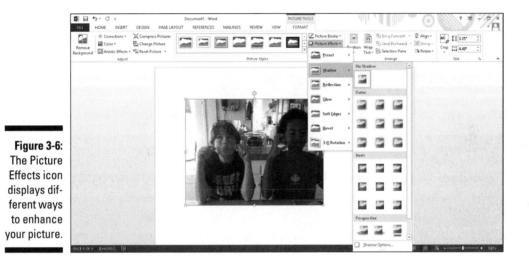

Figure 3-6:
The Picture
Effects icon
displays dif-
ferent ways
to enhance
your picture.

9. **Click a Picture Effects submenu, and then select an option.**

Choosing a picture style

Rather than force you to make individual changes to a picture, Office 2013 provides a collection of predefined picture styles that you can apply to any picture added to a file. To choose a picture style, follow these steps:

1. **Click the picture that you want to modify.**

   The Format tab appears on the Ribbon.

2. **Click a style displayed in the Picture Styles group.**

   The Picture Styles group contains multiple options:

   • To view these options one row at a time, click the up/down arrows in the Picture Styles group, as shown in Figure 3-7.

   • To view all picture styles at once, click the More button, which displays all picture styles, as shown in Figure 3-8.

Up/down arrows   More button

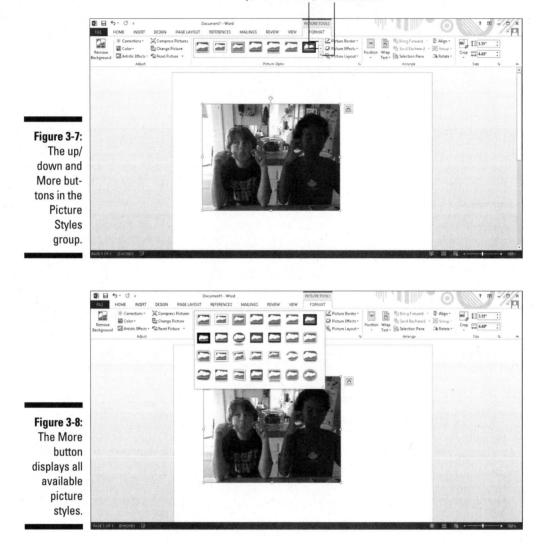

Figure 3-7:
The up/
down and
More but-
tons in the
Picture
Styles
group.

Figure 3-8:
The More
button
displays all
available
picture
styles.

Adding a border around a picture

To help make your picture stand out, you may want to add a border. A border can appear in different colors, thicknesses, and styles (such as a solid line or a dotted line).

To add or modify a border around a picture, follow these steps:

1. **Click the picture that you want to modify.**

   The Format tab appears on the Ribbon.

2. **Click the Picture Border icon.**

   A pull-down menu of different colors and options appears, as shown in Figure 3-9.

Picture Border icon

Figure 3-9:
The Picture Border icon displays a menu.

3. **Choose a color that you want for your border.**

4. **Click the Weight submenu and choose a weight (thickness), as shown in Figure 3-10.**

Weight submenu

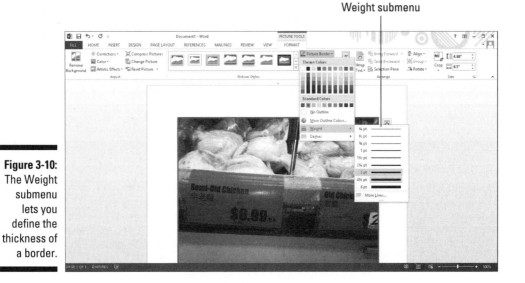

Figure 3-10:
The Weight submenu lets you define the thickness of a border.

5. **Click the Dashes submenu and choose the type of line to use as the border, as shown in Figure 3-11.**

Dashes submenu

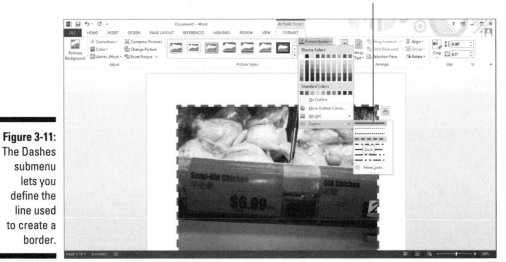

Figure 3-11:
The Dashes submenu lets you define the line used to create a border.

Chapter 4

Getting Help from Office 2013

Microsoft always tries to make each new version of Microsoft Office easier to use than the previous version. Yet it's likely that you'll still have questions about using the features buried in one of the many Office programs.

To answer any questions, Office 2013 provides a Help system, which lets you browse through different help topics until you (hopefully) find the answer you need. There are two ways to use the Help system:

✔ Browse through the various topics displayed until you find the answer you want. This can take time to search but can also show you related help that you may find useful.

✔ Type a query such as **Page margins** or **Font size**. The Help system will then display all topics related to your query. This can be a fast way to search for help, but if you don't type the right terms that the Help system recognizes, this method may not find the exact help you need.

To view the latest help information about Office 2013, make sure that your computer is connected to the Internet.

Browsing the Help Window

Each Office 2013 program comes with its own help files that you can access at any time. To browse through the Help system, follow these steps.

1. **Choose one of the following to display the Help window, as shown in Figure 4-1:**

   • Click the Help icon. (It looks like a question mark sitting in the upper-right corner of the window.)

   • Press F1.

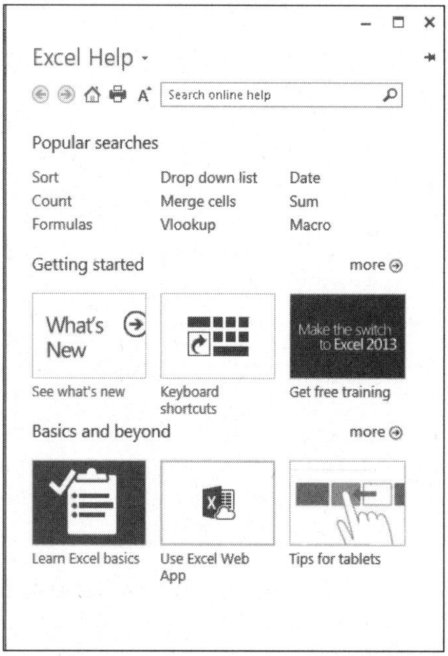

Excel Help ·

Search online help

Popular searches

Sort	Drop down list	Date
Count	Merge cells	Sum
Formulas	Vlookup	Macro

Getting started   more ⊕

What's New →

See what's new

Keyboard shortcuts

Make the switch to Excel 2013

Get free training

Basics and beyond   more ⊕

Learn Excel basics

Use Excel Web App

Tips for tablets

Figure 4-1:
The Help window lets you search for answers to your questions.

2. **Click a topic.**

   The Help window displays a list of Help topics, as shown in Figure 4-2.

3. **Click a Help topic.**

   The Help window displays information about your chosen topic. You may need to click multiple Help topics until you get the answer you want.

4. **Click the Close box when you're done to make the Help window go away.**

If you click the Back icon, you can view the previous text displayed in the Help window. If you click the Forward icon (after clicking the Back icon at least once), you can return forward to the text that you were looking at before you clicked the Back icon. If you click the Home icon, you can view the Help window's list of topics that appear every time you open the Help window.

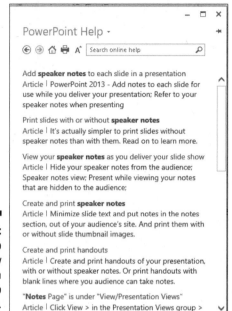

Figure 4-2:
The Help
window
displays a
list of Help
topics.

Searching in the Help Window

Rather than browse through one or more subcategories to find help, you may
want to search for help by typing in one or more keywords. Such keywords
can identify a specific topic, such as *Printing* or *Editing charts.*

If you misspell a topic, the Help system may not understand what you want to
find, so check your spelling.

To search the Help window by typing in a keyword or two, follow these steps:

1. **Choose one of the following methods to display the Help window
   (refer to Figure 4-1):**

   • Click the Help icon.

   • Press F1.

2. **Click in the Search Help list box and type one or more keywords, such
   as** Formatting **or** Aligning text.

   Type as few words as possible. So rather than type "I want to find help
   on printing," just type "Printing." Not only will this make it easier for you
   to search for help, but it will also keep Office 2013 from looking up extra
   words that have nothing to do with your topic, such as "I want to find
   help on. . . ."

3. Click Search or press Enter.

The Help window displays a list of topics, as shown in Figure 4-3.

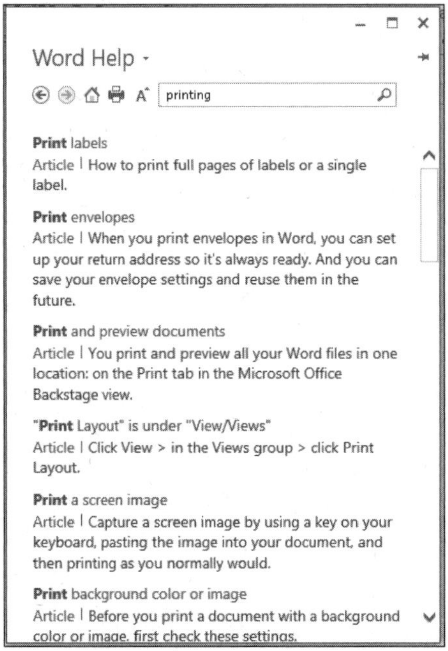

Figure 4-3:
Keywords
let you
view a list
of related
topics right
away.

— ▢ ✕

Word Help ▾

⊙ ⊙ ⌂ 🖨 A͏̌ | printing 🔍

Print labels
Article | How to print full pages of labels or a single
label.

Print envelopes
Article | When you print envelopes in Word, you can set
up your return address so it's always ready. And you can
save your envelope settings and reuse them in the
future.

Print and preview documents
Article | You print and preview all your Word files in one
location: on the Print tab in the Microsoft Office
Backstage view.

"**Print** Layout" is under "View/Views"
Article | Click View > in the Views group > click Print
Layout.

Print a screen image
Article | Capture a screen image by using a key on your
keyboard, pasting the image into your document, and
then printing as you normally would.

Print background color or image
Article | Before you print a document with a background
color or image, first check these settings.

4. Click a Help topic.

The Help window displays information for your chosen topic. You may
need to click additional topics to get the answer you want.

**5. Click the Close box when you're done to make the Help window go
away.**

Making the Help Window Easier to Read

One problem with the Help window is that it may appear too small to read
comfortably. To get around this problem, you have two choices:

✔ Resize the Help window.

✔ Expand the size of the text inside the Help window.

Resizing and pinning the Help window

You can resize the Help window just as you would any other window, by clicking one of the following icons in the upper-right corner (as shown in Figure 4-4):

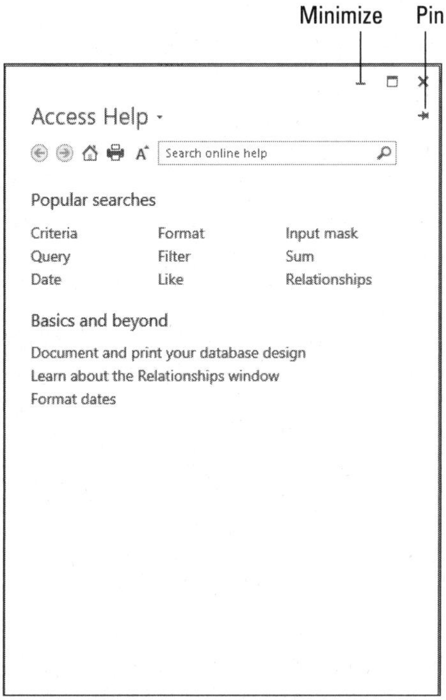

Minimize   Pin

Access Help ·

Search online help

Popular searches

Criteria	Format	Input mask
Query	Filter	Sum
Date	Like	Relationships

Basics and beyond

Document and print your database design
Learn about the Relationships window
Format dates

Figure 4-4:
The Minimize and Pin icons on the Help window.

✔ **Minimize:** Shrinks the Help window to an icon on the Windows taskbar.

✔ **Pin:** Keeps the Help window on the screen so you can read the instructions while still using an Office 2013 program.

To make the Help window disappear if you click away from it, just click the Pin icon a second time to toggle the Help window's behavior.

You can also resize a window by moving the mouse pointer over one edge or bottom corner, holding down the left mouse button, and dragging (moving) the mouse.

Enlarging the text in the Help window

In addition to, or as an alternative to, resizing the Help window, you can enlarge or shrink the text inside the Help window: Make it larger so you can read it easier or smaller so you can cram more text into the limited confines of the Help window. To change the size of the text inside the Help window, follow these steps:

1. **Click the Help icon or press F1 to open the Help window.**

2. **Click the Use Large Text icon.**

   The Help window text changes in size. Each time you click the Use Large Text icon, it toggles between enlarging or shrinking the text.

Printing the text in the Help window

Sometimes you may find the step-by-step instructions in the Help window so useful that you may want to reference them again. Rather than open the Help window each time, you can print the step-by-step instructions so you'll always have them at your fingertips when you need them.

To print the text displayed in the Help window, follow these steps:

1. **Click the Help icon or press F1 to open the Help window.**

2. **Make sure that your printer is connected to your computer and turned on.**

3. **Click the Print icon (refer to Figure 4-4).**

   The Print dialog box appears.

4. **Choose any options in the Print dialog box (such as choosing a printer to use), and then click OK to print the current contents of the Help window.**

Part II
Working with Word

Visit www.dummies.com/extras/office2013 for great Dummies content online.

In this part . . .

- ⌐ Navigating through a document
- ⌐ Checking spelling and grammar
- ⌐ Changing fonts
- ⌐ Coloring text
- ⌐ Organizing text in tables
- ⌐ Dividing text into columns
- ⌐ Visit www.dummies.com/extras/office2013 for great Dummies content online.

Chapter 5

Typing Text in Word

The whole purpose of Microsoft Word is to let you type in text and make it look pretty so you can print or send it for other people to read. So the first step in using Microsoft Word is finding how to enter text in a Word file, called a *document.*

In every document, Word displays a blinking cursor that points to where your text will appear if you type anything. To move the cursor, you can use the keyboard or the mouse.

Moving the Cursor with the Mouse

When you move the mouse, Word turns the mouse pointer into an I-beam pointer. If you move the mouse over an area where you cannot type any text, the mouse pointer turns back into the traditional arrow, pointing up to the left.

To move the cursor with the mouse, just point and click the left mouse button once. The blinking cursor appears where you clicked the mouse.

If you have a blank page or a blank area at the end of your document, you can move the cursor anywhere within this blank area by following these steps.

1. **Move the mouse pointer over any blank area past the end of a document.**

   Word defines the *end* of a document as the spot where no more text appears. (Remember, Word considers blank spaces as text.) To find the end of a document, press Ctrl+End.

   • *In a new document:* The end of the document is in the upper-left corner where the cursor appears.

   • *In a document with existing text:* The end of the document is the last area where text appears (including spaces or tabs).

   Notice that a Left, Left Indent, Center, or Right Justification icon appears to the right or bottom of the I-beam mouse pointer, as shown in Figure 5-1.

2. **Make sure that the correct justification icon appears next to the mouse pointer.**

   For example, if you want to center-justify your text, make sure that the Center Justification icon appears at the bottom of the I-beam pointer.

   Getting the Left, Center, or Right Justification icon to appear in Step 2 can be tricky. The Left Justification icon appears most of the time. If you move the mouse pointer slightly indented from the left margin of the page, the Left Indent icon appears. To make the Center Justification icon appear, move the mouse pointer to the center of the page. To make the Right Justification icon appear, move the mouse pointer to the right edge of the page.

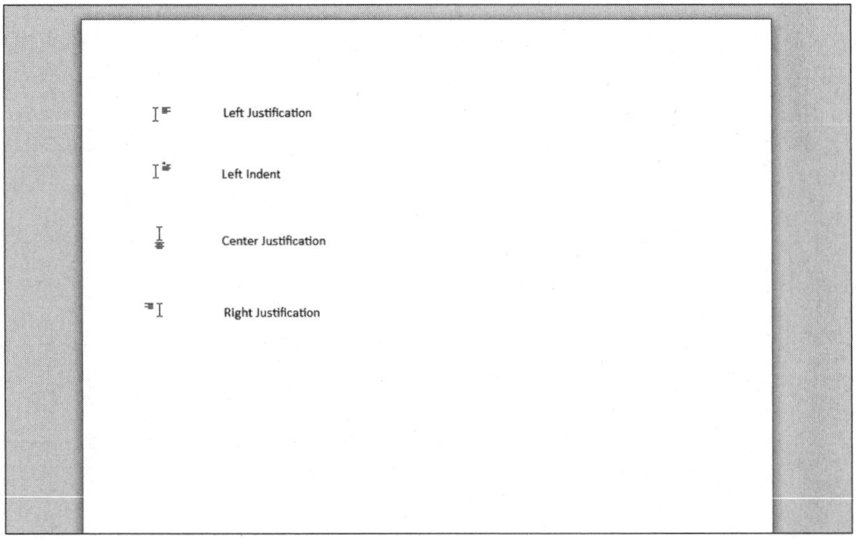

Figure 5-1:
The justification icon appears next to the mouse pointer when you move the mouse pointer past the end of a document.

I ⏸   Left Justification

I ⏸   Left Indent

I   Center Justification

⏸ I   Right Justification

3. Double-click the mouse pointer.

Word displays your cursor in the area you clicked. Any text you type now will appear justified according to the justification icon displayed in Step 3.

Moving the Cursor with the Keyboard

Moving the cursor with the mouse can be fast and easy. However, touch-typists often find that moving the cursor with the keyboard is more convenient (and sometimes faster too). Table 5-1 lists different keystroke combinations you can use to move the cursor.

You can move the cursor with both the keyboard and the mouse.

Table 5-1	Keystroke Shortcuts for Moving the Cursor in Word
Keystroke	*What It Does*
↑	Moves the cursor up one line
↓	Moves the cursor down one line
→	Moves the cursor right one character
←	Moves the cursor left one character
Ctrl+↑	Moves the cursor up to the beginning of the preceding paragraph
Ctrl+↓	Moves the cursor down to the beginning of the next paragraph
Ctrl+→	Moves the cursor right one word
Ctrl+←	Moves the cursor left one word
Home	Moves the cursor to the beginning of the line
End	Moves the cursor to the end of the line
Ctrl+Home	Moves the cursor to the beginning of a document
Ctrl+End	Moves the cursor to the end of a document
Page Up	Moves the cursor up one screen
Page Down	Moves the cursor down one screen
Ctrl+Page Up	Moves the cursor to the top of the preceding page
Ctrl+Page Down	Moves the cursor to the top of the next page

Navigating through a Document

If you have a large document that consists of many pages, you won't be able to see all the pages at the same time. Instead, you'll have to scroll through your document by using either the mouse or the keyboard.

Navigating with the mouse

To scroll through a document with the mouse, you have two choices:

- ✔ Use the vertical scroll bar that appears on the right side of every document window.
- ✔ Use the scroll wheel of your mouse (if your mouse has a scroll wheel).

Using the scroll bar

The scroll bar gives you multiple ways to navigate through a document, as shown in Figure 5-2:

Scroll box

Up arrow

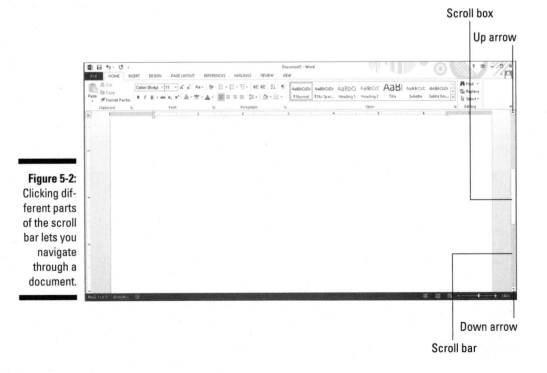

Figure 5-2: Clicking different parts of the scroll bar lets you navigate through a document.

Down arrow

Scroll bar

- ✔ **Up arrow (↑):** Moves up one line at a time.

- ✔ **Down arrow (↓):** Moves down one line at a time.

- ✔ **Scroll box:** Dragging the scroll box up displays different pages. Moving the scroll box up moves closer to the beginning; moving the scroll box down moves closer to the end.

- ✔ **Scroll area:** Clicking above the scroll box moves the document one screen up; clicking below the scroll box moves the document one screen down.

Using a mouse scroll wheel

If your mouse has a scroll wheel, you can use that to scroll through a document in one of two ways:

- ✔ Move the mouse pointer over your document and roll the scroll wheel up or down.

- ✔ Move the mouse pointer over your document and click the scroll wheel; then move the mouse up or down. (The scrolling speeds up the farther up or down you move the mouse from the position where you clicked the scroll wheel.) Click the left mouse button or the scroll wheel to turn off automatic scrolling when you're done.

Using the Go To command

If you know the specific page number of your document that you want to scroll to, you can jump to that page right away by using the Go To command. To use the Go To command, follow these steps:

1. **Click the Home tab.**

2. **Choose one of the following:**

   - Click the downward-pointing arrow to the right of the Find icon and click Go To.

   - Press Ctrl+G.

   The Find and Replace dialog box appears with the Go To tab selected, as shown in Figure 5-3.

3. **Click in the Enter Page Number text box and type a page number.**

If you type a plus sign (+) or a minus sign (–) in front of a number, you can scroll that many pages forward or backward from the currently displayed page. For example, if the displayed page is 5, typing **–2** displays page 3 and typing **+12** displays page 17.

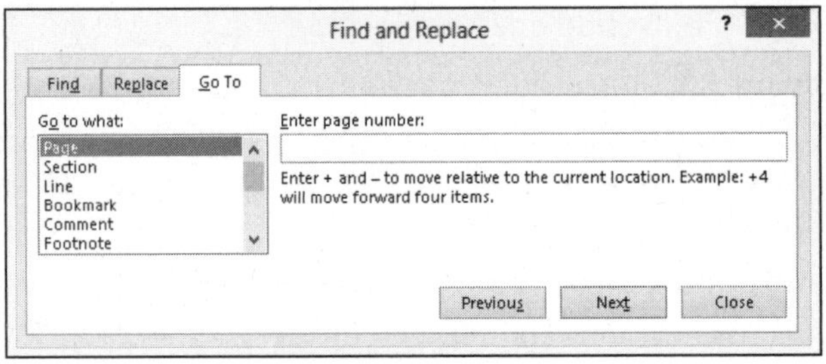

Figure 5-3:
The Go To
tab displays
a menu of
different
searching
options.

Find and Replace

| Find | Replace | Go To |

Go to what:

Page
Section
Line
Bookmark
Comment
Footnote

Enter page number:

Enter + and – to move relative to the current location. Example: +4
will move forward four items.

Previous   Next   Close

4. **Click the Go To button.**

   Word displays your chosen page.

5. **Click Close to make the Find and Replace dialog box disappear.**

Finding and Replacing Text

To help you find text, Word offers a handy Find feature. Not only can this
Find feature search for a word or phrase, but it also offers a Replace option
so you can make Word find certain words and automatically replace them
with other words.

Using the Find command

The Find command can search for a single character, word, or a group of
words. To make searching faster, you can either search an entire document
or just a specific part of a document. To make searching a document more
flexible, Word lets you search for specific words or phrases, headings, or
pages.

To search for words or phrases by using the Find command, follow these
steps:

1. **Click the Home tab.**

2. **Click the Find icon in the Editing group.**

   The Navigation Pane appears in the left side of the screen, as shown in
   Figure 5-4.

   If you click the downward-pointing arrow to the right of the Find icon, a
   menu appears that lets you choose the Find or Go To command.

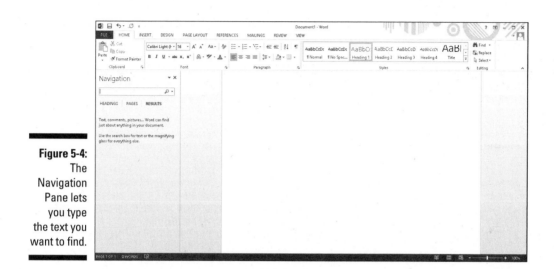

Figure 5-4:
The
Navigation
Pane lets
you type
the text you
want to find.

3. Click in the Navigation text box, type a word or phrase to find, and press Enter.

The Navigation Pane lists all matching text, as shown in Figure 5-5.

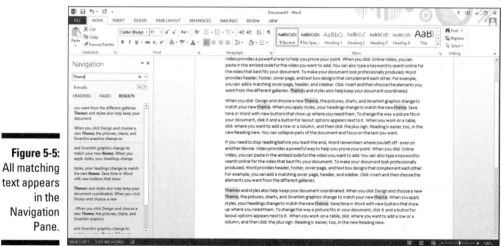

Figure 5-5:
All matching
text appears
in the
Navigation
Pane.

As you type, Word displays all matching text. So if you start typing **he**, Word will find all text that matches "he," such as "hello," "helicopter," or "help."

4. Click any of the text displayed in the Navigation Pane.

Word highlights your chosen text in your document.

5. Click the X icon that appears in the Navigation text box in the Navigation Pane.

Word clears the text you typed in Step 3.

Customizing text searching

If you just want to find a word or phrase, the ordinary Find command works, but if Word finds too much irrelevant text, you may want to take time to customize how Word searches for text. Follow these steps:

1. Click the Home tab.

2. Click the Find icon in the Editing group.

The Navigation Pane appears in the left side of the screen (refer to Figure 5-4).

3. Click the Magnifying Glass icon in the Search Document text box in the Navigation Pane.

A pull-down menu appears, as shown in Figure 5-6.

Pull-down menu

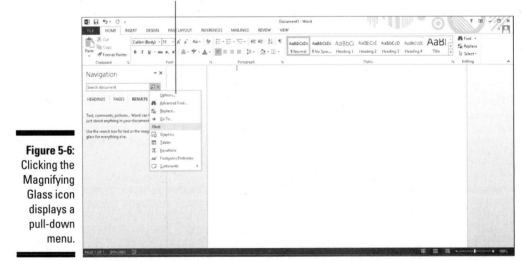

Figure 5-6:
Clicking the
Magnifying
Glass icon
displays a
pull-down
menu.

4. Click Options.

A Find Options dialog box appears, as shown in Figure 5-7.

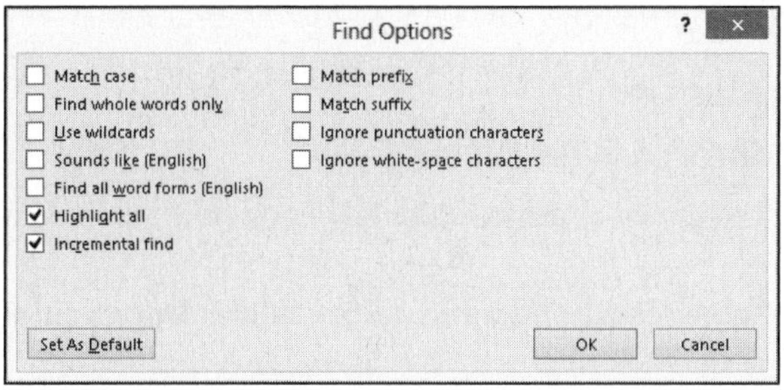

Figure 5-7:
The Find
Options
dialog box
provides
options for
searching
text.

Find Options

☐ Match case   ☐ Match prefix
☐ Find whole words only ☐ Match suffix
☐ Use wildcards   ☐ Ignore punctuation characters
☐ Sounds like (English) ☐ Ignore white-space characters
☐ Find all word forms (English)
☑ Highlight all
☑ Incremental find

Set As Default   OK   Cancel

5. **Select one or more options in the Find Options dialog box.**

   • *Match case:* Finds text that exactly matches the upper- and lower-case letters you type.

   • *Find whole words only:* Finds text that is not part of another word. Searching for *on* will not find words like *onion.*

   • *Use wildcards:* Lets you use the single character (?) or multiple character (*) wildcards, such as searching for *d?g,* which will find *dog* or *dig;* or *b*t,* which will find *but, butt,* or *boost.*

   • *Sounds like:* Searches for words based on their phonetic pronunciation, such as finding *elephant* when searching for *elefant.*

   • *Find all word forms:* Finds all variations of a word, such as finding *run, ran,* and *running.*

   • *Match prefix:* Searches for the prefix of words, such as finding words like *interact* just by searching for *inter.*

   • *Match suffix:* Searches for the suffix of words, such as finding words like *runner* or *keeper* just by searching for *er.*

   • *Ignore punctuation characters:* Ignores punctuation characters in text, such as finding the phrase *Hello, there* when you searched for *Hello there* in the Navigation Pane.

   • *Ignore white-space characters:* Ignores spaces when searching, such as finding the phrase *BotheCat* when you searched for *Bo the Cat* in the Navigation Pane.

6. **Click OK to make the Find Options dialog box disappear.**

   The next time you search for text, Word will use the options you chose.

Searching by headings

Rather than search for a word or phrase, you may want to browse a long document by headings. After you find the heading you want, then you can edit or read the text underneath that heading.

To search by headings, follow these steps:

1. **Click the Home tab.**

2. **Click the Find icon in the Editing group.**

   The Navigation Pane appears in the left side of the screen (refer to Figure 5-4).

3. **Click the Headings tab (underneath the Search Document text box) in the Navigation Pane.**

   A list of headings appears in the Navigation Pane, as shown in Figure 5-8.

List of headings   Heading

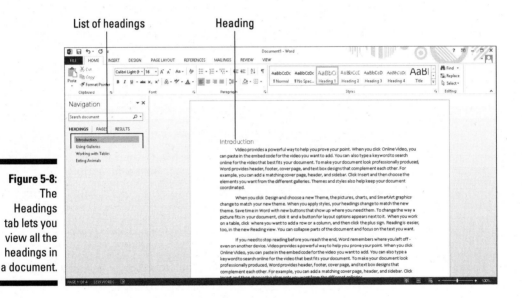

Figure 5-8:
The
Headings
tab lets you
view all the
headings in
a document.

4. **Click a heading in the Navigation Pane.**

   Word displays the heading in your document.

Browsing through pages

In a long document, you often have to scroll or flip through multiple pages to find specific text. To simplify this task, Word can display all pages as thumbnail images. You can browse through these thumbnail images and click the page that you want to view in more detail.

To browse through multiple pages, follow these steps:

1. **Click the Home tab.**

2. Click the Find icon in the Editing group.

The Navigation Pane appears in the left side of the screen (refer to Figure 5-4).

3. Click the Pages tab (the middle tab) in the Navigation Pane.

Word displays thumbnail images of all your pages, as shown in Figure 5-9.

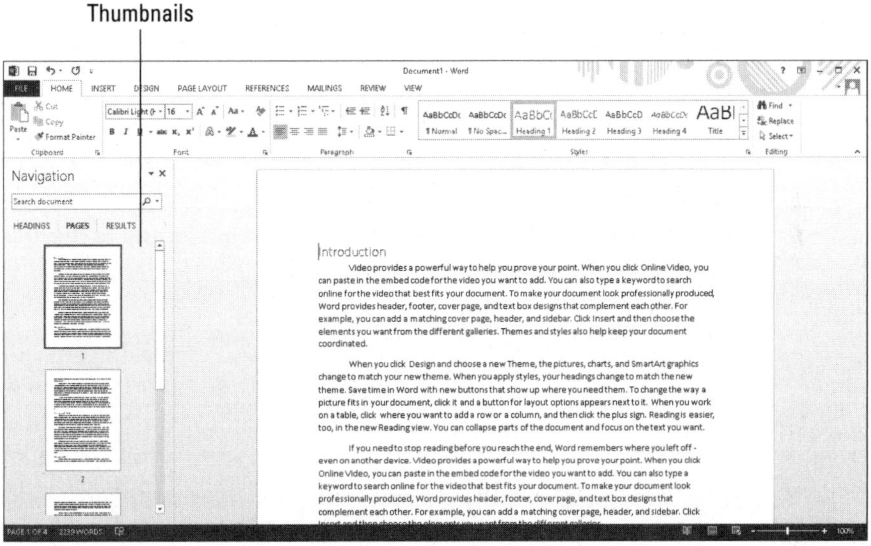

Thumbnails

Figure 5-9: Browsing through thumbnail images of multiple pages.

4. Click the thumbnail image of the page that you want to view.

Word displays your chosen page.

Using the Find and Replace command

Rather than just find a word or phrase, you may want to find that text and replace it with something else. To use the Find and Replace command, follow these steps:

1. Click the Home tab.

2. Click the Replace icon in the Editing group. (You can also press Ctrl+H.)

The Find and Replace dialog box appears, as shown in Figure 5-10.

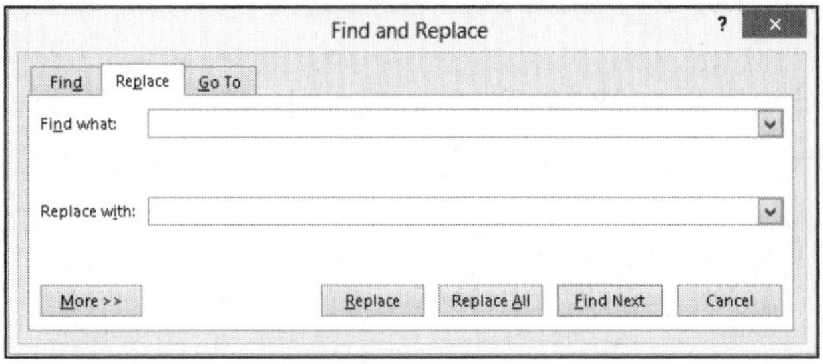

Figure 5-10:
The Find and Replace dialog box provides options for replacing text.

3. **Click in the Find What text box and type a word or phrase to find.**

4. **Click in the Replace With text box and type a word or phrase to replace the text you typed in Step 3.**

5. **(Optional) Click the More button and choose any additional options, as shown in Figure 5-11.**

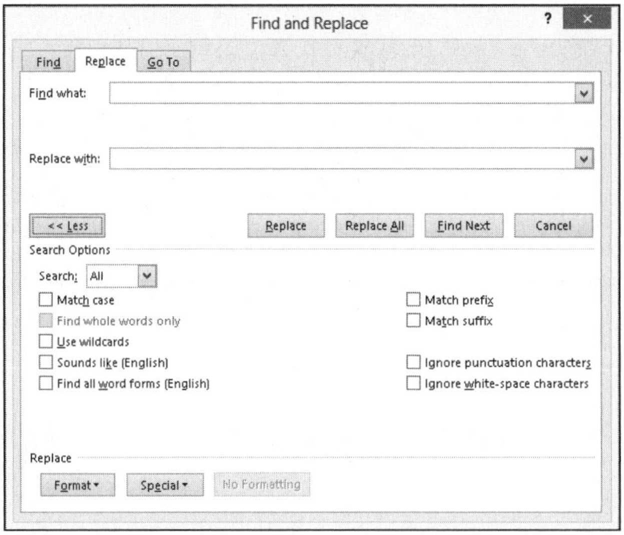

Figure 5-11:
The More button displays additional options in the Find and Replace dialog box.

6. **Click one of the following buttons:**

   • *Replace:* Replaces the currently highlighted text.

   • *Replace All:* Searches and replaces text throughout the entire document.

   • *Find Next:* Searches from the current cursor location to the end of the document.

7. **Click Find Next to search for additional occurrences of the text you typed in Step 3.**

8. **Click Cancel to make the Find and Replace dialog box disappear.**

Checking Your Spelling

As you type, Word tries to correct your spelling automatically. (Try it! Type **tjhe**, and Word will automatically change it to *the* in the blink of an eye.) If you type something that Word doesn't recognize, it underlines it with a red squiggly line.

Just because Word underlines a word doesn't necessarily mean that the word is spelled incorrectly. It could be a proper name, a foreign word, or just a word that Word isn't smart enough to recognize.

To correct any words that Word underlines with a red squiggly line, follow these steps:

1. **Right-click any word underlined with a red squiggly line.**

   A pop-up menu appears, as shown in Figure 5-12.

Pop-up menu

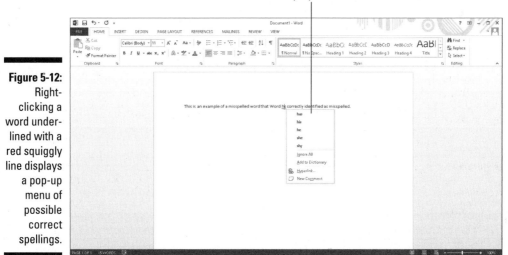

Figure 5-12: Right-clicking a word underlined with a red squiggly line displays a pop-up menu of possible correct spellings.

2. Choose one of the following:

- *The word you want:* Click the correct spelling of the word that appears in bold in the pop-up menu.

- *Ignore All:* This tells Word to ignore this word throughout your document.

- *Add to Dictionary:* This tells Word to remember this word and never flag it again as a misspelled word.

Checking Your Grammar

Sometimes Word may underline one or more words with a green squiggly line to highlight possible grammar errors. To correct any grammar errors, follow these steps:

1. Right-click any text underlined with a green squiggly line.

A pop-up menu appears.

2. Choose Grammar.

A Grammar pane appears on the right side of the window, listing suggested corrections (as shown in Figure 5-13).

Grammar pane

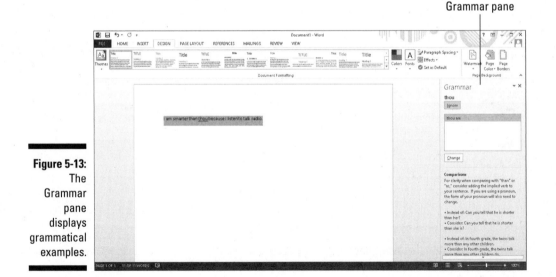

Figure 5-13:
The Grammar pane displays grammatical examples.

Although Word's spell checking and grammar checking can catch most errors, it probably won't catch all of them — and it may even highlight words and sentences that are actually correct. Use spell check and grammar check as a tool, but don't rely on it to do all your proofing for you.

Viewing a Document

Word can display your document in one of five views, which can help you better understand the layout, margins, and page breaks in your document:

- ✔ **Read Mode:** Displays pages that require you to slide them horizontally to view adjacent pages.
- ✔ **Print Layout:** Displays page breaks as thick, dark horizontal bars so you can clearly see where a page ends and begins (this is the default view).
- ✔ **Web Layout:** Displays your document exactly as it would appear if you saved it as a web page.
- ✔ **Outline:** Displays your document as outline headings and subheadings.
- ✔ **Draft:** Displays the document without top or bottom page margins where page breaks appear as dotted lines.

Switching between views

Microsoft Word gives you two ways to switch between different document views, as shown in Figure 5-14:

- ✔ Click the view icons in the bottom-right corner of your document window.

    If you do so, you can choose only Read Mode, Print Layout, and Web Layout.
- ✔ Click the View tab and then click the view you want to use, such as Print Layout or Draft view.

Print Layout view can help you edit and create the design of your pages. If you just want to focus on writing and not see your page margins or headers and footers, you may be happier switching to Draft view instead. The two most unusual views are Read Mode and Outline views.

Document1 - Word
FILE
HOME
INSERT
DESIGN
PAGE LAYOUT
REFERENCES
MAILINGS
REVIEW
VIEW
Read Mode
Web Layout
Print Layout

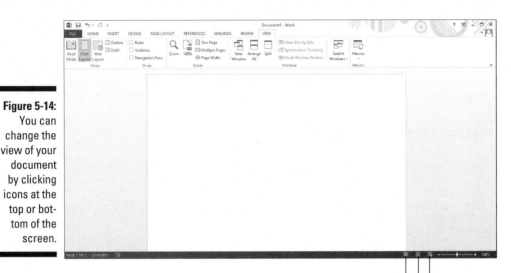

Figure 5-14: You can change the view of your document by clicking icons at the top or bottom of the screen.

Using Read Mode view

Read Mode can be handy for making text easier to read just the way you'd see it a book, as shown in Figure 5-15. To "turn the pages" of a document displayed in Read Mode view, click the Previous Screen or Next Screen button on the left and right edges of the screen.

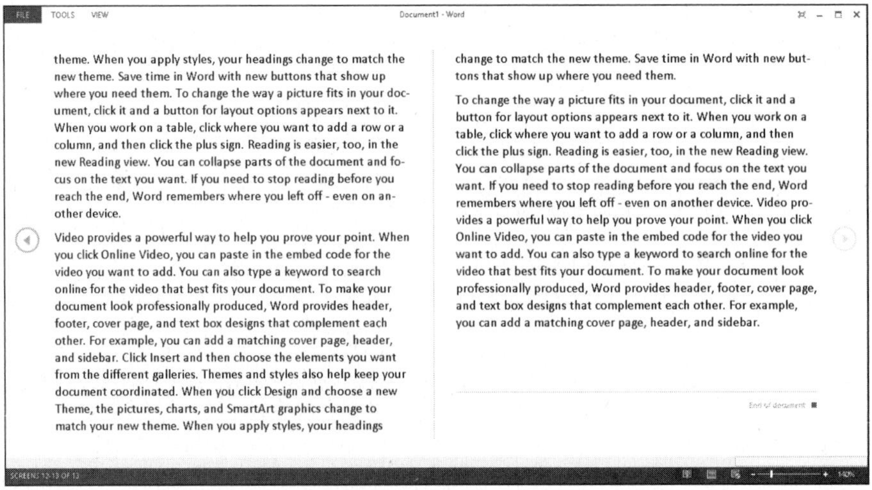

FILE TOOLS VIEW
Document1 - Word
theme. When you apply styles, your headings change to match the new theme. Save time in Word with new buttons that show up where you need them. To change the way a picture fits in your document, click it and a button for layout options appears next to it. When you work on a table, click where you want to add a row or a column, and then click the plus sign. Reading is easier, too, in the new Reading view. You can collapse parts of the document and focus on the text you want. If you need to stop reading before you reach the end, Word remembers where you left off - even on another device.
Video provides a powerful way to help you prove your point. When you click Online Video, you can paste in the embed code for the video you want to add. You can also type a keyword to search online for the video that best fits your document. To make your document look professionally produced, Word provides header, footer, cover page, and text box designs that complement each other. For example, you can add a matching cover page, header, and sidebar. Click Insert and then choose the elements you want from the different galleries. Themes and styles also help keep your document coordinated. When you click Design and choose a new Theme, the pictures, charts, and SmartArt graphics change to match your new theme. When you apply styles, your headings
change to match the new theme. Save time in Word with new buttons that show up where you need them.
To change the way a picture fits in your document, click it and a button for layout options appears next to it. When you work on a table, click where you want to add a row or a column, and then click the plus sign. Reading is easier, too, in the new Reading view. You can collapse parts of the document and focus on the text you want. If you need to stop reading before you reach the end, Word remembers where you left off - even on another device. Video provides a powerful way to help you prove your point. When you click Online Video, you can paste in the embed code for the video you want to add. You can also type a keyword to search online for the video that best fits your document. To make your document look professionally produced, Word provides header, footer, cover page, and text box designs that complement each other. For example, you can add a matching cover page, header, and sidebar.

Figure 5-15: Read Mode view lets you read a document in the form of an open book.

To exit Full Screen Reading view, choose one of the following:

- ✔ Press Esc.
- ✔ Click the Print Layout or Web Layout button in the bottom-right corner of the screen.

Using Outline view

Outline view divides a document into sections defined by headings and text. A *heading* represents a main idea. Text contains one or more paragraphs that are "attached" to a particular heading. A *subheading* lets you divide a main idea (heading) into multiple parts. A typical outline may look like Figure 5-16.

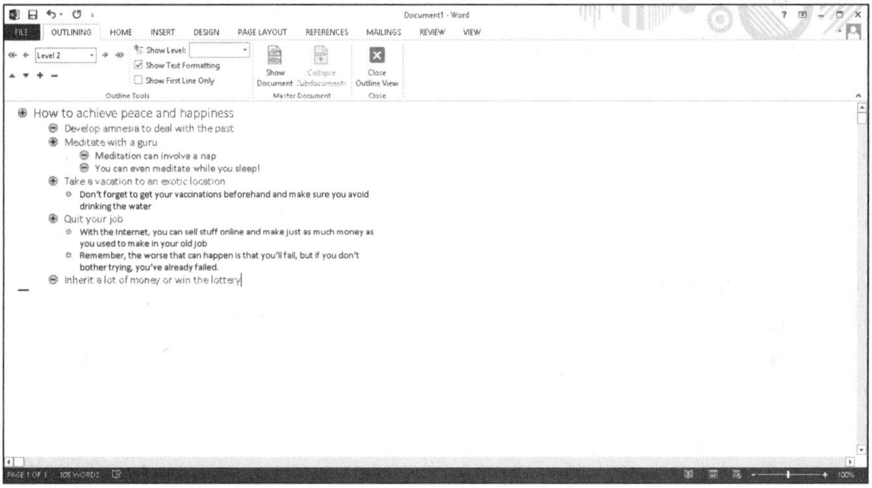

Figure 5-16: A typical outline consists of headings, subheadings, and text that you can expand or collapse to hide subheadings or text from view.

Within Outline view, you can

- ✔ **Collapse headings** to hide parts (subheadings and text) temporarily from view.
- ✔ **Rearrange headings** to move subheadings and text easily within a large document.

Moving a heading automatically moves all subheadings and text. Instead of cutting and pasting multiple paragraphs, Outline view lets you rearrange a document by just moving headings around.

To switch to Outline view, click the View tab and then click the Outline icon.

Defining a heading

Outline view considers each line as either a heading or text. To define a line as either a heading style (Level 1 to Level 9) or text, make sure you have switched to Outline view and then follow these steps:

1. **Move the cursor on the line that you want to define as a heading or text.**

2. **Click in the Outline Level list box and choose a heading level, such as Level 2.**

Word displays Level 1 headings in large type justified to the far-left margin. Level 2 headings appear in smaller type that's slightly indented to the right, Level 3 headings appear in even smaller type that's indented farther to the right, and so on, as shown in Figure 5-17.

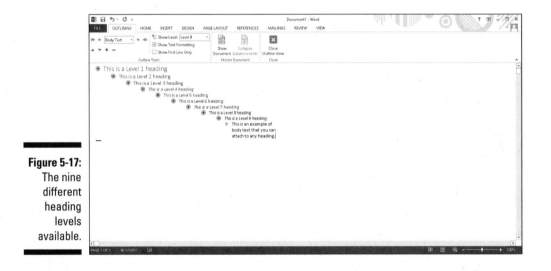

Figure 5-17: The nine different heading levels available.

To create a heading quickly, move the cursor to the end of an existing heading and press Enter to create an identical heading. For example, if you put the cursor at the end of a Level 3 heading and press Enter, Word creates a new blank Level 3 heading.

Promoting and demoting a heading

After you define a heading (such as a Level 1 or Level 3 heading), you can always change its level, such as changing a Level 1 heading to a Level 2 heading or vice versa:

✔ When you raise a heading from one level to another (such as from Level 3 to Level 2), that's *promoting*.

✔ When you lower a heading (such as from Level 4 to Level 5), that's *demoting*.

A Level 1 heading cannot be promoted because Level 1 is the highest heading. Likewise, a Level 9 heading cannot be demoted because Level 9 is the lowest heading.

To promote or demote a heading to a different level, follow these steps:

1. **Using either the mouse or the keyboard, move the cursor to the heading you want to promote or demote.**

2. **Choose one of the following methods:**

   • Click the Outline Level list box and click a level (such as Level 2).

   • Press Tab (to promote) or Shift+Tab (to demote) the heading.

   • Click the Promote or Demote arrow.

   • Move the mouse pointer over the circle that appears to the left of the heading, hold down the left mouse button, drag the mouse right or left, and then release the left mouse button.

Promoting or demoting a heading automatically promotes or demotes any subheadings or text attached to the promoted or demoted heading. That way the subheadings or text maintain the same relationship to the heading.

Moving headings up and down

You can move headings up or down within a document.

To move a heading, follow these steps:

1. **Using either the mouse or the keyboard, move the cursor to the heading you want to promote or demote.**

2. **Choose one of the following methods:**

   • Click the Move Up or Move Down arrow.

   • Press Alt+Shift+↑ or Alt+Shift+↓.

   • Move the mouse pointer over the circle that appears to the left of the heading, hold down the left mouse button, drag the mouse up or down, and then release the left mouse button.

If you collapse a heading before moving it, you can move any subheadings or text underneath that heading.

Creating text

Text can consist of a single sentence, multiple sentences, or several paragraphs. Text always appears indented underneath a heading (or subheading). To create text, follow these steps:

1. **Move the cursor to the end of a heading or subheading.**

   This is the heading (or subheading) that your text will be attached to if you move the heading (or subheading).

2. **Press Enter.**

   Word creates a blank heading.

3. **Click the Demote to Body Text button (or click in the Outline Level list box and choose Body Text).**

   Word displays a bullet point, indented underneath the heading you chose in Step 1.

4. **Type your text.**

Collapsing and expanding headings and subheadings

If a heading or subheading contains any subheadings or text underneath, you can collapse that heading. *Collapsing* a heading simply hides any indented subheadings or text from view temporarily. *Expanding* a heading displays any previously hidden subheadings or text.

To collapse a heading along with all subheadings or body text underneath it, double-click the plus (+) icon that appears to the left of the heading.

If you just want to collapse the subheading or body text immediately underneath a heading, choose one of the following:

  ✔ Move the cursor anywhere in the heading that you want to collapse, and then click the Collapse button.

  ✔ Press Alt+Shift++ (plus-sign key).

To expand a collapsed heading to reveal all subheadings and body text, double-click the plus icon that appears to the left of the heading.

If you just want to expand the subheading or body text immediately underneath a collapsed heading, choose one of the following:

  ✔ Move the cursor anywhere in the heading that you want to expand, and then click the Expand button.

  ✔ Press Alt+Shift+– (minus-sign key).

Chapter 6

Formatting Text

- -

- -

*A*fter you type text into a document, edit it, and check it for spelling and grammatical errors, you're ready to make it look pretty — a process known as *formatting text*. A properly formatted document can make your text easy to read, while a poorly formatted document can make even the best writing difficult or confusing to read.

The Home tab groups Word's formatting tools into three categories:

✔ **Font:** Defines the font, font size, color, highlighting, and style (bold, italic, underline, strikethrough, superscript, subscript, and case)

✔ **Paragraph:** Defines justification (left, center, or right), line spacing, shading, borders, indentation, formatting symbols, and list style (bullets, numbered, and outline)

✔ **Styles:** Displays predefined formatting that you can apply to your text

To format any text, follow these steps:

1. **Select the text you want to format.**

2. **Choose a formatting tool.**

When you choose certain formatting commands such as italics, bold, or underline, the command you've chosen stays on until you turn it off by choosing the same command again.

As soon as you select text by dragging the mouse, Word displays the most commonly used formatting tools in a floating toolbar. You can click any icon on this floating toolbar rather than click the same icon stored on the Ribbon.

Changing the Font

The most common way to format text is to change the font. The font defines the uniform style and appearance of letters; examples include Baskerville, Old English, and **STENCIL.**

To change the font, follow these steps:

1. **Click the Home tab.**

2. **Select the text you want to change.**

3. **Click the Font list box.**

   A list of the fonts available on your computer appears, as shown in Figure 6-1.

4. **Move the mouse pointer over each font.**

   Word temporarily changes your selected text (from Step 2) so you can see how the currently highlighted font will look.

5. **Click the font you want to use.**

   Word changes your text to appear in your chosen font.

As a general rule, try not to use more than three fonts in a document. If you use too many fonts, the overall appearance can be annoying and distracting.

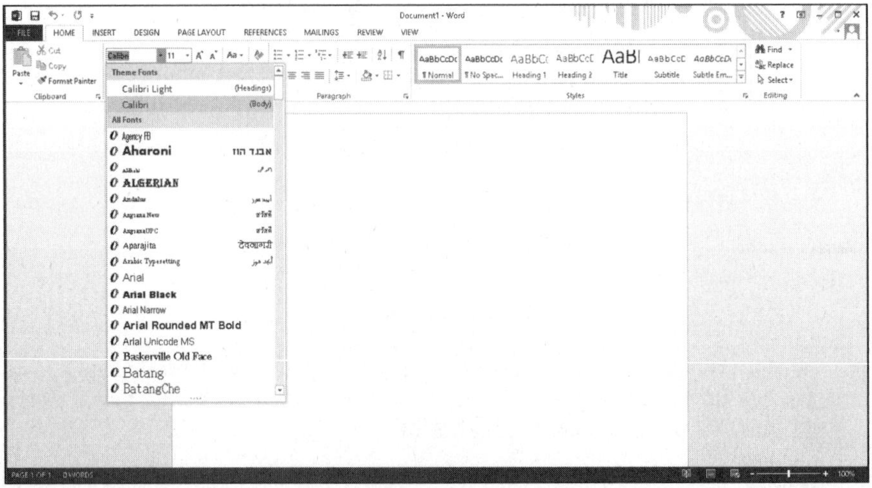

Figure 6-1:
The Font list box displays the appearance of each font.

Not all computers have the same lists of fonts, so if you plan on sharing documents with others, stick with common fonts that everybody's computers can display. The more bizarre the font, the less likely everybody will have that font on their computers.

Changing the Font Size

The *font* changes the appearance of text, but the *font size* defines how big (or small) the text may look. To change the font size, you have two choices:

- ✔ Select a numeric size from the Font Size list box.
- ✔ Choose the Grow Font/Shrink Font commands.

You can use both methods to change the font size of text. For example, you may use the Font Size list box to choose an approximate size for your text, and then use the Grow Font/Shrink Font commands to fine-tune the font size.

To change the font size, follow these steps:

1. **Click the Home tab.**

2. **Select the text you want to change.**

3. **Choose one of the following:**

    - Click the Font Size list box and then click a number, such as 12 or 24, as shown in Figure 6-2.

    - Click the Grow Font or Shrink Font icon.

Sizes

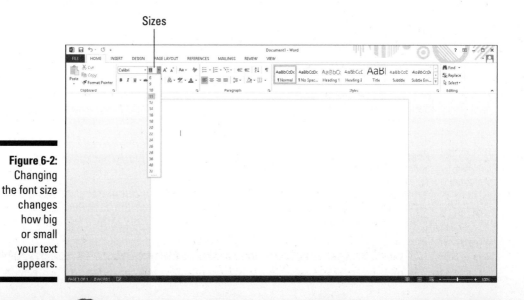

Figure 6-2:
Changing the font size changes how big or small your text appears.

Changing the Text Style

The text style defines the appearance of text in one or more of the following ways:

- **Bold:** Press Ctrl+B.
- *Italic:* Press Ctrl+I.
- <u>Underline</u>: Press Ctrl+U.
- ~~Strikethrough~~: This formatting draws a line through text.
- Subscript: Use this to create text that falls below the text line, as in the 2 in H_2O.
- Superscript: Use this to create text that sits higher than the top of the text line, as in the 2 in $E = mc^2$.

To change the style of text, follow these steps:

1. **Click the Home tab.**
2. **Select the text you want to change.**
3. **Click a Style icon, such as Bold or Underline.**
4. **Repeat Step 3 for each additional style you want to apply to your text (such as *italic* and <u>underlining</u>).**

If you select any style change without selecting any text, Word applies your style changes to any new text you type from the cursor's current position.

Changing Colors

Color can emphasize text. There are two ways to use color:

- Change the color of the text (Font color).
- Highlight the text with a different color (Text Highlight color).

Changing the color of text

When you change the color of text, you're physically displaying a different color for each letter. Normally Word displays text in black, but you can change the color to anything you want, such as bright red or dark green.

If you choose a light color for your text, it may be hard to read against a white background.

To change the color of text, follow these steps:

1. **Click the Home tab.**
2. **Select the text you want to color.**
3. **Click the downward-pointing arrow to the right of the Font Color icon.**

   A color palette appears, as shown in Figure 6-3.
4. **Click a color.**

   Word displays your selected text (from Step 2) in your chosen color.

Color palette

Figure 6-3:
Coloring text
in different
ways can
emphasize
parts of your
document.

After you choose a color, that color appears directly on the Font Color icon. Now you can select text and click directly on the Font Color icon (not the downward-pointing arrow) to color your text.

Highlighting text with color

Highlighting text mimics coloring chunks of text with a highlighting marker that students often use to emphasize passages in a book. To highlight text, follow these steps.

1. **Click the Home tab.**

2. **Select the text you want to highlight.**

3. **Click the downward-pointing arrow to the right of the Text Highlight Color icon.**

   A color palette appears, as shown in Figure 6-4.

Color palette

4. **Click a color.**

   Word highlights your selected text (from Step 2) in your chosen color.

5. **Press Esc (or click the Text Highlight Color icon again) to turn off the Text Highlight Color command.**

To remove a highlight, select the text and choose the same color again or choose No Color.

If no text is selected and the Text Highlight Color currently displays a color you want to use (such as yellow), you can click the Text Highlight Color icon (not its downward-pointing arrow). This turns the mouse pointer into a marker icon. Now you can select and highlight text in one step.

Using Text Effects

If you want a fast way to format text to make it appear colorful like a neon sign, then you can use Text Effects by following these steps:

1. **Click the Home tab.**

2. **Select the text you want to modify.**

3. **Click the Text Effects icon.**

   A menu of different effects appears, as shown in Figure 6-5.

Text Effects

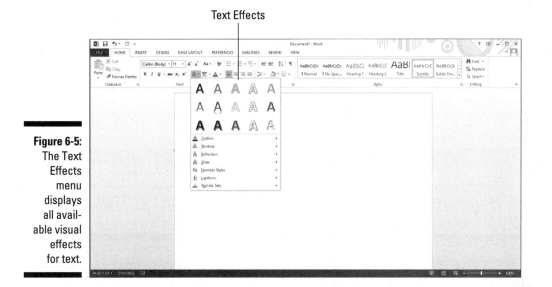

Figure 6-5:
The Text
Effects
menu
displays
all avail-
able visual
effects
for text.

4. **Click an effect.**

   Word changes your selected text (from Step 2) in your chosen visual effect.

Text Effects are a special feature of recent versions of Office. If you save your document in an older Word file format (such as Word 97-2003), you won't be able to use Text Effects.

Justifying Text Alignment

Word can align text in one of four ways, as shown in Figure 6-6:

- ✔ **Left:** Text appears flush against the left margin but ragged on the right margin.
- ✔ **Center:** Every line appears centered within the left and right margins.
- ✔ **Right:** Text appears flush against the right margin but ragged on the left margin.
- ✔ **Justified:** Text appears flush against both the left and right margins.

Justified

Right aligned

Centered

Left aligned

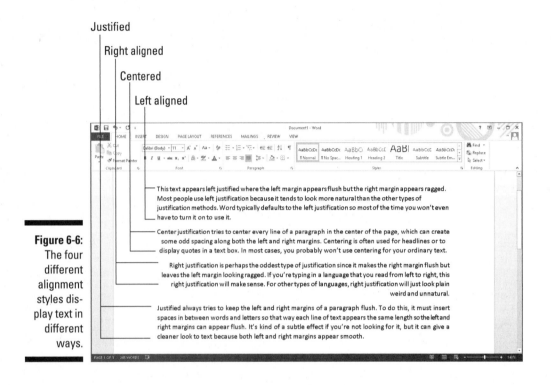

Figure 6-6:
The four
different
alignment
styles dis-
play text in
different
ways.

This text appears left justified where the left margin appears flush but the right margin appears ragged. Most people use left justification because it tends to look more natural than the other types of justification methods. Word typically defaults to the left justification so most of the time you won't even have to turn it on to use it.

Center justification tries to center every line of a paragraph in the center of the page, which can create some odd spacing along both the left and right margins. Centering is often used for headlines or to display quotes in a text box. In most cases, you probably won't use centering for your ordinary text.

Right justification is perhaps the oddest type of justification since it makes the right margin flush but leaves the left margin looking ragged. If you're typing in a language that you read from left to right, this right justification will make sense. For other types of languages, right justification will just look plain weird and unnatural.

Justified always tries to keep the left and right margins of a paragraph flush. To do this, it must insert spaces in between words and letters so that way each line of text appears the same length so the left and right margins can appear flush. It's kind of a subtle effect if you're not looking for it, but it can give a cleaner look to text because both left and right margins appear smooth.

To align text, follow these steps:

1. **Click the Home tab.**

2. **Move the cursor anywhere in the text you want to align.**

3. **Click one of the alignment icons, such as Center or Justify.**

Rather than click an alignment icon, you can use one of the alignment key-stroke shortcuts as follows: Align Left (Ctrl+L), Center (Ctrl+E), Align Right (Ctrl+R), or Justify (Ctrl+J).

Adjusting Line Spacing

Line spacing defines how close lines appear stacked on top of each other. To change the line spacing of text, follow these steps:

1. **Click the Home tab.**

2. **Select the text where you want to adjust the line spacing.**

3. **Click the Line Spacing icon.**

    A pull-down menu appears, as shown in Figure 6-7.

4. **Click the line spacing you want, such as 1 (single spacing) or 3 (triple spacing).**

Line spacing menu

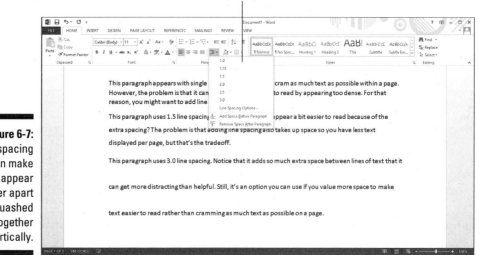

Figure 6-7:
Line spacing
can make
text appear
farther apart
or squashed
together
vertically.

If you click the Line Spacing Options in the pull-down menu, you can precisely define your own line spacing, such as 2.75 or 3.13. Line spacing depends on the largest font used in your text. Larger fonts will create different line spacing from that of smaller fonts, even if the setting for line spacing (say, 2.0) is identical.

By default, Word automatically adds a blank line between paragraphs regardless of the line spacing you choose. To get rid of this extra space between paragraphs, click the Page Layout tab, click in the After text box in the Paragraph group, and type **0** (zero). (The default value may be 8 or 10 pt.)

Making Lists

Word can organize and arrange text in three types of lists:

✔ Bullets (like this list)

✔ Numbering

✔ Multilevel list

You can create a list from scratch or convert existing text into a list. To create a list from scratch, follow these steps:

1. **Click the Home tab.**
2. **Move the cursor where you want to create a list.**
3. **Click the Bullets, Numbering, or Multilevel List icon.**

   Word creates your list (bulleted or numbered).

4. **Type your text and press Enter to create another blank item in your list.**
5. **Repeat Step 4 for each additional bullet or numbered item you want to make.**

If you have existing text, you can convert it into a list by following these steps:

1. **Click the Home tab.**
2. **Select the text you want to convert into a list.**
3. **Click the Bullets, Numbering, or Outline Numbering icon.**

   Word converts your selected text into your chosen list where each paragraph appears as a separate item in the list.

Indenting list items

After you create a list, you may want to indent one list item underneath another one. To indent an item in a list, follow these steps:

1. **Move the cursor anywhere in the text in the list item you want to indent.**
2. **Press the Home key to move the cursor to the front of the line.**
3. **Press the Tab key to indent an item to the right (or press the Shift+Tab keystroke combination to indent an item to the left).**

   When you indent a list, Word changes the number or bullet style to set the line apart from the rest of your list.

Converting list items back into text

If you have a list, you may want to convert one or more items back into ordinary text. To convert a list item into plain text, follow these steps:

1. **Click the Home tab.**

2. **Select the list items you want to convert into plain text.**

3. **Click the appropriate Bullets, Numbering, or Outline Numbering icon.**

   If you want to convert a bullet list item into text, click the Bullets icon.

Customizing a list

When you create a bullet or numbered list, you can choose from a variety of different styles. To choose a numbering style, follow these steps:

1. **Click the downward-pointing arrow to the right of a list icon, such as the Bullet or Numbering icon.**

   Make sure that you don't click the Numbering icon itself.

   A pull-down menu appears, listing all the different numbering styles available, as shown in Figure 6-8.

Numbering styles

Figure 6-8:
The different numbering styles you can choose for creating numbered lists.

2. **Click the numbering style you want.**

   The next time you click the Numbering icon, Word will use the numbering style you chose.

The changes you make to the numbering or bullet style will apply only to your current document.

Renumbering numbered lists

Numbered lists can cause special problems when you're dividing or copying them because the numbering may get out of sequence, or you may want to start numbering from a number other than one.

To change the starting number of a numbered list, follow these steps:

1. **Right-click the item that you want to renumber.**

    If you want to renumber your entire list, right-click the first item at the top of the numbered list.

    A pop-up menu appears, as shown in Figure 6-9.

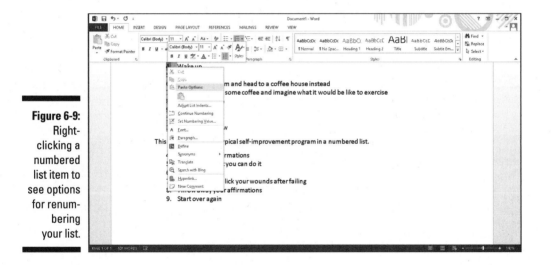

Figure 6-9:
Right-clicking a numbered list item to see options for renumbering your list.

2. **Choose one of the following:**

    • *Adjust List Indents:* Defines the indentation of your text and number in a numbered list.

- *Continue Numbering:* Changes the number of the current list item to one greater than the last numbered list item earlier in the document.

- *Set Numbering Value:* Displays the Set Numbering Value dialog box, shown in Figure 6-10, so you can change the current list item to a specific number such as 34 or 89.

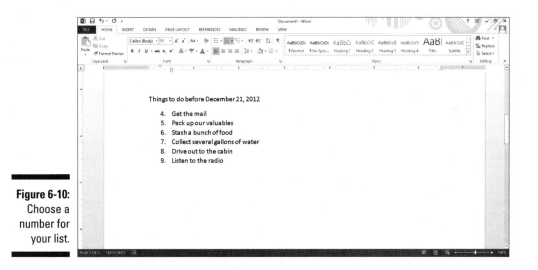

Figure 6-10:
Choose a
number for
your list.

Using the Ruler

When you create a document, Word creates page margins automatically. However, if you want to adjust the left and right page margins, or define how far the Tab key indents text, you need to use the Ruler.

By default, Word hides the Ruler to avoid cluttering up the screen. To display (or hide) the Ruler, follow these steps:

1. **Click the View tab.**

2. **Select (or clear) the Ruler check box in the Show group.**

   The Ruler appears at the top and left margin of your document, as shown in Figure 6-11.

Ruler

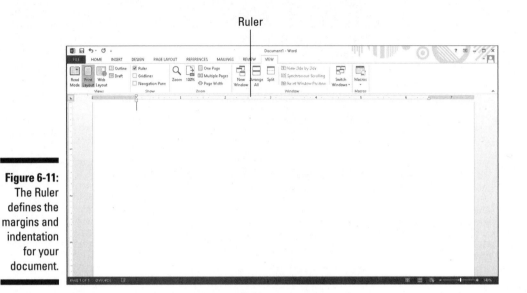

Figure 6-11:
The Ruler
defines the
margins and
indentation
for your
document.

Adjusting left and right paragraph margins

The Ruler defines the left and right margins for your paragraphs. To change these paragraph margins, follow these steps:

1. **Make sure that the Ruler appears visible.**

2. **Select any text.**

3. **Move the mouse pointer over the Left Indent icon on the Ruler (the top icon), hold down the left mouse button, and drag (move) the mouse to the right to adjust the left paragraph margin.**

   Word displays a dotted vertical line to show you where the paragraph's new left margin will be, as shown in Figure 6-12.

4. **Release the left mouse button when you're happy with the position of the left paragraph margin.**

5. **Move the mouse pointer over the Right Indent icon on the Ruler, hold down the left mouse button, and drag (move) the mouse to the left to adjust the right paragraph margin.**

   Word displays a dotted vertical line to show you where the new right paragraph margin will be.

6. **Release the left mouse button when you're happy with the position of the right paragraph margin.**

Left Indent icon

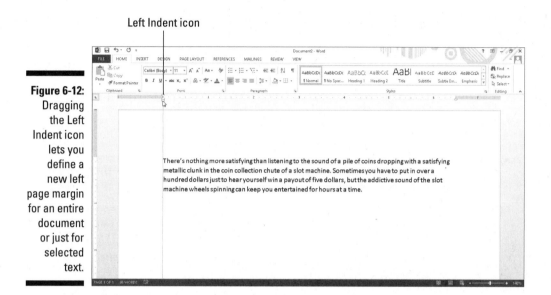

Figure 6-12:
Dragging
the Left
Indent icon
lets you
define a
new left
page margin
for an entire
document
or just for
selected
text.

Defining indentation with the Ruler

The two icons on the Ruler that define indentation are the First Line Indent
and the Hanging Indent icons. The First Line Indent icon defines the position
of (what else?) the first line of every paragraph. The Hanging Indent icon
defines the position of every line of text except for the first line, as shown in
Figure 6-13.

First Line Indent

Hanging Indent

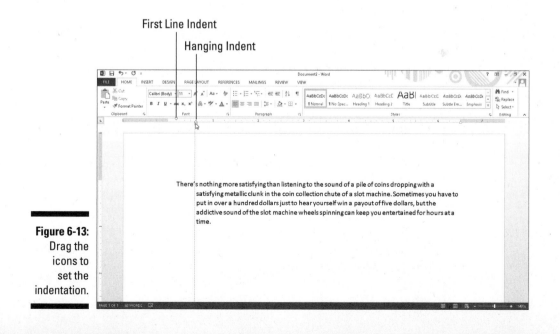

Figure 6-13:
Drag the
icons to
set the
indentation.

To define the first line and hanging indent, follow these steps:

1. **Make sure that the Ruler appears visible.**

2. **Select any text.**

3. **Move the mouse pointer over the Left Indent icon on the Ruler, hold down the left mouse button, and drag (move) the mouse to the right.**

   Word displays a dotted vertical line to show you where the new indentation margin will be.

4. **Release the left mouse button when you're happy with the position of the left indentation of your text.**

5. **Move the mouse pointer over the First Line Indent icon on the Ruler, hold down the left mouse button, and drag (move) the mouse to the right (or left).**

   Word displays a dotted vertical line to show you where the new first line indentation will be.

6. **Release the left mouse button when you're happy with the position of the first line indent position.**

Using Format Painter

Formatting can be simple, such as underlining text, or fairly complicated, such as underlining text while also changing its font and font size. After you format one chunk of text a certain way, you may want to format other parts of your document the exact same way.

Although you can take time to format text manually, it's much easier to use Format Painter instead. Format Painter tells Word, "See the way I formatted that chunk of text over there? Apply that same formatting to a new chunk of text."

To use Format Painter, follow these steps:

1. **Click the Home tab.**

2. **Select the text that contains the formatting you want to copy.**

3. **Click the Format Painter icon, as shown in Figure 6-14.**

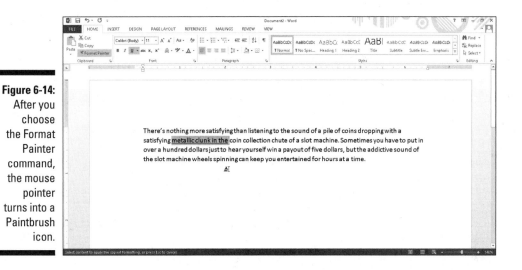

Figure 6-14:
After you
choose
the Format
Painter
command,
the mouse
pointer
turns into a
Paintbrush
icon.

4. **Select the text that you want to format. (Move the mouse pointer over the beginning of the text you want to format, hold down the left mouse button, and drag the mouse until you reach the end of the text you want to format.)**

Word applies your formatting to your selected text.

If you double-click the Format Painter icon on the Home tab, you can select and format multiple chunks of text. When you're finished formatting text, just click the Format Painter icon again to turn off this Format Painter feature.

Using Styles

As an alternative to choosing fonts, font sizes, and text styles (such as bold) individually, Word offers several predefined formatting styles. To apply a style to your text, follow these steps:

1. **Click the Home tab.**

2. **Select the text that you want to format.**

3. **Click the up/down arrows of the Styles scroll bar to scroll through the different styles available. Or click the More button to display**

a pull-down menu of all the Quick Formatting styles, as shown in Figure 6-15.

4. Move the mouse pointer over a style.

Word displays what your text will look like if you choose this style.

5. Click the style you want to use, such as Heading 1, Title, or Quote.

Word formats your text.

Figure 6-15: Clicking the More button displays a menu of all available styles.

Using Templates

In case you need to format an entire document a certain way, you may want to use templates instead. *Templates* act like preformatted documents. Word comes with several templates, but Microsoft offers several through its website as well.

To create a new document from a template, follow these steps:

1. Click the File tab and then choose New.

All available templates appear, as shown in Figure 6-16.

2. Double-click a template.

Word creates a blank document with "dummy" text to show you how the formatting looks.

3. Type new text into your newly created document.

You may need to be connected to the Internet to download some of the available templates.

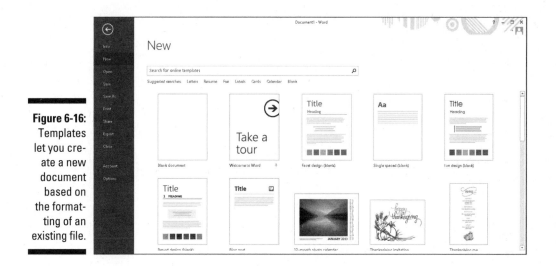

Figure 6-16:
Templates
let you cre-
ate a new
document
based on
the format-
ting of an
existing file.

Removing Formatting from Text

After you format text, you can always remove that formatting. The simplest way to do this is to apply the same formatting you want to remove. For example, if you underline text, you can remove the underlining by highlighting all the underlined text and choosing the underline command (by pressing Ctrl+U or by clicking the Underline icon).

If you want to remove multiple formatting from text, you can remove each formatting style one by one, but it's much easier just to use the Clear Formatting command instead, which removes all formatting from text, no matter how much formatting there may be.

To use the Clear Formatting command, follow these steps:

1. **Click the Home tab.**
2. **Select the text that contains the formatting you want to remove.**
3. **Click the Clear Formatting icon, as shown in Figure 6-17.**

    Word removes all formatting from your selected text.

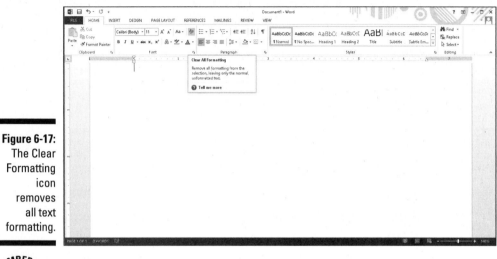

Figure 6-17:
The Clear
Formatting
icon
removes
all text
formatting.

The Clear Formatting command will not remove any highlighting you
may have applied over your text.

Chapter 7

Designing Your Pages

*T*he Insert, Design, and Page Layout tabs contain the most frequently used commands for designing the layout and appearance of your pages. You can add columns or headers and footers that display titles or page numbers, or add colors and pictures to your pages.

The Insert tab provides commands for inserting items into a document, such as new pages, tables, pictures, and headers and footers.

The Design tab provides commands for choosing spacing, colors, borders, and themes.

The Page Layout tab provides commands for defining how your pages look, such as creating columns; defining top, bottom, left, and right page margins; as well as defining how text wraps around pictures or other objects you place in the middle of a page.

Inserting New Pages

Word automatically adds new pages to your document as you write. However, Word also gives you the option of adding a new page anywhere in your document, such as in the middle or the beginning.

To insert a new, blank page into your document, follow these steps:

1. **Click the Insert tab.**

2. **Move the cursor to where you want to insert the new page.**

3. **Click the Blank Page icon in the Pages group.**

    Word adds a blank page to your document where the cursor appears. So if you put the cursor between two sentences and insert a blank page, the first sentence will appear on one page, a blank page will appear next, and the second sentence will appear after the blank page.

You don't need to add a page to the end of a document if you're still creating new text. Just move the cursor to the end of your document (Ctrl+End), start typing, and Word automatically adds new pages at the end of your document.

Adding (and Deleting) a Cover Page

Rather than add more pages on which to type text, you can just add a *cover page* that is the first page anyone can read in the document. A cover page typically displays a title and any additional information, such as your company name and a date.

To create a cover page, follow these steps:

1. **Click the Insert tab.**

2. **Click the Cover Page icon in the Pages group.**

    Word displays a list of cover-page designs, as shown in Figure 7-1.

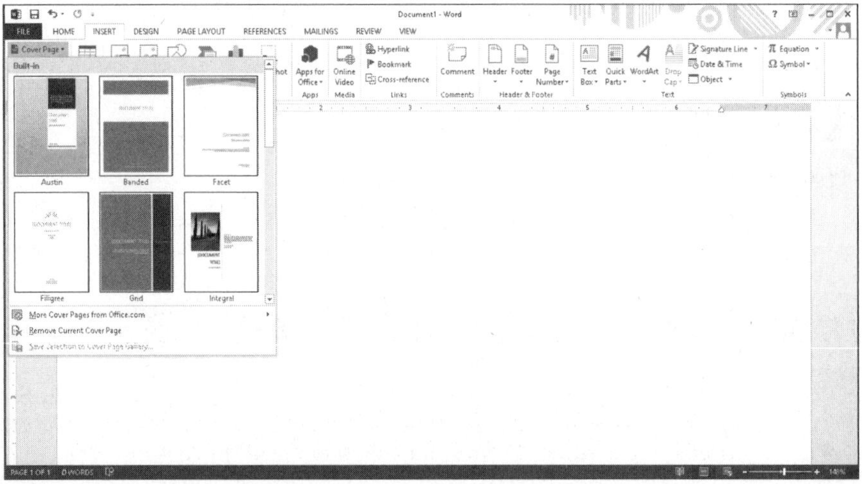

Figure 7-1:
Word can insert a variety of preformatted cover pages into your document.

3. **Click a cover-page design.**

   Word adds your chosen cover page as the first page of your document.

A document can have only one cover page at a time. If you choose another cover page, Word deletes your current cover page and replaces it with the new one you chose.

After you add a cover page, you may want to delete it later. To delete a cover page, follow these steps:

1. **Click the Insert tab.**
2. **Click Cover Page in the Pages group.**

   A pull-down menu appears (refer to Figure 7-1).

3. **Choose Remove Current Cover Page.**

   Word deletes your cover page.

Inserting Page Breaks

Rather than insert a new page, you may want to break text on an existing page into two pages. To insert a page break into your document, follow these steps:

1. **Move the cursor where you want to break your document into two pages.**
2. **Click the Insert tab.**
3. **Click the Page Break icon in the Pages group.**

   Word breaks your document into two pages.

To delete a page break, move the cursor to the top of the page directly following the page break you want to delete. Then press Backspace until Word deletes the page break.

As an alternative to following Steps 2 and 3 in the preceding step list, you can just press Ctrl+Enter to create a page break at the cursor's current location.

Inserting Headers and Footers

Headers and footers appear at the top (headers) and bottom (footers) on one or more pages of your document. Headers and footers can display information such as titles, chapter names, dates, and page numbers.

Creating a header (or footer)

To create a header or footer, follow these steps:

1. **Click the Insert tab.**

2. **Click the Header or Footer icon in the Header & Footer group.**

   A pull-down menu appears.

3. **Click Edit Header (or Edit Footer).**

   Word displays your header or footer.

   You can click a predefined header (or footer) that's already formatted to look pretty so you don't have to spend time formatting it yourself.

   Headers and footers are visible only when you display a document in Print Layout view.

4. **Type, edit, or delete any text you want to change.**

5. **(Optional) Click the Date & Time or Page Number icons of the Design contextual tools to insert the date and time or page numbers, respectively.**

6. **Click the Close Header and Footer icon.**

   Word dims your header and footer text.

Defining which pages display a header (or footer)

Usually when you define a header or footer, Word displays that header or footer on every page of your document. However, Word gives you the option of displaying a different header and footer for your first page only, or displaying different headers and footers for odd- and even-numbered pages.

Creating a unique header or footer for your first page

Often you want a header or footer to display page numbers and document or chapter titles — just not on the first page of your document. To create a unique header or footer that appears only on your first page, follow these steps:

1. **Click the Insert tab, click the Header icon in the Header & Footer group, and choose Edit Header.**

   The Header & Footer Tools Design tab appears, as shown in Figure 7-2.

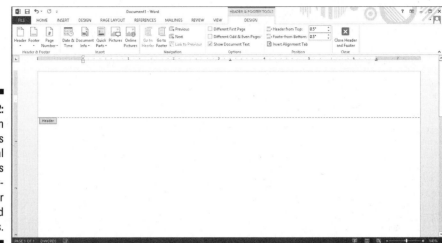

Figure 7-2:
The Design
tab provides
additional
commands
for modify-
ing your
headers and
footers.

2. **Select the Different First Page check box in the Options group.**

   Word displays a header or footer with the name First Page Header
   or First Page Footer.

3. **Click the Close Header and Footer icon.**

   Word dims your header and footer text.

Creating unique headers and footers for odd and even pages

Sometimes you may want different headers or footers to appear on even or
odd pages. In most books, even page numbers (even headers) appear in the
upper-left corner; odd page numbers (odd headers) appear in the upper-right
corner. To create this effect in your own documents, you need to create different headers to appear on odd- and even-numbered pages.

To create a different header or footer for odd- and even-numbered pages,
follow these steps:

1. **Click the Insert tab, click the Header icon in the Header & Footer
   group, and choose Edit Header.**

   The Header & Footer Tools Design tab appears.

2. **Select the Different Odd & Even Pages check box in the Options group.**

   Word displays a header or footer with the name Odd Page Header or
   Even Page Footer.

3. **Click the Close Header and Footer icon.**

4. **Switch to another page.**

5. **Repeat Steps 2 through 4 to define the other odd or even header.**

   If an odd page number originally appeared in Step 2, switch to an even page number (or vice versa) for Step 5.

Deleting a header (or footer)

In case you want to get rid of a header or footer, you can always delete it by following these steps:

1. **Click the Insert tab.**

2. **Click the Header or Footer icon in the Header & Footer group.**

   A pull-down menu appears.

3. **Click Remove Header (or Remove Footer).**

   Word removes your header or footer.

Organizing Text in Tables

Tables organize text into rows and columns, which can make the text easy to type, edit, and format while spacing it correctly in your document. Tables organize text into cells, where a *cell* is the intersection of a row and a column.

Word provides four ways to create a table:

- Click the Insert tab, click the Table icon, and then highlight the number of rows and columns for your table (up to a maximum of eight rows and ten columns).
- Use the Insert Table dialog box.
- Draw the size and position of the table with the mouse.
- Convert existing text (divided by a delimiter character such as a Tab or comma).

Creating a table by highlighting rows and columns

Creating a table by highlighting rows and columns can be fast, but it limits the size of your table to a maximum of eight rows and ten columns. To create a table by highlighting rows and columns, follow these steps:

1. **Click the Insert tab.**
2. **Move the cursor where you want to insert a table in your document.**
3. **Click the Table icon.**

   A pull-down menu appears, as shown in Figure 7-3.

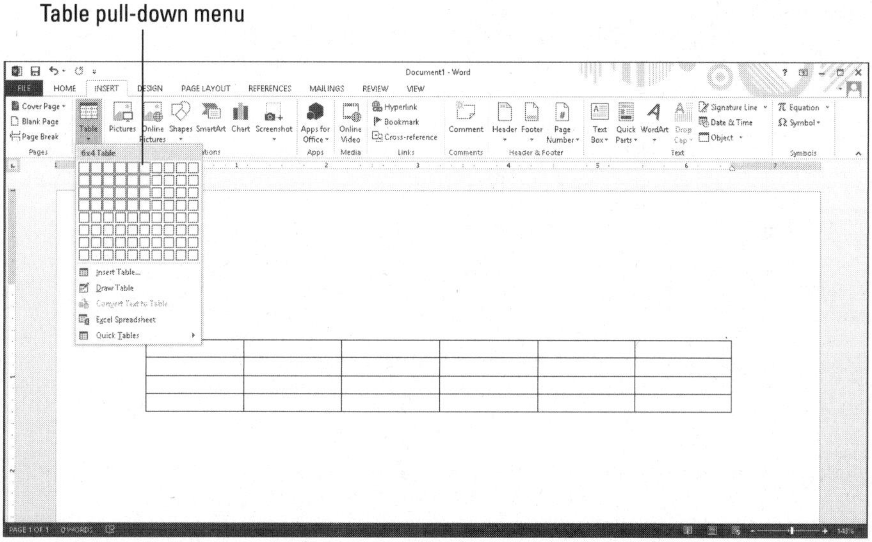

Table pull-down menu

Figure 7-3:
The Table pull-down menu displays squares that represent the number of rows and columns for your table.

4. **Move the mouse pointer to highlight the number of rows and columns you want to create for your table.**

   When you highlight rows and columns, Word displays your table directly in your document so you can see exactly what your table will look like.

5. **Click the left mouse button when you're happy with the size of your table.**

Creating a table with the Insert Table dialog box

Creating a table by highlighting the number of rows and columns can be fast, but it limits the size of your table to a maximum of eight rows and ten columns. To create a table by defining a specific number of rows and columns (up to a maximum of 63 columns), follow these steps:

1. **Click the Insert tab.**
2. **Move the cursor where you want to insert a table.**

3. **Click the Table icon.**

   A pull-down menu appears (refer to Figure 7-3).

4. **Click Insert Table.**

   The Insert Table dialog box appears, as shown in Figure 7-4.

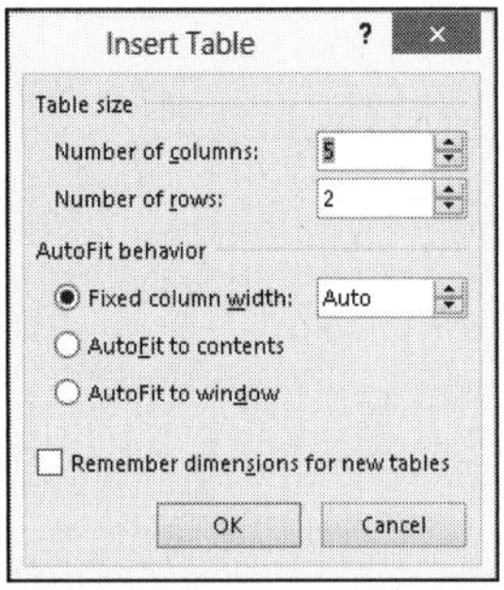

Figure 7-4:
The Insert Table dialog box lets you specify an exact number of rows and columns.

5. **Click in the Number of Columns text box and type a number between 1 and 63, or click the up/down arrows to define the number of columns.**

6. **Click in the Number of Rows text box and type a number or click the up/down arrows to define the number of rows.**

7. **Select one of the following radio buttons in the AutoFit Behavior group:**

   • *Fixed Column Width:* Defines a fixed size for the column widths, such as 0.3 inches

   • *AutoFit to Contents:* Defines the width of a column based on the width of the largest item stored in that column

   • *AutoFit to Window:* Expands (or shrinks) the table to fit within the current size of the document window

8. **Click OK.**

   Word draws the table in your document.

Creating a table with the mouse

Drawing a table can be especially useful when you want to place a table in the middle of a page and create rows and columns of different sizes, as shown in Figure 7-5.

Drawn table

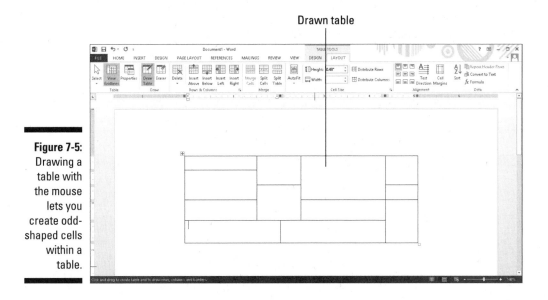

Figure 7-5:
Drawing a
table with
the mouse
lets you
create odd-
shaped cells
within a
table.

To draw a table in your document, follow these steps:

1. **Click the Insert tab.**

2. **Click the Table icon.**

   A pull-down menu appears.

3. **Click Draw Table.**

   The mouse pointer turns into a Pencil icon.

4. **Move the mouse pointer where you want to draw your table, hold down the left mouse button, and drag (move) the mouse to draw your table.**

   Word draws a rectangular dotted box to show you where your table will appear.

5. **Release the left mouse button when you're happy with the size and position of your table.**

6. **Move the mouse pointer to the top/bottom or left/right side of the table, hold down the left mouse button, and drag (move) the mouse up and down (or right and left) to draw the boundaries for your table's rows and columns.**

7. **Press Esc or double-click to turn the mouse pointer from a Pencil icon back to an I-beam pointer.**

TIP

If you need to draw new lines on a table later, click anywhere inside that table, and the Table Tools Layout tab appears. Then click the Draw Table icon to turn the mouse pointer into a Pencil icon. Now you can draw new lines in your table.

Creating a table from existing text

If you have existing text that you'd like to turn into a table, you need to first separate text into chunks so Word knows how to place the text into individual cells in a table. To separate text, you need to use a unique character such as

- ✔ **Paragraphs:** The invisible Return character separates text.

- ✔ **Tabs:** The invisible Tab character separates text.

- ✔ **Commas:** Commas separate text.

- ✔ **Other:** You can define other characters to separate text, such as the # or @ characters.

By using the same unique character to divide text, you can define how you want Word to define how much text to display in each individual cell of a table.

To convert existing text into a table, follow these steps:

1. **Click the Insert tab.**

2. **Select the text that you want to convert into a table.**

3. **Click the Table icon.**

    A pull-down menu appears (refer to Figure 7-3).

4. **Click the Convert Text to Table command.**

    The Convert Text to Table dialog box appears, as shown in Figure 7-6.

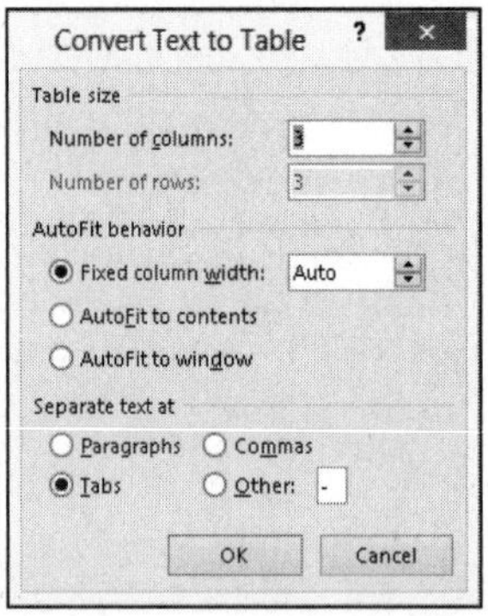

Figure 7-6: The Convert Text to Table dialog box defines how to convert your text into a table.

Convert Text to Table   ?   ×

Table size
Number of columns: 3
Number of rows: 3
AutoFit behavior
◉ Fixed column width: Auto
○ AutoFit to contents
○ AutoFit to window
Separate text at
○ Paragraphs   ○ Commas
◉ Tabs   ○ Other: -

OK   Cancel

5. **(Optional) Select a radio button in the Separate Text At group, such as Paragraphs, Tabs, or Commas.**

    You must choose the option that corresponds to the way you divided your text. So if you divided your text by tabs, you would select the Tabs radio button.

6. **Click OK.**

    Word converts your text into a table.

You can also convert a table into text. To convert a table into text, follow these steps:

1. **Click anywhere inside the table you want to convert into text.**

    The Layout tab appears.

2. **Click the Table Tools Layout tab.**

3. **Click Convert to Text.**

    The Convert Table to Text dialog box appears, as shown in Figure 7-7.

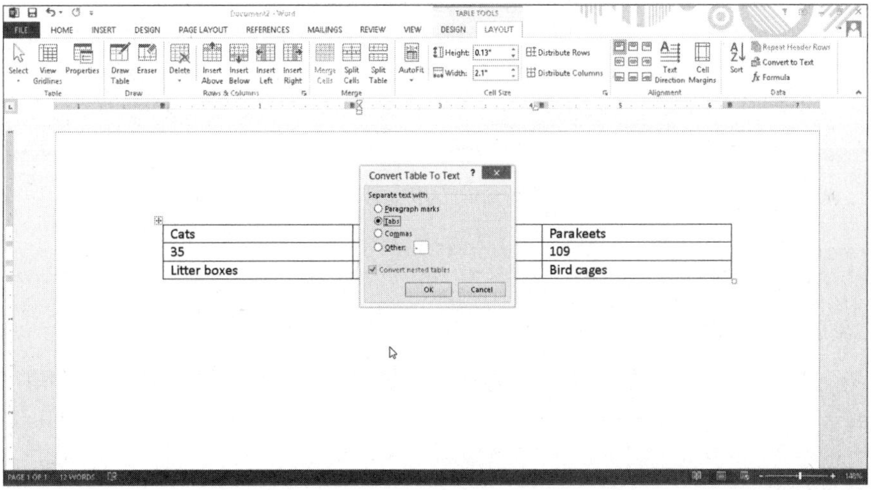

Figure 7-7: The Convert Table to Text dialog box lets you specify how to divide up a table.

4. **Select a radio button to define how you want to divide your table into text, such as by Commas, Tabs, Paragraph Marks, or other symbol.**

5. **Click OK.**

Formatting and Coloring a Table

After you create a table, you can format individual *cells* (spaces formed by the intersection of a row and a column) — or format entire rows and columns — by aligning text in cells, resizing columns and rows, and adding borders, shading, or colors. All these changes can make the text inside the cells easier to read.

Selecting all or part of a table

To format and color a table, you must first select the table, row, column, or cell that you want to modify. To select all or part of a table, follow these steps:

1. **Click in the table, row, column, or cell you want to modify.**

   The Table Tools tab appears.

2. **Click the Table Tools Layout tab.**

3. **Click Select in the Table group.**

   A pull-down menu appears, as shown in Figure 7-8.

4. **Choose an option, such as Select Row or Select Column.**

   Word highlights your chosen item in the table. At this point, you can choose a command to modify the selected row or column (as when you choose a color or alignment).

Pull-down menu

Figure 7-8: The Select icon displays a pull-down menu.

Aligning text in a table cell

You can align text in a table cell in nine different ways: Top Left (the default alignment), Top Center, Top Right, Center Left, Center, Center Right, Bottom Left, Bottom Center, and Bottom Right, as shown in Figure 7-9.

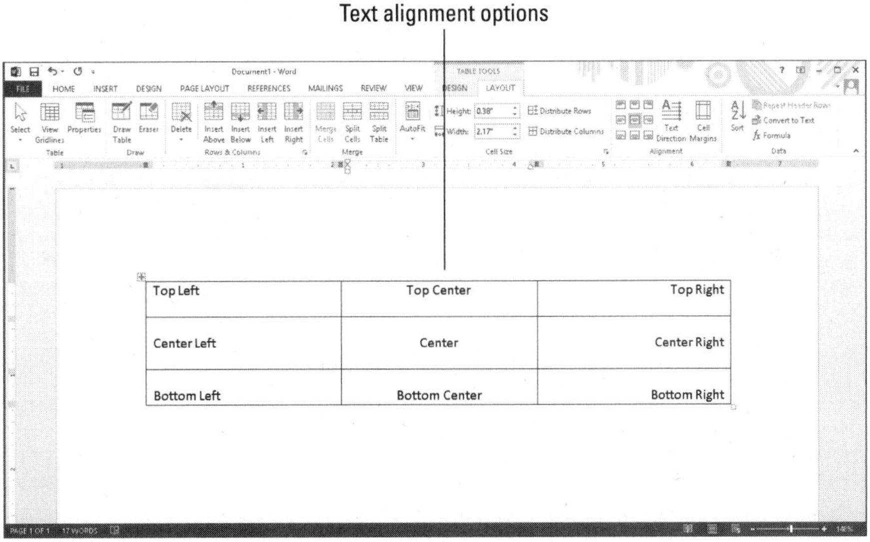

Text alignment options

Figure 7-9: Tables can align text within cells in nine different ways.

To align one or more cells, follow these steps:

1. **Click in the cell (or select multiple cells) that contains text you want to align.**

   The Table Tools tabs appear.

2. **Click the Table Tools Layout tab.**

3. **Click an alignment icon in the Alignment group (refer to Figure 7-9) such as Top Right or Bottom Center.**

   Word aligns your text. If you changed the alignment of blank cells, any new text you type in those blank cells will appear according to the alignment you chose.

Picking a table style

By coloring rows or columns and adding borders, you can customize the appearance of your tables. However, it can be much faster to use a predesigned table style instead, which can automatically format your text, color rows, and add borders to your tables.

To choose a table style, follow these steps:

1. **Move the cursor inside the table you want to modify.**

2. **Click the Table Tools Design tab.**

3. **(Optional) select or clear check boxes under the Table Style Options group, such as the Header Row or Last Column check box.**

4. **Click the More button on the Table Styles group.**

   A pull-down menu of all available styles appears, as shown in Figure 7-10. As you move the mouse pointer over a table style, Word displays a live preview of how your table will look.

Table styles

Figure 7-10:
The Table Styles group displays different ways to format your table.

5. **Click a table style.**

   Word formats your table according to the style you chose.

Resizing columns and rows

You may need to resize a column or row in your table to expand or shrink it so your text doesn't appear crowded or surrounded by empty space. You can resize a column or row by using the mouse or by defining row heights and column widths.

To resize a row or column with the mouse, follow these steps:

1. **Move the mouse over the row or column border that you want to resize.**

   The mouse pointer turns into a two-way pointing arrow.

2. **Hold the left mouse button down and drag (move) the mouse to resize the row or column.**

3. **Release the left mouse button when you're happy with the size of the row or column.**

Using the mouse to resize a row or column can be fast, but if you want to resize a row or column to a specific height or width, you can type in the specific dimensions by following these steps:

1. **Select the row, column, or table that you want to modify. (If you select the entire table, you can adjust the width or height of rows and columns for your entire table.)**

2. **Click the Table Tools Layout tab.**

3. **Click the Table Column Width text box and type a value (or click the up/down arrows to choose a value).**

4. **Click the Table Row Height text box and type a value (or click the up/down arrows to choose a value).**

5. **(Optional) Click AutoFit and choose one of the following, as shown in Figure 7-11:**

   • *AutoFit Contents:* Shrinks your columns or rows to largest cell.

   • *AutoFit Window:* Expands the table to fit the width of the current document window.

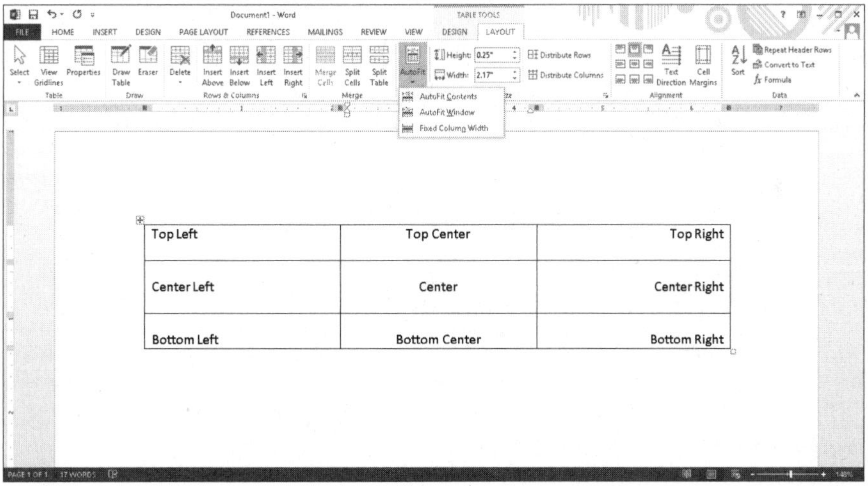

Figure 7-11:
The AutoFit menu.

Sorting a Table

Tables not only can organize data, but they can also sort your data alphabetically. To sort a table, you need to specify a single column of data to sort. When Word sorts the data in this column, it automatically sorts every row in the table as well, as shown in Figure 7-12.

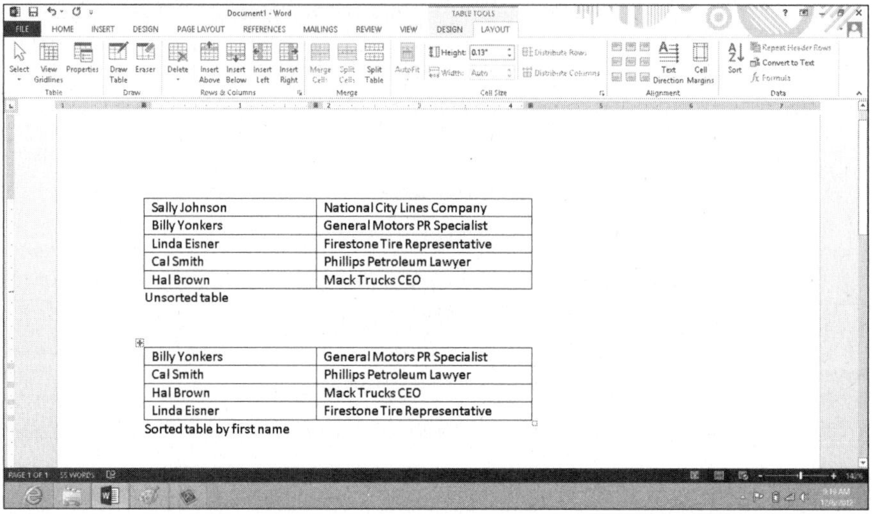

Figure 7-12:
Sorting data
in a column
rearranges
every row in
a table.

To sort a table, follow these steps:

1. **Select the column that contains the data you want to sort.**

2. **Click the Layout tab under the Table Tools tab.**

3. **Click the Sort icon in the Data group.**

   The Sort dialog box appears, as shown in Figure 7-13.

4. **Click in the top Type list box and choose the type of data you want to sort: Text, Number, or Date.**

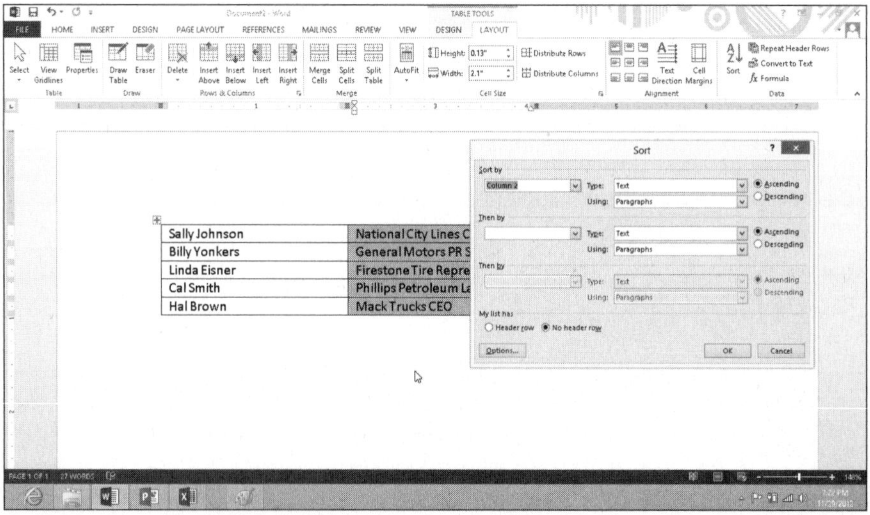

Figure 7-13:
The Sort
dialog box
lets you
specify
whether
to sort by
ascending
or descend-
ing order.

5. **Select either the Ascending or Descending radio button.**
6. **(Optional) Click the Header Row or No Header Row radio button.**

   If you select the Header Row, Word won't sort the top row of your table.
7. **Click OK.**

   Word sorts your entire table based on the data in the column you selected.

Deleting Tables

After you create a table, you can delete the entire table, delete one or more rows or columns, or just delete individual cells along with their data.

Deleting an entire table

Sometimes you may need to delete an entire table along with all the data stored inside that table. To delete both your table and all the data stored in it at the same time, follow these steps:

1. **Move the cursor into the table you want to wipe out.**
2. **Click the Layout tab under the Table Tools tab.**
3. **Click the Delete icon in the Rows & Columns group.**

   A pull-down menu appears, as shown in Figure 7-14.
4. **Choose Delete Table.**

   Word wipes out your table and all the data stored in it.

Table example - Word
TABLE TOOLS
FILE
HOME
INSERT
DESIGN
PAGE LAYOUT
REFERENCES
MAILINGS
REVIEW
VIEW
DESIGN
LAYOUT
Delete Cells...
Delete Columns
Delete Rows
Delete Table
Delete Entire Table
Sally Johnson
National City Lines Company
Billy Yonkers
General Motors PR Specialist
Linda Eisner
Firestone Tire Representative
Cal Smith
Phillips Petroleum Lawyer
Hal Brown
Mack Trucks CEO

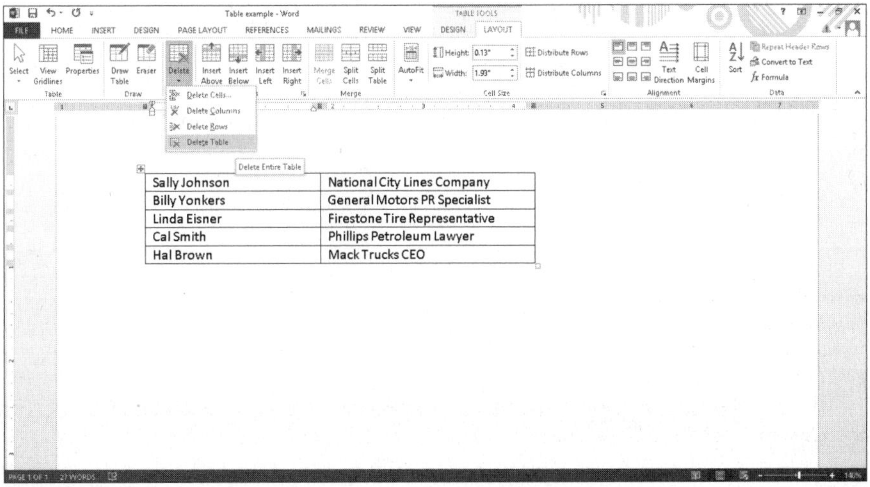

Figure 7-14: The Delete icon displays commands for deleting parts of a table.

Deleting rows and columns

Rather than delete an entire table, you can also delete rows and columns. When you delete a row or column, you wipe out any data stored inside that row or column.

To delete a row or column, follow these steps:

1. **Move the cursor into the row or column you want to delete.**
2. **Click the Layout tab under the Table Tools tab.**
3. **Click the Delete icon.**

   A pull-down menu appears (refer to Figure 7-14).

4. **Choose Delete Columns or Delete Rows.**

   Word deletes your chosen column or row.

Deleting cells

You can delete data in cells just by selecting the data and pressing the Delete key. If you want to delete data and the cell itself, you have two options:

- **Delete a cell and shift adjacent rows or columns.** This creates an odd-shaped table.
- **Delete the data and cell borders.** This keeps the table symmetrical but often merges cells.

To delete a cell and change the physical layout of a table, follow these steps:

1. **Select the cell or cells you want to delete.**
2. **Click the Layout tab under the Table Tools tab.**
3. **Click the Delete icon in the Rows & Columns group.**

   A pull-down menu appears (refer to Figure 7-14).

4. **Choose Delete Cells.**

   The Delete Cells dialog box appears, as shown in Figure 7-15.

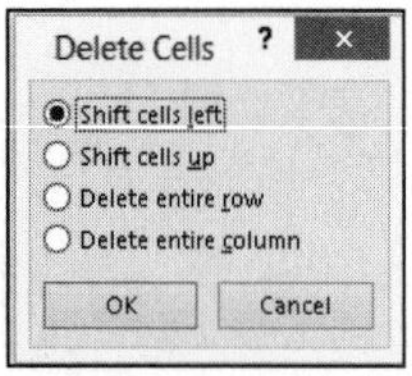

Figure 7-15: The Delete Cells dialog box.

Delete Cells

- ● Shift cells left
- ○ Shift cells up
- ○ Delete entire row
- ○ Delete entire column

OK   Cancel

5. **Select the radio button for Shift Cells Left or Shift Cells Up.**

6. **Click OK.**

   Word deletes your chosen cells and shifts cells left or up, creating an odd-shaped table with missing cells, as shown in Figure 7-16.

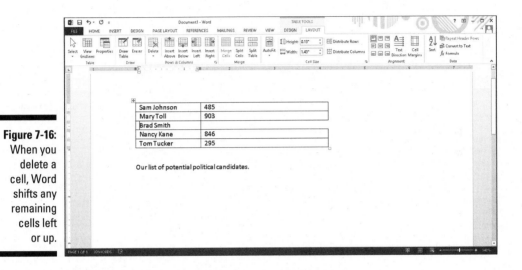

Figure 7-16: When you delete a cell, Word shifts any remaining cells left or up.

Sam Johnson	485
Mary Toll	903
Brad Smith	
Nancy Kane	846
Tom Tucker	295

Our list of potential political candidates.

Deleting cell borders

Word also lets you delete individual cell lines by using the mouse. By using the mouse, you can delete borders and merge adjacent cells at the same time.

To use the mouse to delete cell lines, follow these steps:

1. **Move the cursor into the table you want to modify.**

2. **Click the Layout tab under the Table Tools tab.**

3. **Click the Eraser icon in the Rows & Columns group.**

   The mouse pointer turns into an eraser icon.

4. **Choose one of the following:**

   Click a cell border to delete it.

   or

   a. *Move the mouse pointer near a cell line to delete, hold down the left mouse button, and drag (move) the mouse to highlight one or more cell lines.*

   Word highlights any cell lines you select.

       b. Release the left mouse button.

       Word deletes the selected cell lines and any data stored in adjacent cells.

5. **Press Esc or double-click the mouse to turn off the Eraser and convert the mouse pointer back into an I-beam cursor.**

Making Text Look Artistic

To spice up the appearance of individual paragraphs, Word lets you add drop caps, text boxes, or WordArt. *Drop caps* make the first letter of a paragraph appear huge. *WordArt* displays text as graphical images. Text boxes let you display chunks of text in separate boxes that you can arrange anywhere in your document.

Creating drop caps

To create a drop cap, follow these steps:

1. **Click the Insert tab.**

2. **Move the cursor anywhere inside the paragraph for which you want to create a drop cap.**

3. **Click Drop Cap.**

    The Drop Cap menu appears, as shown in Figure 7-17.

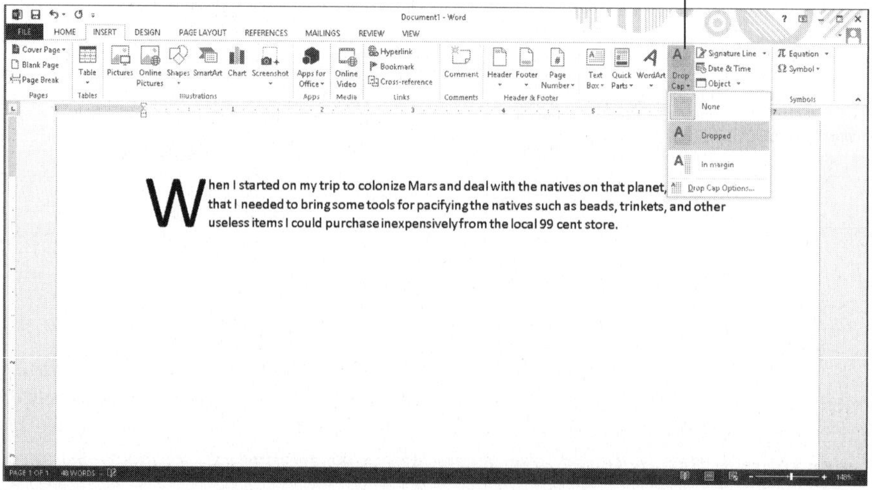

Drop Cap menu

Figure 7-17:
The Drop Cap menu lists different drop cap styles you can choose.

4. **Move the mouse pointer over the drop-cap style you want to use.**

   Word shows you what your drop cap will look like.

5. **Click the drop cap style you want to use.**

Creating WordArt

WordArt is Microsoft's fancy term for displaying text in different graphical styles that you can stretch or resize on a page. You can create WordArt from scratch or from existing text.

To create WordArt, follow these steps:

1. **(Optional) Select the text you want to convert into WordArt.**

   If you skip this step, you have to type in text later.

2. **Click the Insert tab.**

3. **Click WordArt.**

   The WordArt menu appears, as shown in Figure 7-18.

4. **Click a WordArt style.**

   A WordArt text box appears in your document, as shown in Figure 7-19.

5. **(Optional) To resize your WordArt, move the mouse pointer over a WordArt handle (on the edge or the corner), hold down the left mouse button, and drag (move) the mouse.**

WordArt menu

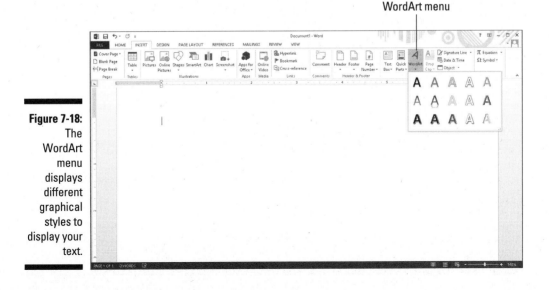

Figure 7-18: The WordArt menu displays different graphical styles to display your text.

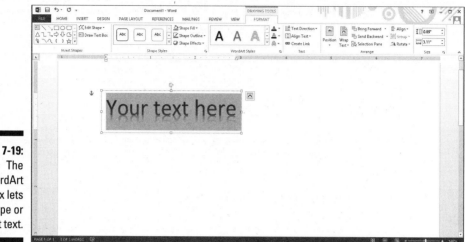

Figure 7-19:
The
WordArt
text box lets
you type or
edit text.

6. **Type or edit text, and then click outside of the WordArt text box.**

   Word displays your text as WordArt.

   To edit your WordArt text, just click that text.

   You can delete WordArt by clicking its border and then pressing Delete.

Dividing Text into Columns

When you type, Word normally displays your text to fill the area defined by the left and right margins. However, you can also divide a page into two or three columns, which can be especially handy for printing newsletters.

To divide a document into columns, follow these steps:

1. **Click the Page Layout tab.**

2. **Select the text that you want to divide into columns. (Press Ctrl+A to select your entire document.)**

3. **Click the Columns icon.**

   A pull-down menu appears that lists different column styles, as shown in Figure 7-20.

4. **Click a column style (such as Two).**

   Word changes your document to display columns.

Columns menu

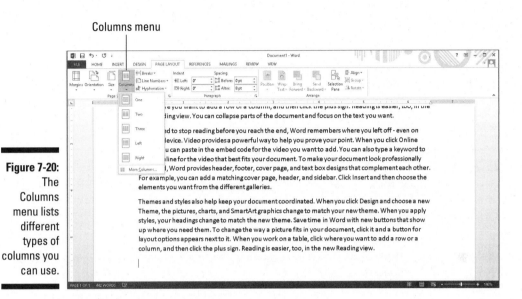

Figure 7-20:
The
Columns
menu lists
different
types of
columns you
can use.

Editing columns

After you create two or three columns in your document, you may want to modify their widths, modify the spacing between columns, and choose whether to display a vertical line between columns. To edit columns, follow these steps:

1. **Move the cursor to the text divided into columns that you want to modify.**

2. **Click the Page Layout tab.**

3. **Click the Columns icon.**

   A pull-down menu appears (refer to Figure 7-20).

4. **Click More Columns.**

   The Columns dialog box appears, as shown in Figure 7-21.

5. **(Optional) Click in the Number of Columns text box and click the up/down arrows to define how many columns you want (from 1 to 9).**

6. **(Optional) Click in the Width text box and type a value or click the up/down arrows to define a width for column 1.**

7. **(Optional) Click in the Spacing text box and type a value or click the up/down arrows to define the spacing width to the right of column 1.**

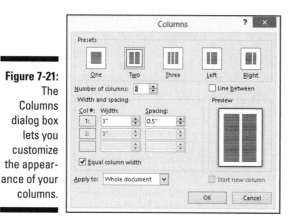

Figure 7-21:
The
Columns
dialog box
lets you
customize
the appear-
ance of your
columns.

8. **(Optional) Repeat Steps 6 and 7 for each additional column you want to modify.**

9. **(Optional) Select the Line Between check box to display a vertical line between your columns.**

10. **(Optional) Click the Apply To list box and choose Whole Document or This Point Forward (to define how columns appear from the current cursor position to the end of the document).**

11. **Click OK.**

Word displays the changes for your columns.

Removing columns

If you decide you don't want to display text in columns anymore, you can remove columns — throughout your entire document or just from the current cursor position to the end of the document.

To remove columns, follow these steps:

1. **Move the cursor to the page from which you want to remove columns to the end of a document.**

2. **Click the Page Layout tab.**

3. **Click the Columns icon.**

    A pull-down menu appears (refer to Figure 7-20).

4. **Click One.**

    Word removes columns from the current cursor position to the end of the document.

Previewing a Document before Printing

Before you print your document, you may want to preview how it will look so you don't waste paper printing something you can't use anyway. After you see that your pages will look perfect, then you can finally print out your document for everyone to read.

Defining page size and orientation

If you need to print your document on different sizes of paper, you may need to define the page size and paper orientation. By doing this, Word can accurately show you what your text may look like when printed on an 8.5" x 11" page compared with an 8.27" x 11.69" page.

To define the Page Size, follow these steps:

1. **Click the Page Layout tab.**
2. **Click the Size icon in the Page Setup group.**

    A pull-down menu appears, as shown in Figure 7-22.

3. **Click the page size you want.**

    Word displays your document based on the new page size.

Size menu

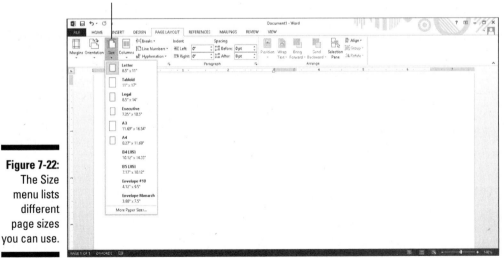

Figure 7-22:
The Size
menu lists
different
page sizes
you can use.

Normally Word assumes that you want to print in *portrait orientation,* where the height of the paper is greater than its width. However, you may want to print in *landscape orientation,* where the height of the paper is less than its width.

To define the orientation, follow these steps:

1. **Click the Page Layout tab.**

2. **Click the Orientation icon in the Page Setup group.**

   A pull-down menu appears, as shown in Figure 7-23.

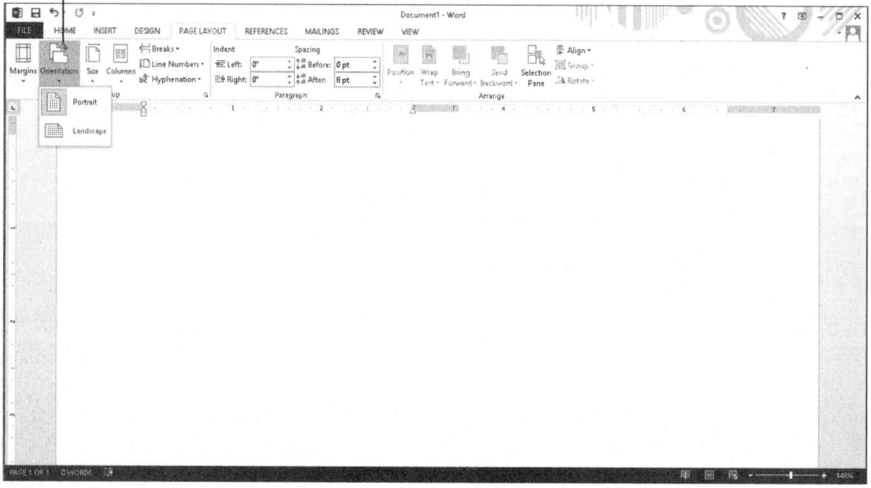

Page orientation

Figure 7-23:
Choose a page orientation.

3. **Click either Portrait or Landscape orientation.**

   Word displays your document based on the new paper orientation.

Using Print Preview

Print Preview lets you browse through your document so you can see how every page will look, including any headers and footers, cover pages, and pictures you may have added. To use Print Preview, follow these steps:

1. **Click the File tab.**

2. Click Print.

Word displays various print settings in the middle pane and a preview of your document in the right pane, as shown in Figure 7-24.

Print Preview

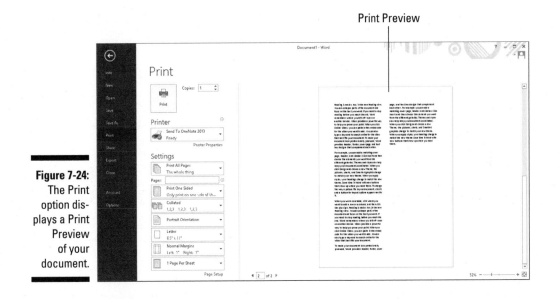

Figure 7-24: The Print option displays a Print Preview of your document.

3. (Optional) Click the various options in the middle pane, such as choosing a printer to use or how many copies to print.

4. (Optional) Click Next Page/Previous Page or use the vertical scroll bar to browse through all the pages of your document.

If you drag the Magnifier slider in the bottom-right corner, you can zoom in or zoom out so you can examine the details of your document.

5. Press Esc to return to your document, or click Print to start printing.

You can also start printing by just pressing Ctrl+P.

Part III

Playing the Numbers with Excel

Visit www.dummies.com/extras/office2013 for great Dummies content online.

In this part . . .

- ✔ Typing and formatting data
- ✔ Searching a spreadsheet
- ✔ Creating formulas
- ✔ Conditional formatting
- ✔ Creating a chart
- ✔ Modifying the parts of a chart
- ✔ Visit www.dummies.com/extras/office2013 for great Dummies content online.

Chapter 8

The Basics of Spreadsheets: Numbers, Labels, and Formulas

*E*veryone needs to perform simple math. Businesses need to keep track of sales and profits, and individuals need to keep track of budgets. In the old days, people not only had to write down numbers on paper, but they also had to do all their calculations by hand (or with the aid of a calculator).

That's why people use Excel. Instead of writing numbers on paper, they can type numbers on the computer. Instead of adding or subtracting columns or rows of numbers by hand, they can let Excel do it faster. By using Excel, you can focus on typing in the correct numbers and let Excel worry about calculating accurate results quickly.

Besides calculating numbers, spreadsheets can also store lists of data organized in rows and columns.

Understanding Spreadsheets

Excel organizes numbers in rows and columns. An entire page of rows and columns is called a *spreadsheet* or a *worksheet*. (A collection of one or more worksheets is stored in a file called a *workbook*.) Each row is identified by a number such as 1 or 249; and each column is identified by letters, such as A,

G, or BF. The intersection of each row and column defines rectangular spaces called *cells,* each of which contains one of three items:

- ✔ Numbers
- ✔ Text (labels)
- ✔ Formulas

Numbers provide the data, and *formulas* calculate that data to produce a useful result, such as adding sales results for the week. Of course, just displaying numbers on the screen may be confusing if you don't know what those numbers mean, so labels simply identify what numbers represent. Figure 8-1 shows the parts of a typical spreadsheet.

Formulas usually appear as numbers, so at first glance, it may be difficult to tell the difference between ordinary numbers and numbers that represent a calculation by a formula.

The strength of spreadsheets comes by playing "What-if?" games with your data, such as "What if I gave myself a $20-per-hour raise and cut everyone else's salary by 25%? How much money would that save the company every month?" Because spreadsheets can rapidly calculate new results, you can experiment with different numbers to see how they create different answers.

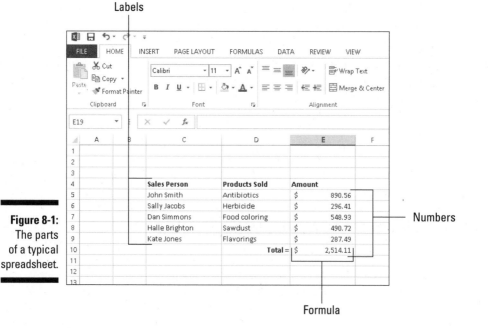

Labels

Numbers

Formula

Figure 8-1: The parts of a typical spreadsheet.

Storing Stuff in a Spreadsheet

Every cell can contain a number, a label, or a formula. To type anything into a spreadsheet, you must first select or click in the cell (or cells) and then type a number or text.

Typing data into a single cell

To type data in a single cell, follow these steps:

1. **Choose one of the following to select a single cell:**

   • Click a cell.

   • Press the up/down/right/left arrow keys to highlight a cell.

2. **Type a number (such as** 34.29 **or** 198**), a label (such as** Tax Returns**), or a formula.**

   You can see how to create formulas in Chapter 9.

Typing data in multiple cells

After you type data in a cell, you can press one of the following four keystrokes to select a different cell:

✔ **Enter:** Selects the cell below in the same column

✔ **Tab:** Selects the cell to the right in the same row

✔ **Shift+Enter:** Selects the cell above in the same column

✔ **Shift+Tab:** Selects the cell to the left in the same row

If you type data in cell A1 and press Enter, Excel selects the next cell below, which is A2. If you type data in A2 and press Tab, Excel selects the cell to the right, which is B2.

However, what if you want to type data in a cell such as A1 and then have Excel select the next cell to the right (B1)? Or what if you want to type data in cells A1 and A2 but then jump back to type additional data in cells B1 and B2?

To make this easy, Excel lets you select a *range* of cells, which essentially tells Excel, "See all the cells I just highlighted? I only want to type data in those cells." After you select multiple cells, you can type data and press

Enter. Excel selects the next cell down in that same column. When Excel reaches the last cell in the column, it selects the top cell of the column to the right.

To select multiple cells for typing data in, follow these steps:

1. **Highlight multiple cells by choosing one of the following:**

    • Move the mouse pointer over a cell, hold down the left mouse button, and drag (move) the mouse to highlight multiple cells. Release the left mouse button when you've selected enough cells.

    • Hold down the Shift key and press the up/down/right/left arrow keys to highlight multiple cells. Release the Shift key when you've selected enough cells.

    Excel selects the cell that appears in the upper-left corner of your selected cells.

2. **Type a number, label, or formula.**

3. **Press Enter.**

    Excel selects the cell directly below the preceding cell. If the preceding cell appeared at the bottom of the selected column, Excel highlights the top cell in the column that appears to the right.

    You can also move backward by pressing Shift+Enter instead.

4. **Repeat Steps 2 and 3 until you fill your selected cells with data.**

5. **Click outside the selected cells or press an arrow key to tell Excel not to select the cells anymore.**

Typing in sequences with AutoFill

If you need to type the names of successive months or days in a row or column (such as January, February, March, and so on), Excel offers a short-cut to save you from typing all the day or month names yourself. With this shortcut, you just type one month or day and then drag the mouse to high-light all the adjacent cells. Then Excel types the rest of the month or day names in those cells automatically.

To use this shortcut, follow these steps:

1. **Click a cell and type a month (such as** January **or just** Jan**) or a day (such as** Monday **or just** Mon**).**

    The Fill Handle, a block box, appears in the bottom-right corner of the cell.

TIP

You can also type in a sequence of numbers in Step 1. So if you typed the numbers 2, 4, and 6 in adjacent cells, highlighted all these adjacent cells, and grabbed the Fill Handle, Excel is smart enough to detect the pattern and display the numbers 8, 10, and 12 in the next three adjacent cells.

2. **Move the mouse pointer over the Fill Handle until the mouse pointer turns into a black crosshair icon.**

3. **Hold down the left mouse button and drag (move) the mouse down a column or across the row.**

   As you drag the mouse, Excel automatically types in the remaining month or day names, as shown in Figure 8-2.

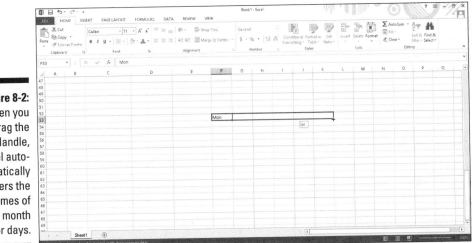

Figure 8-2:
When you drag the Fill Handle, Excel automatically enters the names of the month or days.

Formatting Numbers and Labels

When you first create a spreadsheet, numbers and labels appear as plain text. Plain labels may look boring, but plain numbers (such as 8495 or 0.39) can be difficult to read and understand if the numbers are supposed to represent currency amounts ($8,495) or percentages (39%).

To make labels visually interesting and numbers appear more descriptive of what they actually represent, you need to format your data after you type it into a spreadsheet.

REMEMBER

You can format a cell or range of cells after you've already typed in data or before you type in any data. If you format cells before typing any data, any data you type in that cell will appear in your chosen format.

Formatting numbers

To format the appearance of numbers, follow these steps:

1. **Select one or more cells by using the mouse or keyboard.**

   To select multiple cells, drag the mouse or hold the Shift key while pressing the arrow keys.

2. **Click the Home tab.**

3. **Click the Number Format list box in the Number group.**

   A pull-down menu appears, as shown in Figure 8-3.

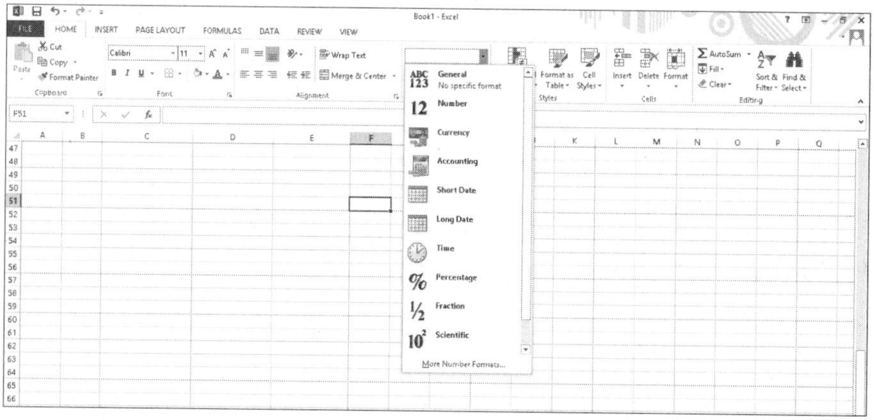

Figure 8-3: The Number Format list box lists the different ways you can format the appearance of numbers.

The Number group also displays three icons that let you format numbers as Currency, Percentage, or with Commas in one click, as shown in Figure 8-4. If you click the downward-pointing arrow to the right of the Accounting Number Format icon, you can choose different currency symbols to use, such as $, £, or €.

4. **Click a number format style, such as Percentage or Scientific.**

   Excel displays your numbers in your chosen format.

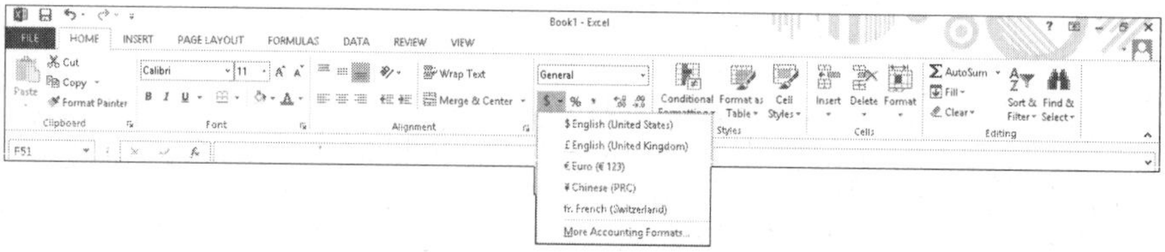

Figure 8-4: The different ways you can format money.

Displaying negative numbers

Because many people use spreadsheets for business, they often want negative numbers to appear highlighted so they can see them easier. Excel can display negative numbers in parentheses (–23) or in red so you can't miss them.

To define how negative numbers appear in your spreadsheet, follow these steps:

1. **Select the cell or range of cells that you want to modify.**

2. **Click the Home tab.**

3. **Click the Format icon in the Cells group.**

   A menu appears, as shown in Figure 8-5.

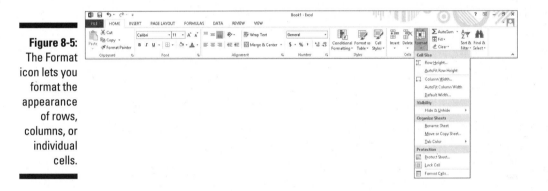

Figure 8-5:
The Format icon lets you format the appearance of rows, columns, or individual cells.

4. **Choose Format Cells.**

   The Format Cells dialog box appears, as shown in Figure 8-6.

5. **Choose Currency or Number from the Category list.**

   You can choose how to format negative numbers only if you format your numbers by using the Currency or Number category.

6. **Click a negative number format and then click OK.**

   If any of your numbers become negative in the cell or cells you selected in Step 1, Excel automatically displays those negative numbers in the negative number format you chose.

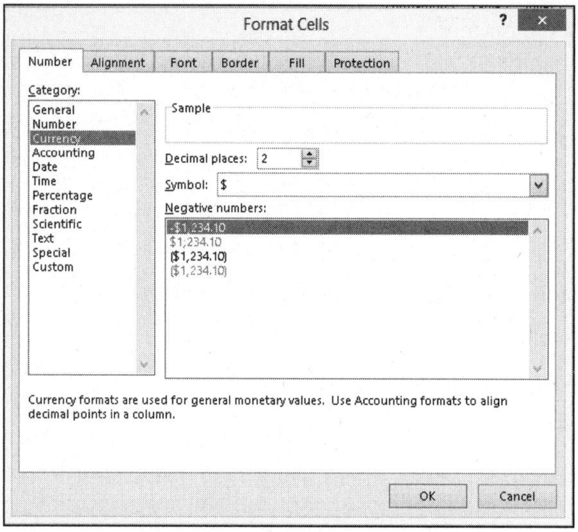

Figure 8-6:
The Format
Cells dialog
box lets you
customize
the appear-
ance of your
numbers.

Formatting decimal numbers

If you format cells to display numbers with decimal places, such as 23.09 or 23.09185, you can modify how many decimal places appear. To define the number of decimal places, follow these steps:

1. **Select the cell or cells that contain the numbers you want to format.**

2. **Click the Home tab.**

3. **Click in the Number Format list box (refer to Figure 8-3) and choose a format that displays decimal places, such as Number or Percentage.**

   Excel formats the numbers in your chosen cells.

You can click the Increase Decimal (increases the number of decimal places displayed) or Decrease Decimal icon (decreases the number of decimal places displayed) in the Number group on the Home tab, as shown in Figure 8-7.

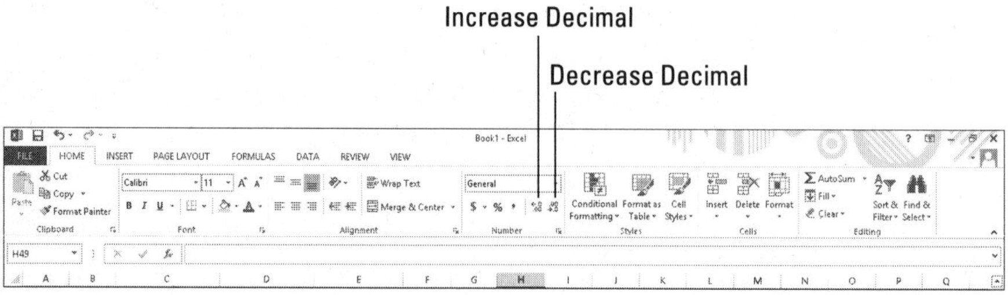

Increase Decimal

Decrease Decimal

Figure 8-7:
A click
quickly
changes
the number
of decimal
places
displayed.

Formatting cells

To make your data look prettier, Excel can format the appearance of cells to change the font, background color, text color, or font size used to display data in a cell.

Excel provides two ways to format cells: You can use Excel's built-in formatting styles, or you can apply different types of formatting individually. Some of the individual formatting styles you can choose include

- ✔ Font and font size
- ✔ Text styles (underlining, italic, and bold)
- ✔ Text and background color
- ✔ Borders
- ✔ Alignment
- ✔ Text wrapping and orientation

Formatting cells with built-in styles

Excel provides a variety of predesigned formatting styles that you can apply to one or more cells. To format cells with a built-in style, follow these steps:

1. **Select the cell or cells that you want to format with a built-in style.**

2. **Click the Home tab.**

3. **Click the Cell Styles icon in the Styles group.**

   A pull-down menu appears listing all the different styles you can choose, as shown in Figure 8-8.

4. **Move the mouse pointer over a style.**

   Excel displays a Live Preview of how your selected cells will look with that particular style.

5. **Click the style you want.**

   Excel applies your chosen style to the selected cells.

Formatting fonts and text styles

Different fonts can emphasize parts of your spreadsheet, such as using one font to label columns and rows and another font or font size to display the actual data. Text styles (bold, underline, and italic) can also emphasize data that appears in the same font or font size.

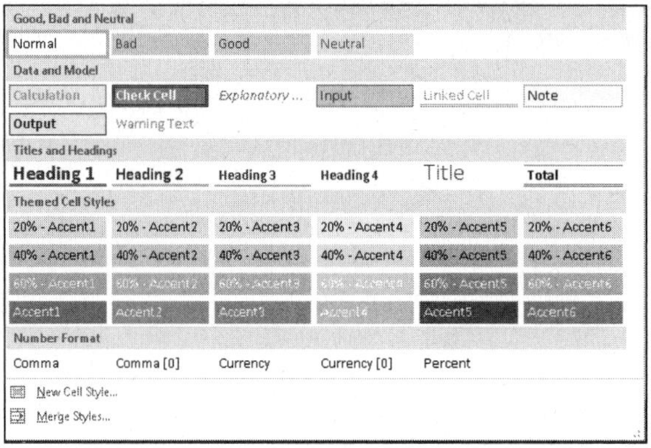

Figure 8-8:
The Cell
Styles menu
offers dif-
ferent ways
to format
your cells
quickly.

To change the font, font size, and text style of one or more cells, follow these steps:

1. **Select the cell or cells that you want to change the font and font size.**

2. **Click the Home tab.**

3. **Click the Font list box.**

   A pull-down menu of different fonts appears.

4. **Click the font you want to use.**

5. **Choose one of the following methods to change the font size:**

   • Click the Font Size list box and then choose a font size, such as 12 or 16.

   • Click the Font Size list box and type a value, such as 7 or 15.

   • Click the Increase Font Size or Decrease Font Size icon until your data appears in the size you want.

6. **Click one or more text style icons (Bold, Italic, Underline).**

Formatting with color

Each cell displays data in a Font color and a Fill color. The *Font color* defines the color of the numbers and letters that appear inside a cell. (The default Font color is black.) The *Fill color* defines the color that fills the background of the cell. (The default Fill color is white.)

To change the Font and Fill colors of cells, follow these steps:

1. **Select the cell or cells that you want to color.**

2. **Click the Home tab.**

3. **Click the downward-pointing arrow that appears to the right of the Font Color icon.**

A color palette appears, as shown in Figure 8-9.

Fill Color icon

Font Color icon

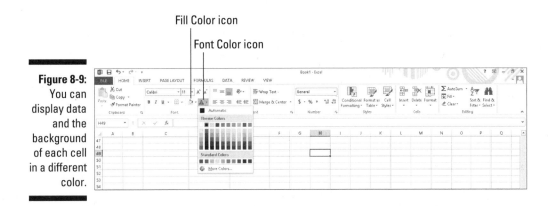

Figure 8-9:
You can display data and the background of each cell in a different color.

4. **Click the color you want to use for your text.**

The color you select appears directly on the Font Color icon. The next time you want to apply this same color to a cell, you can click the Font Color icon directly instead of the downward-pointing arrow to the right of the Font Color icon.

5. **Click the downward-pointing arrow that appears to the right of the Fill Color icon.**

A color palette appears.

6. **Click a color to use to fill the background of your cell.**

The color you select appears directly on the Fill Color icon. The next time you want to apply this same color to a cell, you can click the Fill Color icon directly instead of the downward-pointing arrow to the right of the Fill Color icon.

Adding borders

For another way to highlight one or more cells, you can add borders. Borders can surround the entire cell or just the top, bottom, left, or right side of a cell. To add borders to a cell, follow these steps:

1. **Select one or more cells.**

2. **Click the Home tab.**

3. **Click the downward-pointing arrow to the right of the Border icon.**

A pull-down menu appears, as shown in Figure 8-10.

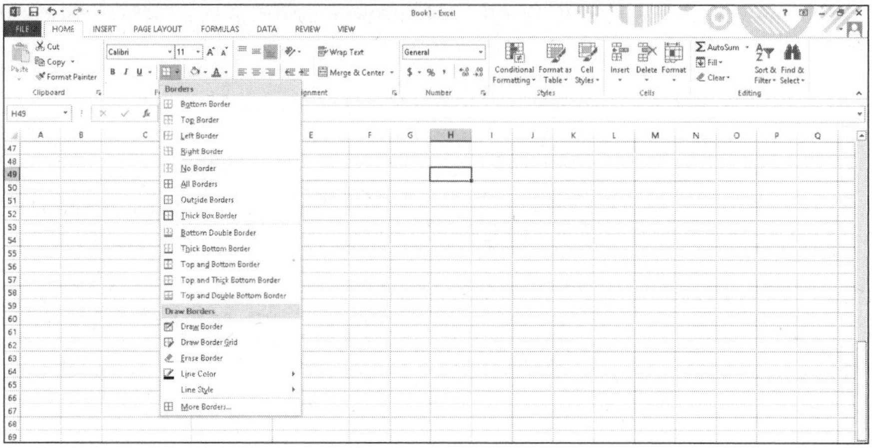

Figure 8-10:
The Border
menu lists
different
ways to
place bor-
ders around
cells.

4. Click a border style.

Excel displays your chosen borders around the cells you selected in Step 1.

Navigating a Spreadsheet

If you have a large spreadsheet, chances are good that some information may be hidden by the limitations of your computer screen. To help you view and select cells in different parts of your spreadsheet, Excel offers various ways to navigate a spreadsheet by using the mouse and keyboard.

Using the mouse to move around in a spreadsheet

To navigate a spreadsheet with the mouse, you can click the onscreen scroll bars or use the scroll wheel on your mouse (if it has one). To use the scroll bars, you have three choices:

- ✔ **Click the up/down or right/left arrows on the horizontal or vertical scroll bars.**

  This moves the spreadsheet one row (up or down) or column (right or left) at a time.

- ✔ **Drag the scroll box of a scroll bar.**

- ✔ **Click the scroll area (any area to the left/right or above/below the scroll box on the scroll bar).**

  This moves the spreadsheet one screen left/right or up/down.

If your mouse has a scroll wheel, you can use this wheel to move through a spreadsheet by two methods:

✔ Roll the mouse's scroll wheel forward or back to scroll your spreadsheet up or down.

✔ Press the scroll wheel to display a four-way pointing arrow, and then move the mouse up, down, right, or left. (When you're done, click the scroll wheel again.)

Using the keyboard to move around a spreadsheet

Using the mouse can be a faster way to jump from one place in a spreadsheet to another, but sometimes trying to line up the mouse just right can be frustrating. For that reason, you can also use the keyboard to move around a spreadsheet. Some of the common ways to move around a spreadsheet are shown in Table 8-1.

Table 8-1   Using the Keyboard to Navigate a Spreadsheet

Pressing This	*Does This*
Up arrow (↑)	Moves up one row
Down arrow (↓)	Moves down one row
Left arrow (←)	Moves left one column
Right arrow (→)	Moves right one column
Ctrl+↑	Jumps up to the top of a column that contains data
Ctrl+↓	Jumps down to the bottom of a column that contains data
Ctrl+←	Jumps to the left of a row that contains data
Ctrl+→	Jumps to the right of a row that contains data
Page Up	Moves up one screen
Page Down	Moves down one screen
Ctrl+Page Up	Displays the previous worksheet
Ctrl+Page Down	Displays the next worksheet
Home	Moves to the A column of the current row
Ctrl+Home	Moves to the A1 cell
Ctrl+End	Moves to the bottom-right cell of your spreadsheet

If you know the specific cell you want to move to, you can jump to that cell by using the Go To command. To use the Go To command, follow these steps:

1. **Click the Home tab.**

2. **Click the Find & Select icon in the Editing group.**

   A pull-down menu appears.

3. **Click Go To.**

   The Go To dialog box appears, as shown in Figure 8-11.

   You can also choose the Go To command by pressing Ctrl+G.

Figure 8-11:
The Go To
dialog box
lets you
jump to a
specific cell.

Go To	?	✕

Go to:

Reference:

Special... | OK | Cancel

4. **Click in the Reference text box and type the cell you want to move to, such as C13 or F4.**

   If you've used the Go To command before, Excel lists the last cell references you typed. Now you can just click one of those cell references to jump to that cell.

5. **Click OK.**

   Excel highlights the cell you typed in Step 4.

Naming cells

One problem with the Go To command is that most people won't know which cell contains the data they want to find. For example, if you want to view the cell that contains the total amount of money you owe for your income taxes, you probably don't want to memorize that this cell is G68 or P92.

To help you identify certain cells, Excel lets you give them descriptive names. To name a cell or range of cells, follow these steps:

1. **Select the cell or cells that you want to name.**

2. **Click in the Name box, which appears directly above the A column heading, as shown in Figure 8-12.**

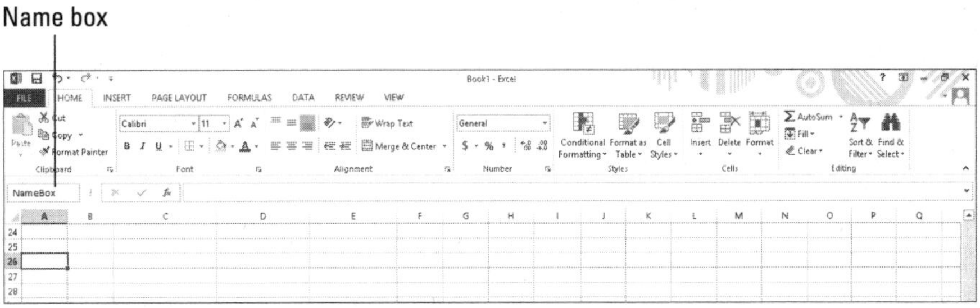

Name box

Figure 8-12:
You can type
a descrip-
tive name
for your
cells in the
Name box.

3. **Type a descriptive name without any spaces and then press Enter.**

After you name a cell, you can jump to it quickly by following these steps:

1. **Click the downward-pointing arrow to the right of the Name box.**

   A list of named cells appears.

2. **Click the named cell you want to view.**

   Excel displays your chosen cell.

Eventually, you may want to edit or delete a name for your cells. To delete or edit a name, follow these steps:

1. **Click the Formulas tab.**

2. **Click the Name Manager icon.**

   The Name Manager dialog box appears, as shown in Figure 8-13.

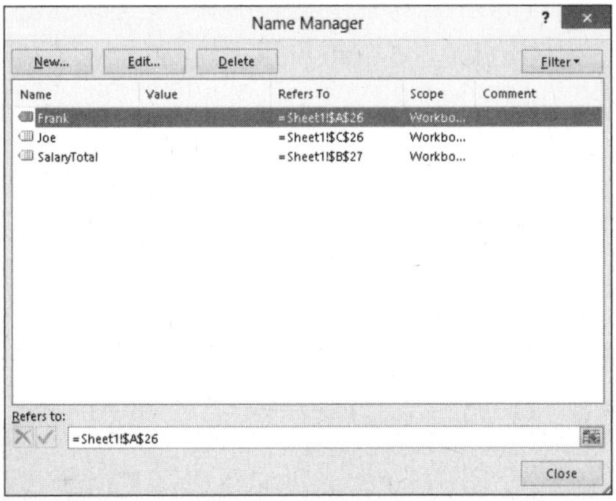

Figure 8-13:
The Name
Manager
dialog box
lets you
rename or
delete previ-
ously named
cells.

3. **Edit or delete the named cell as follows:**

- To edit the name, click the cell name you want to edit and then click the Edit button. An Edit Name dialog box appears, where you can change the name or the cell reference.

- To delete the name, click the cell name you want to delete and then click the Delete button.

4. **Click Close.**

Searching a Spreadsheet

Rather than search for a specific cell, you may want to search for a particular label or number in a spreadsheet. Excel lets you search for the following:

- ✔ Specific text or numbers
- ✔ All cells that contain formulas
- ✔ All cells that contain conditional formatting

Searching for text

You can search for a specific label or number anywhere in your spreadsheet. To search for text or numbers, follow these steps:

1. **Click the Home tab.**

2. **Click the Find & Select icon in the Editing group.**

   A pull-down menu appears.

3. **Click Find.**

   The Find and Replace dialog box appears, as shown in Figure 8-14.

   If you click the Replace tab, you can define the text or number to find and new text or numbers to replace it.

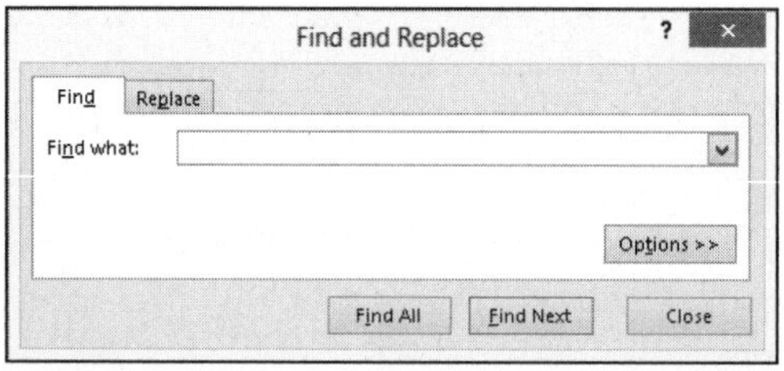

Figure 8-14:
The Find and Replace dialog box lets you search your worksheet.

Find and Replace	?	✕

Find | Replace

Find what: [   ] ▼

Options >>

Find All | Find Next | Close

4. Click in the Find What text box and type the text or number you want to find.

If you click the Options button, the Find and Replace dialog box expands to provide additional options for searching, such as searching in the displayed sheet or the entire workbook.

5. Click one of the following:

- *Find Next:* Finds and selects the first cell, starting from the currently selected cell that contains the text you typed in Step 4.

- *Find All:* Finds and lists all cells that contain the text you typed in Step 4, as shown in Figure 8-15.

Figure 8-15:
The Find All button names all the cells that contain the text or number you want to find.

Find and Replace	?	×

Find | Replace

Find what: Antibiotics

Options >>

Find All | Find Next | Close

Book	Sheet	Name	Cell	Value	Formula
Book1	Sheet1		D5	Antibiotics	

1 cell(s) found

6. Click Close to make the Find and Replace dialog box go away.

Searching for formulas

Formulas appear just like numbers; to help you find which cells contain formulas, Excel gives you two choices:

✔ Display formulas in your cells (instead of numbers)

✔ Highlight the cells that contain formulas

To display formulas in a spreadsheet, press Ctrl+` (an accent grave character, which appears on the same key as the ~ sign, often to the left of the number 1 key near the top of a keyboard). Figure 8-16 shows what a spreadsheet looks like when formulas appear inside of cells.

Figure 8-16:
By display-
ing formulas
in cells, you
can identify
which cells
display cal-
culations.

	A	B	C	D	E	F
1						
2						
3						
4			Sales Person	Products Sold	Amount	
5			John Smith	Antibiotics	890.56	
6			Sally Jacobs	Herbicide	296.41	
7			Dan Simmons	Food coloring	548.93	
8			Halle Brighton	Sawdust	490.72	
9			Kate Jones	Flavorings	287.49	
10				Total =	=SUM(E5:E9)	
11						
12						
13						

Formula

To highlight all cells that contain formulas, follow these steps:

1. **Click the Home tab.**

2. **Click the Find & Select icon in the Editing group.**

    A pull-down menu appears.

3. **Click Formulas.**

    Excel highlights all the cells that contain formulas.

Editing a Spreadsheet

The two ways to edit a spreadsheet are

- ✔ Edit the data itself, such as the labels, numbers, and formulas that make up a spreadsheet.

- ✔ Edit the physical layout of the spreadsheet, such as adding or deleting rows and columns, or widening or shrinking the width or height of rows and columns.

Editing data in a cell

To edit data in a single cell, follow these steps:

1. **Double-click the cell that contains the data you want to edit.**

    Excel displays a cursor in your selected cell.

2. **Edit your data by using the Backspace or Delete key, or by typing new data.**

If you click a cell, Excel displays the contents of that cell in the Formula bar. You can click and edit data directly in the Formula bar, which can be more convenient for editing large amounts of data such as a formula.

Changing the size of rows and columns with the mouse

Using the mouse can be a quick way to modify the sizes of rows and columns. To change the height of a row or the width of a column, follow these steps:

1. **Move the mouse pointer over the bottom line of a row heading, such as the 2 or 18 heading. (Or move the mouse pointer over the right line of the column heading, as for column A or D.)**

   The mouse pointer turns into a two-way pointing arrow.

2. **Hold down the left mouse button and drag (move) the mouse.**

   Excel resizes your row or column.

3. **Release the left mouse button when you're happy with the size of your row or column.**

Typing the size of rows and columns

If you need to resize a row or column to a precise value, it's easier to type a specific value into the Row Height or Column Width dialog box instead. To type a value into a Row Height or Column Width dialog box, follow these steps:

1. **Click the Home tab.**

2. **Click the row or column heading that you want to resize.**

   Excel highlights your entire row or column.

3. **Click the Format icon that appears in the Cells group.**

   A pull-down menu appears, as shown in Figure 8-17.

4. **Click Row Height (if you selected a row) or Column Width (if you selected a column).**

   The Row Height or Column Width dialog box appears.

5. **Type a value and then click OK.**

   Excel resizes your row or column.

Excel measures column width in characters. (A cell defined as 1 character width can display a single letter or number.) Excel measures row height by points where 1 point equals $\frac{1}{72}$ inch.

Figure 8-17:
The Format
icon lets
you adjust
the size of
rows and
columns.

Adding and deleting rows and columns

After you type in labels, numbers, and formulas, you may suddenly realize that you need to add or delete extra rows or columns. To add a row or
column, follow these steps:

1. **Click the Home tab.**

2. **Click the row or column heading where you want to add another row
   or column.**

   Excel highlights the entire row or column.

3. **Click the bottom half of the Insert icon in the Cells group.**

   A menu appears.

4. **Choose Insert Sheet Rows or Insert Sheet Columns.**

   Excel inserts a new row above the selected row or inserts a column to
   the left of the selected column.

To delete a row or column, follow these steps:

1. **Click the Home tab.**

2. **Click the row or column heading that you want to delete.**

3. **Click the bottom half of the Delete icon in the Cells group.**

   A menu appears.

4. **Choose Delete Sheet Rows or Delete Sheet Columns.**

Deleting a row or column deletes any data stored in that row or column.

Adding sheets

For greater flexibility, Excel lets you create individual spreadsheets that you can save in a single workbook (file). When you load Excel, it automatically provides you with a sheet, but you can add more if you need them.

To add a new sheet, choose one of the following:

- ✔ Click the New sheet icon (it looks like a plus sign inside a circle) that appears to the right of your existing tabs (or press Shift+F11), as shown in Figure 8-18.
- ✔ Click the Home tab, click the bottom half of the Insert icon in the Cells group, and when a menu appears, choose Insert Sheet.

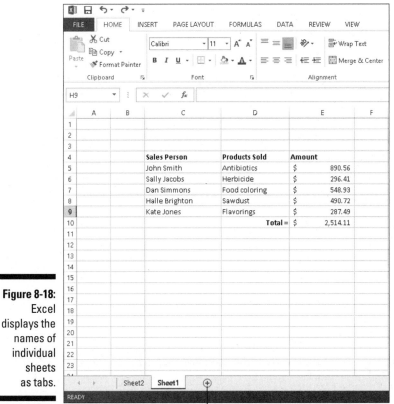

Figure 8-18: Excel displays the names of individual sheets as tabs.

Insert Worksheet icon

Renaming sheets

By default, Excel gives each sheet a generic name such as Sheet1. To give your sheets a more descriptive name, follow these steps:

1. **Choose one of the following:**

    • *Double-click the sheet tab that you want to rename.*

    Excel highlights the entire sheet name.

    • *Click the sheet tab you want to rename, click the Home tab, click the Format icon in the Cells group, and choose Rename Sheet.*

    • *Right-click the sheet tab you want to rename; when a pop-up menu appears, choose Rename Sheet.*

2. **Type a new name for your sheet and press Enter when you're done.**

    Your new name appears on the sheet tab.

Rearranging sheets

You can rearrange the order that your sheets appear in your workbook. To rearrange a sheet, follow these steps:

1. **Move the mouse pointer over the sheet tab that you want to move.**

2. **Hold down the left mouse button and drag (move) the mouse.**

    The downward-pointing black arrow points where Excel will place your sheet.

3. **Release the left mouse button to place your sheet in a new order.**

Deleting a sheet

Using multiple sheets may be handy, but you may want to delete a sheet if you don't need it.

If you delete a sheet, you also delete all the data stored on that sheet.

To delete a sheet, follow these steps:

1. **Click on the sheet that you want to delete.**

2. **Choose one of the following:**

   - *Right-click the tab of the sheet you want to delete. When a pop-up menu appears, click Delete.*

   - *Click the Home tab, click the bottom of the Delete icon in the Cells group; when a menu appears, choose Delete Sheet.*

   If your sheet is empty, Excel deletes the sheet right away. If your sheet contains data, a dialog box appears to warn you that you'll lose any data stored on that sheet.

3. **Click Delete.**

   Excel deletes your sheet along with any data on it.

Clearing Data

After you create a spreadsheet, you may need to delete data, formulas, or just the formatting that defines the appearance of your data. To clear out one or more cells of data, formatting, or both data and formatting, follow these steps:

1. **Click the Home tab.**

2. **Select the cell or cells that contain the data you want to clear.**

3. **Click the Clear icon in the Editing group.**

   A pull-down menu appears, as shown in Figure 8-19.

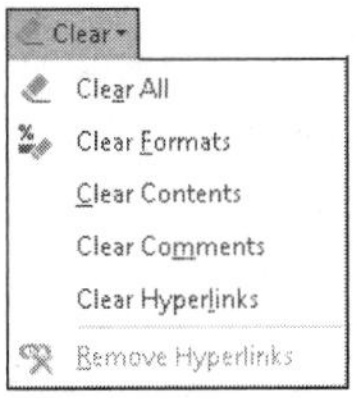

Figure 8-19:
The Clear menu provides different ways to clear out a cell.

Clear
- Clear All
- Clear Formats
- Clear Contents
- Clear Comments
- Clear Hyperlinks
- Remove Hyperlinks

4. **Choose one of the following:**

   - *Clear All:* Deletes the data and any formatting applied to that cell or cells.

   - *Clear Formats:* Leaves the data in the cell but strips away any formatting.

- *Clear Contents:* Leaves the formatting in the cell but deletes the data.

- *Clear Comments:* Leaves data and formatting but deletes any comments added to the cell.

- *Clear Hyperlinks:* Leaves data and formatting but deletes any hyperlinks connecting one cell to another cell.

Printing Workbooks

After you create a spreadsheet, you can print it out for others to see. When printing spreadsheets, you need to take special care how your spreadsheet appears on a page because a large spreadsheet will likely get printed on two or more sheets of paper.

This can cause problems if an entire spreadsheet prints on a one page but a single row of numbers appears on a second page, which can make reading and understanding your spreadsheet data confusing. When printing spreadsheets, take time to align your data so that it prints correctly on every page.

Using Page Layout view

Excel can display your spreadsheets in two ways: Normal view and Page Layout view. Normal view is the default appearance, which simply fills your screen with rows and columns so you can see as much of your spreadsheet as possible.

Page Layout view displays your spreadsheet exactly as it will appear if you print it. Not only can you see where your page breaks occur, but you can also add any headers to the top of your spreadsheet.

To switch back and forth from Normal view to Page Layout view, follow these steps:

1. **Click the View tab.**

2. **Click the Normal or Page Layout View icon in the Workbook Views group, as shown in Figure 8-20.**

You can also click the Normal or Page Layout View icons in the bottom-right corner of the Excel window.

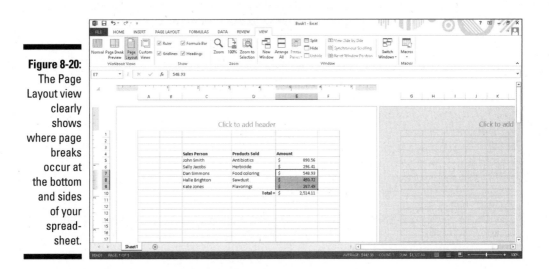

Figure 8-20:
The Page
Layout view
clearly
shows
where page
breaks
occur at
the bottom
and sides
of your
spread-
sheet.

Adding a header (or footer)

Headers and footers are useful when printing out your spreadsheet. A header
may explain the information in the spreadsheet, such as *2014 Tax Return
Information,* and a footer may display page numbers. To create a header or
footer, follow these steps:

1. **Click the Insert tab.**

2. **Click the Header & Footer icon in the Text group.**

   Excel displays the Design tab and creates a text box for your header and
   footer, as shown in Figure 8-21.

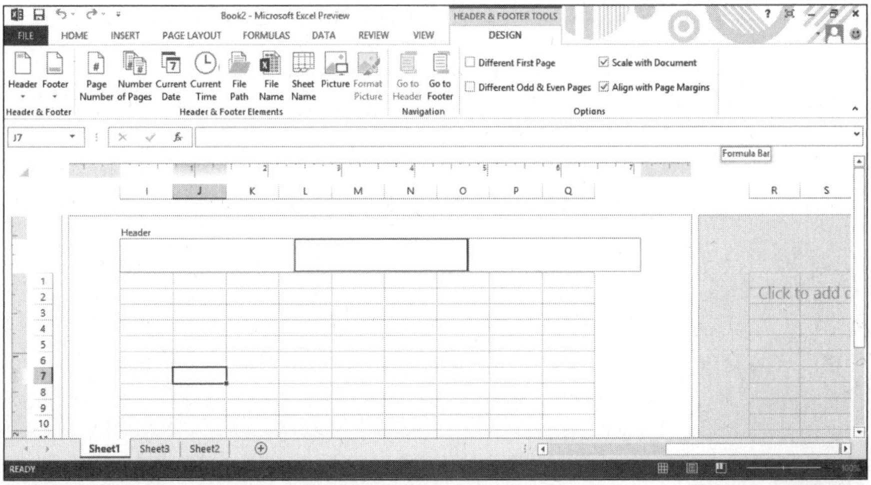

Figure 8-21:
The Design
tab provides
tools for
creating a
header or
footer.

3. **Type your header text in the header text box.**

4. **Click the Go To Footer icon in the Navigation group.**

    Excel displays your footer text box.

5. **Type your footer text in the footer text box.**

TIP

If you switch to Page Layout view, you can click directly in the header or footer box at the top or bottom of the page.

Printing gridlines

Gridlines appear on the screen to help you align data in rows and columns. However, when you print your worksheet, you can choose to omit gridlines or print them to make your data easier to understand.

To print gridlines and/or row and column headings, follow these steps:

1. **Click the Page Layout tab.**

2. **(Optional) Select the Print check box under the Gridlines category.**

3. **(Optional) Select the Print check box under the Heading category.**

Defining a print area

Sometimes you may not want to print your entire spreadsheet but just a certain part of it, called the *print area*. To define the print area, follow these steps:

1. **Select the cells that you want to print.**

2. **Click the Page Layout tab.**

3. **Click the Print Area icon in the Page Setup group.**

    A pull-down menu appears, as shown in Figure 8-22.

Figure 8-22:
The Print Area menu lets you define or clear the printable cells.

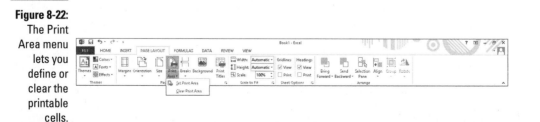

4. **Choose Set Print Area.**

   Excel displays a line around your print area.

5. **Click the File tab and then click Print.**

   A print preview image of your chosen print area appears.

6. **Click Print.**

After you define a print area, you can see which cells are part of your print area by clicking the downward-pointing arrow of the Name box and choosing Print_Area.

After you define a print area, you can always add to it by following these steps:

1. **Select the cells adjacent to the print area.**

2. **Click the Page Layout tab.**

3. **Click the Print Area icon in the Page Setup group.**

   A pull-down menu appears.

4. **Choose Add to Print Area.**

   Excel displays a line around your newly defined print area.

After you define the print area, you can always remove it by following these steps:

1. **Click the Page Layout tab.**

2. **Click Print Area.**

   A pull-down menu appears (refer to Figure 8-22).

3. **Choose Clear Print Area.**

Inserting (and removing) page breaks

One problem with large spreadsheets is that when you print them out, parts may get cut off when printed on separate pages. To correct this problem, you can tell Excel exactly where page breaks should occur.

To insert page breaks, follow these steps:

1. **Move the cursor in the cell to define where the vertical and horizontal page breaks will appear.**

2. **Click the Page Layout tab.**

3. Click the Breaks icon in the Page Setup group.

A pull-down menu appears, as shown in Figure 8-23.

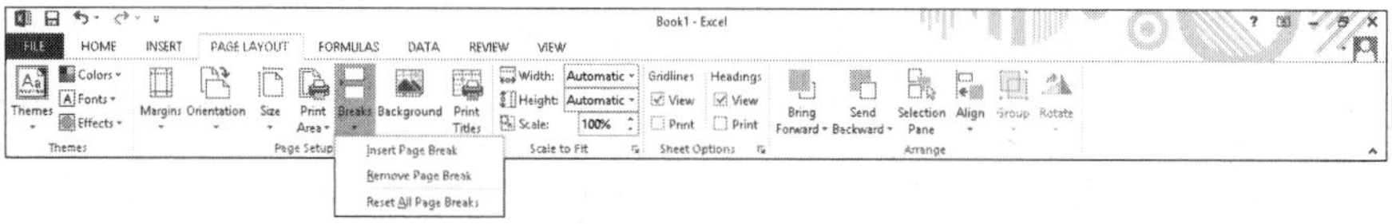

Figure 8-23:
The Breaks
menu lets
you insert a
page break.

4. Choose Insert Page Break.

Excel inserts a horizontal page directly above the cell you selected in Step 1, as well as a vertical page break to the left of that cell.

To remove a page break, follow these steps:

1. Choose one of the following:

- *To remove a horizontal page break:* Click in any cell that appears directly below that horizontal page break.

- *To remove a vertical page break:* Click in any cell that appears directly to the right of that horizontal page break.

- *To remove both a vertical and horizontal page break:* Click in the cell that appears to the right of the vertical page break and directly underneath the horizontal page break.

2. Click the Page Layout tab.

3. Click the Breaks icon in the Page Setup group.

A pull-down menu appears (refer to Figure 8-23).

4. Choose Remove Page Break.

Excel removes your chosen page break.

Printing row and column headings

If you have a large spreadsheet that fills two or more pages, Excel may print your spreadsheet data on separate pages. Although the first page may print your labels to identify what each row and column may represent, any additional pages that Excel prints won't bear those same identifying labels. As a result, you may wind up printing rows and columns of numbers without any labels that identify what those numbers mean.

To fix this problem, you can define labels to print on every page by following these steps:

1. **Click the Page Layout tab.**

2. **Click the Print Titles icon in the Page Setup group.**

   The Page Setup dialog box appears, as shown in Figure 8-24.

3. **Click the Collapse/Expand button that appears to the far right of the Rows to Repeat at Top text box.**

   The Page Setup dialog box shrinks.

4. **Click in the row that contains the labels you want to print at the top of every page.**

5. **Click the Collapse/Expand button again.**

   The Page Setup dialog box reappears.

6. **Click the Collapse/Expand button that appears to the far right of the Columns to Repeat at Left text box.**

   The Page Setup dialog box shrinks.

7. **Click in the column that contains the labels you want to print on the left of every page.**

8. **Click the Collapse/Expand button again.**

   The Page Setup dialog box reappears.

9. **Click OK.**

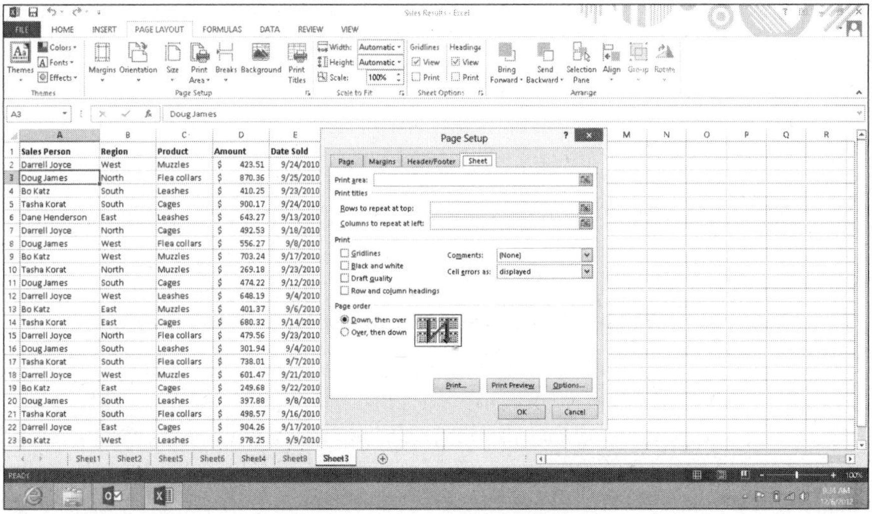

Figure 8-24: The Page Setup dialog box lets you define the row and column headings to print on every page.

Defining printing margins

To help you squeeze or expand your spreadsheet to fill a printed page, you can define different margins for each printed page. To define margins, follow these steps:

1. **Click the Page Layout tab.**

2. **Click the Margins icon in the Page Setup group.**

   A pull-down menu appears, as shown in Figure 8-25.

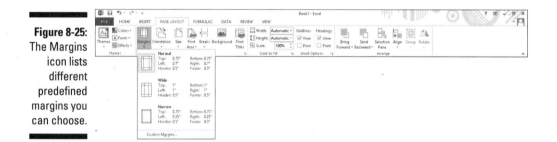

Figure 8-25: The Margins icon lists different predefined margins you can choose.

3. **Choose a page margin style you want to use.**

If you choose Custom Margins in Step 3, you can define your own margins for a printed page.

Defining paper orientation and size

Paper *orientation* can be either *landscape* (the paper width is greater than its height) or *portrait* mode (the paper width is less than its height). Paper *size* defines the physical dimensions of the page.

To change the paper orientation and size, follow these steps:

1. **Click the Page Layout tab.**

2. **Click the Orientation icon in the Page Setup group.**

   A pull-down menu appears.

3. **Choose Portrait or Landscape.**

4. **Click the Size icon in the Page Setup group.**

   A pull-down menu appears, as shown in Figure 8-26.

Figure 8-26:
The Size
menu lists
different
paper sizes
you can use.

5. **Click a paper size.**

Printing in Excel

When you finish defining how to print your spreadsheet, you'll probably want to print it eventually. To print a worksheet, follow these steps:

1. **Click the File tab.**

   The Backstage View appears.

2. **Click Print.**

   The Print Preview appears in the right pane.

3. **Click the Print icon near the top of the middle pane.**

Chapter 9

Playing with Formulas

. . . .

. . . .

*W*hat makes Excel useful is its ability to manipulate data by using for-mulas. Formulas can be as simple as adding two or more numbers together or as complicated as calculating a second-order differential equation.

Formulas use data, stored in other cells, to calculate a new result that appears in another cell. To create even more complicated spreadsheets, you can even make a formula use data from other formulas so that changes in a single cell can ripple throughout an entire spreadsheet.

Creating a Formula

Formulas consist of three crucial bits of information:

▶ An equal sign (=)

▶ One or more cell references

▶ The type of calculation to do on the data (addition, subtraction, and so on)

The equal sign (=) simply tells Excel not to treat the formula as text but as instructions for calculating something.

A *cell reference* is simply the unique row and column heading that identifies a single cell, such as A4 or D9.

The four common calculations that a formula can use are addition (+), subtraction (–), multiplication (*), and division (/). Table 9-1 lists other mathematical operators you can use in a formula.

Table 9-1	Common Mathematical Operators Used to Create Formulas		
Operator	**What It Does**	**Example**	**Result**
+	Addition	=5+3.4	8.4
–	Subtraction	=54.2-2.1	52.1
*	Multiplication	=1.2*4	4.8
/	Division	=25/5	5
%	Percentage	=42%	0.42
^	Exponentiation	=4^3	64
=	Equal	=6=7	False
>	Greater than	=7>2	True
<	Less than	=9<8	False
>=	Greater than or equal to	=45>=3	True
<=	Less than or equal to	=40<=2	False
<>	Not equal to	=5<>7	True
&	Text concatenation	="Bo the "& "Cat"	Bo the Cat

A simple formula uses a single mathematical operator and two cell references such as:

=A4+C7

This formula consists of three parts:

- ✔ **The = sign:** This identifies your formula. If you typed just **A4+C7** into a cell, Excel would treat it as ordinary text.
- ✔ **Two cell references:** In this example, A4 and C7.
- ✔ **The addition (+) mathematical operator.**

To type a formula in a cell, follow these steps:

1. **Click in the cell where you want to store the formula.**

   You can also select a cell by pressing the arrow keys.

   Excel highlights your selected cell.

2. **Type the equal sign (=).**

   This tells Excel that you are creating a formula.

3. **Type your formula that includes one or more cell references that identify cells that contain data, such as A4 or E8.**

   For example, if you want to add the numbers stored in cells A4 and E8, you would type =A4+E8.

4. **Press Enter.**

Typing cell references can get cumbersome because you have to match the row and column headings of a cell correctly. As a faster alternative, you can use the mouse to click any cell that contains data; then Excel types that cell reference into your formula automatically.

To use the mouse to click cell references when creating a formula, follow these steps:

1. **Click in the cell where you want to store the formula. (You can also select the cell by pressing the arrow keys.)**

   Excel highlights your selected cell.

2. **Type the equal sign (=).**

   This tells Excel that anything you type after the equal sign is part of your formula.

3. **Type any mathematical operators and click any cells that contain data, such as A4 or E8.**

   If you want to create the formula =A4+E8, you would do the following:

   a. *Type =.*

      This tells Excel that you're creating a formula.

   b. *Click cell A4.*

      Excel types the A4 cell reference in your formula automatically.

   c. *Type +.*

   d. *Click cell E8.*

      Excel types in the E8 cell reference in your formula automatically.

4. **Press Enter.**

After you finish creating a formula, you can type data into the cell references used in your formula to calculate a new result.

Organizing formulas with parentheses

Formulas can be as simple as a single mathematical operator such as =D3*E4. However, you can also use multiple mathematical operators, such as

=A4+A5*C7/F4+D9

There are two problems with using multiple mathematical operators. First, they make a formula harder to read and understand. Second, Excel calculates mathematical operators from left to right, based on precedence, which means a formula may calculate results differently from what you intended.

Precedence tells Excel which mathematical operators to calculate first, as listed in Table 9-2. For example, Excel calculates multiplication before it calculates addition. If you had a formula such as

=A3+A4*B4+B5

Excel first multiplies A4*B4 and then adds this result to A3 and B5.

Table 9-2	Operator Precedence in Excel
Mathematical Operator	*Description*
: (colon) (single space) , (comma)	Reference operators
–	Negation
%	Percent
^	Exponentiation
* /	Multiplication and division
+ –	Addition and subtraction
&	Text concatenation
= < > <= >= <>	Comparison

Typing parentheses around cell references and mathematical operators not only organizes your formulas, but also tells Excel specifically how you want to calculate a formula. In the example =A3+A4*B4+B5, Excel multiplies A4 and B4 first. If you want Excel to first add A3 and A4, then add B4 and B5, and finally multiply the two results together, you have to use parentheses, like this:

=(A3+A4)*(B4+B5)

Copying formulas

In many spreadsheets, you may need to create similar formulas that use different data. For example, you may have a spreadsheet that needs to add the same number of cells in adjacent columns.

You can type nearly identical formulas in multiple cells, but that's tedious and error-prone. For a faster way, you can copy a formula and paste it in another cell; then Excel automatically changes the cell references, as shown in Figure 9-1.

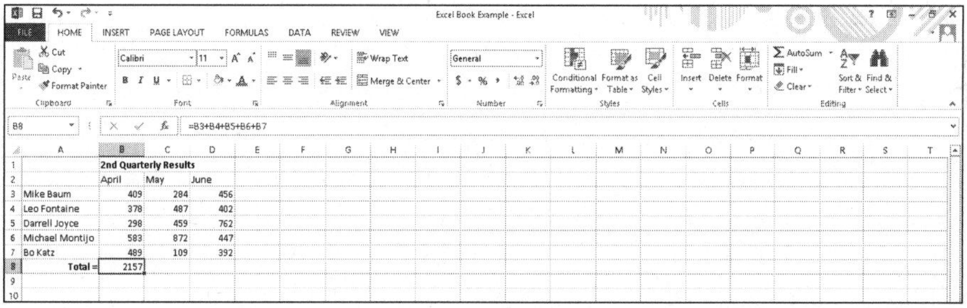

Figure 9-1: Rather than type repetitive formulas over and over again, Excel can copy a formula but automatically change the cell references.

From Figure 9-1, you can see that cell B8 contains the formula =B3+B4+B5+B6+B7, which simply adds the numbers stored in the five cells directly above the cell that contains the formula (B8). If you copy this formula to another cell, that new formula will also add the six cells directly above it. Copy and paste this formula to cell C8, and Excel changes the formula to =C3+C4+C5+C6+C7.

To copy and paste a formula so that each formula changes cell references automatically, follow these steps:

1. **Select the cell that contains the formula you want to copy.**

2. **Press Ctrl+C (or click the Copy icon under the Home tab).**

   Excel displays a dotted line around your selected cell.

3. **Select the cell (or cells) where you want to paste your formula.**

   If you select multiple cells, Excel pastes a copy of your formula in each of those cells.

4. **Press Ctrl+V (or click the Paste icon under the Home tab).**

   Excel pastes your formula and automatically changes the cell references.

5. **Press Esc or double-click away from the cell with the dotted line to make the dotted line go away.**

Using Functions

Creating simple formulas is easy, but creating complex formulas is hard. To make complex formulas easier to create, Excel comes with prebuilt formulas called *functions*. Table 9-3 lists some of the many functions available.

Table 9-3	Common Excel Functions
Function Name	*What It Does*
AVERAGE	Calculates the average value of numbers stored in two or more cells
COUNT	Counts how many cells contain a number instead of a label (text)
MAX	Finds the largest number stored in two or more cells
MIN	Finds the smallest number stored in two or more cells
ROUND	Rounds a decimal number to a specific number of digits
SQRT	Calculates the square root of a number
SUM	Adds the values stored in two or more cells

Excel provides hundreds of functions that you can use by themselves or as part of your own formulas. A *function* typically uses one or more cell references:

✔ **Single cell references** such as =ROUND(C4,2), which rounds the number found in cell C4 to two decimal places.

✔ *Contiguous* **(adjacent) cell ranges** such as =SUM(A4:A9), which adds all the numbers found in cells A4, A5, A6, A7, A8, and A9.

✔ **Noncontiguous cell ranges** such as =SUM(A4,B7,C11), which adds all the numbers found in cells A4, B7, and C11.

To use a function, follow these steps:

1. **Click in the cell where you want to create a formula using a function.**

2. **Click the Formulas tab.**

3. **Click one of the following function icons in the Function Library group:**

   • *Financial:* Calculates business-related equations, such as the amount of interest earned over a specified time period.

   • *Logical:* Provides logical operators to manipulate True and False (also known as *Boolean)* values.

   • *Text:* Searches and manipulates text.

   • *Date & Time:* Provides date and time information.

   • *Lookup & Reference:* Provides information about cells, such as their row headings.

   • *Math & Trig:* Offers mathematical equations.

   • *More Functions:* Provides access to statistical and engineering functions.

4. **Click a function category, such as Financial or Math & Trig.**

   A pull-down menu appears, as shown in Figure 9-2.

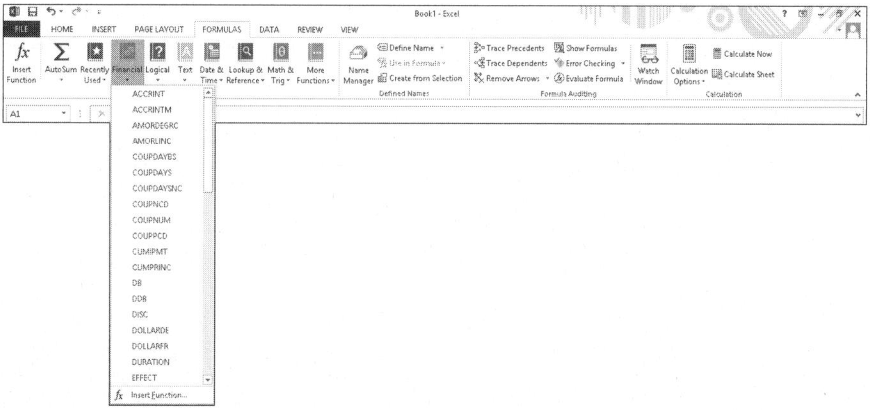

Figure 9-2: Clicking a function library icon displays a menu of available functions you can use.

5. Click a function.

The Function Arguments dialog box appears, as shown in Figure 9-3.

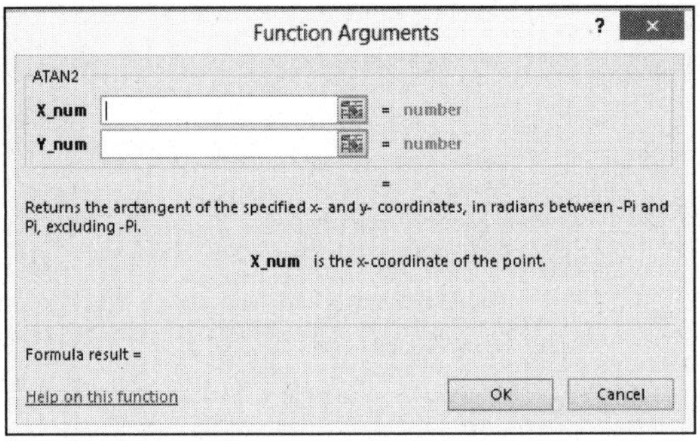

Figure 9-3:
Specify
which cell
references
contain the
data your
function
needs to
calculate a
result.

6. Click the cell references you want to use.

7. Repeat Step 6 as many times as necessary.

8. Click OK.

Excel displays the calculation of your function in the cell you selected in Step 1.

Using the AutoSum command

One of the most useful and commonly used commands is the AutoSum command. The *AutoSum command* uses the SUM function to add two or more cell references without making you type those cell references yourself. The most common use for the AutoSum function is to add a column or row of numbers.

To add a column or row of numbers with the AutoSum function, follow these steps:

1. Create a column or row of numbers that you want to add.

2. Click at the bottom of the column or the right of the row.

3. Click the Formulas tab.

4. Click the AutoSum icon in the Function Library group.

Excel automatically creates a SUM function in the cell you chose in Step 2 and highlights all the cells where it will retrieve data to add, as shown in Figure 9-4. (If you accidentally click the downward-pointing arrow under the AutoSum icon, a pull-down menu appears. Just choose Sum.)

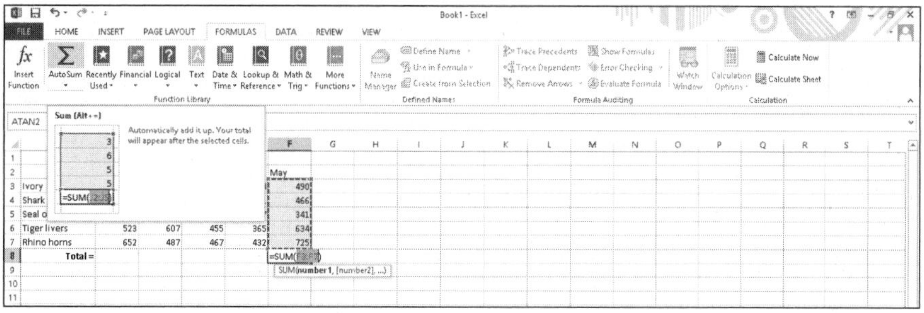

Figure 9-4:
The
AutoSum
command
auto-
matically
creates cell
references
for the SUM
function.

5. **Press Enter.**

   Excel automatically sums all the cell references.

   The AutoSum icon also appears on the Home tab in the Editing group.

Using recently used functions

Digging through all the different function library menus can be cumbersome, so Excel tries to make your life easier by creating a special Recently Used list that contains (what else?) a list of the functions you've used most often. From this menu, you can see just a list of your favorite functions and ignore the other hundred functions that you may never need in a million years.

To use the list of recently used functions, follow these steps:

1. **Click the cell where you want to store a function.**

2. **Click the Formulas tab.**

3. **Click the Recently Used icon in the Function Library group.**

   A pull-down menu appears, as shown in Figure 9-5.

Figure 9-5:
The
Recently
Used menu
lists the
functions
you've used
most often.

4. Choose a function.

The more functions you use, the more your list will vary from what you see in Figure 9-5.

Editing a Formula

After you create a formula, you can always edit it later. You can edit a formula in two places:

- ✔ In the Formula bar
- ✔ In the cell itself

To edit a formula in the Formula bar, follow these steps:

1. **Select the cell that contains the formula you want to edit.**

   Excel displays the formula in the Formula bar.

2. **Click in the Formula bar and edit your formula by using the Backspace and Delete keys.**

To edit a formula in the cell itself, follow these steps:

1. **Double-click in the cell that contains the formula you want to edit.**

   Excel displays a cursor in the cell you selected.

2. **Edit your formula by using the Backspace and Delete keys.**

Because formulas display their calculations in a cell, it can be hard to tell the difference between cells that contain numbers and cells that contain formulas. To make formulas visible, press Ctrl+` (an *accent grave* character, which appears on the same key as the tilde, the ~ symbol).

Conditional Formatting

A formula in a cell can display a variety of values, depending on the data that the formula receives. Because a formula can display any type of a number, you may want to use conditional formatting as a way to highlight certain types of values.

Suppose you have a formula that calculates your monthly profits. You can change the formatting to emphasize the results:

  ✔ If your result is zero or a loss, display that value in *red*.

  ✔ If you make a profit under $1,000, display that value in *yellow*.

  ✔ If the profit is at least $100,000, display that value in *green*.

Conditional formatting simply displays data in a formula in various ways, depending on the value that the formula calculates.

Comparing data values

The simplest type of conditional formatting displays different colors or icons based on adjacent values, which makes it easy to compare, at a glance, different numbers.

Excel offers three types of conditional formatting for identifying values, as shown in Figure 9-6:

  ✔ **Data Bars:** Higher values display more color while lower values display less color.

  ✔ **Color Scales:** Different colors identify different ranges of values.

  ✔ **Icon Sets:** Different icons identify different ranges of values.

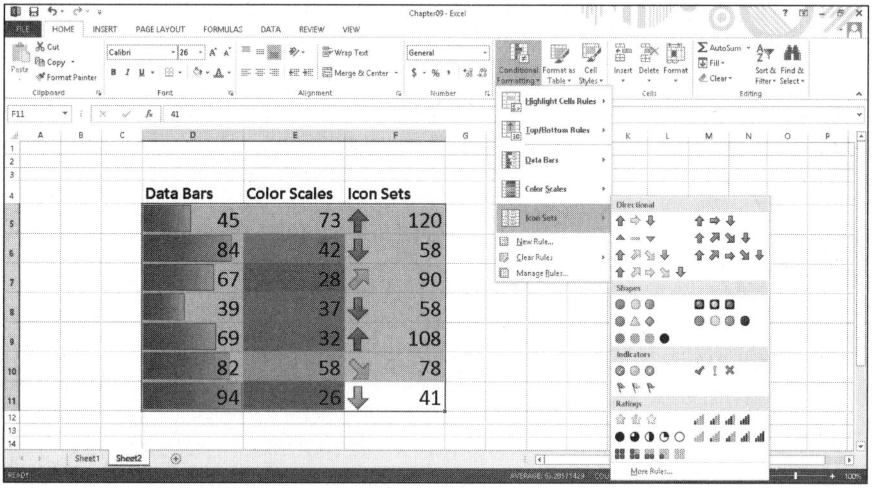

Figure 9-6: Conditional formatting can identify values of different cells.

To apply conditional formatting, follow these steps:

1. **Select the cells that you want to apply conditional formatting.**

2. **Click the Home tab and then click the Conditional Formatting icon in the Styles group.**

   A menu appears (refer to Figure 9-6).

3. **Move the mouse over Data Bars, Color Scales, or Icon Sets.**

   A menu appears.

4. **Click the type of conditional formatting you want.**

   Excel applies your conditional formatting over the cells you chose in Step 1.

Creating conditional formatting rules

Using colors or icons to identify ranges of values may be nice, but you may want to define your own rules for how conditional formatting should work, such as displaying all negative values in red and all values above 1,000 in green.

To define your own rules for formatting values, follow these steps:

1. **Select the cells that you want to apply conditional formatting.**

2. **Click the Home tab and then click the Conditional Formatting icon in the Styles group.**

   A menu appears (refer to Figure 9-6).

3. **Move the mouse over Highlight Cells Rules.**

   A menu appears, as shown in Figure 9-7.

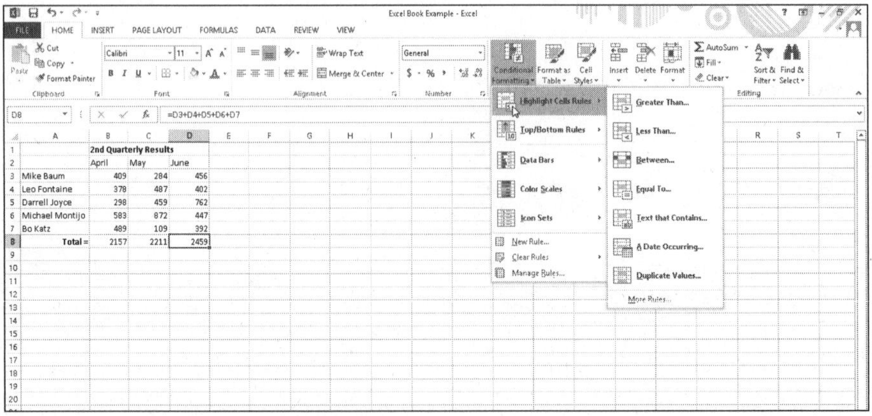

Figure 9-7: The Highlight Cells Rules displays a variety of options.

4. Click an option, such as Greater Than or Between.

A dialog box appears, which lets you define one or more values and choose a color for formatting your selected cells, as shown in Figure 9-8.

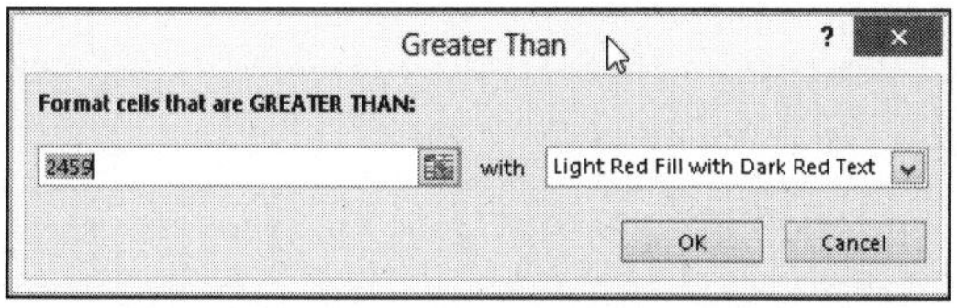

Figure 9-8:
A dialog box lets you define a value and color to format cells.

Greater Than ? ✕

Format cells that are GREATER THAN:

| 2459 | with | Light Red Fill with Dark Red Text ▾ |

OK   Cancel

5. Type a value, choose a color for formatting, and click OK.

Excel displays conditional formatting only to those selected cells that meet the criteria you defined.

TIP

If you click the Conditional Formatting icon on the Home tab and choose Top/Bottom Rules, Excel can apply conditional formatting to your top (or bottom) ten values or those values above or below the average, as shown in Figure 9-9.

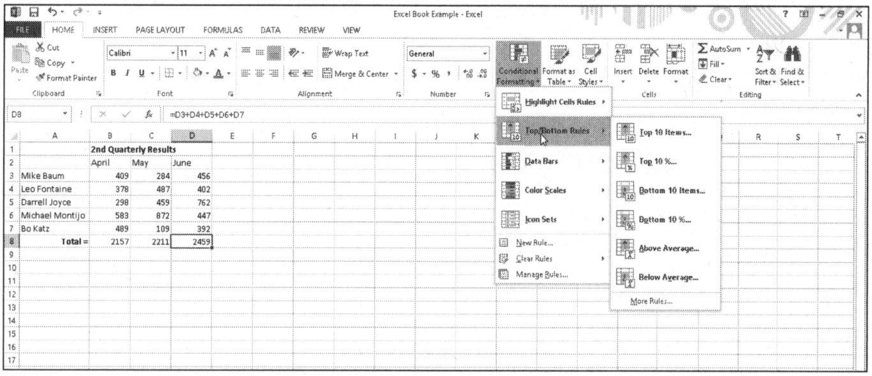

Figure 9-9:
The Top/Bottom Rules menu can identify the top/bottom values or those above/below the average.

Data Validation

Because formulas are only as accurate as the data they receive, it's important that your spreadsheet contains only valid data. Examples of invalid data may be a negative number (such as –9) for a price or a decimal number (such as 4.39) for the number of items a customer bought.

To keep your spreadsheet from accepting invalid data, you can define a cell to accept only certain types of data, such as numbers that fall between 30 and 100. The moment someone tries to type invalid data into a cell, Excel immediately warns you, as shown in Figure 9-10.

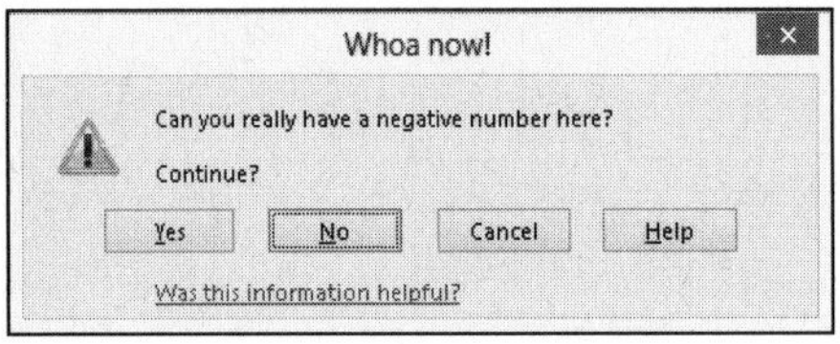

Figure 9-10:
Excel warns
you if you
type invalid
data in
a cell.

Whoa now!

Can you really have a negative number here?

Continue?

Yes   No   Cancel   Help

Was this information helpful?

To define valid types of data for a cell, follow these steps:

1. **Click a cell that contains data used by a formula.**

2. **Click the Data tab.**

3. **Click the top of the Data Validation icon in the Data Tools group.**

   The Data Validation dialog box appears, as shown in Figure 9-11.

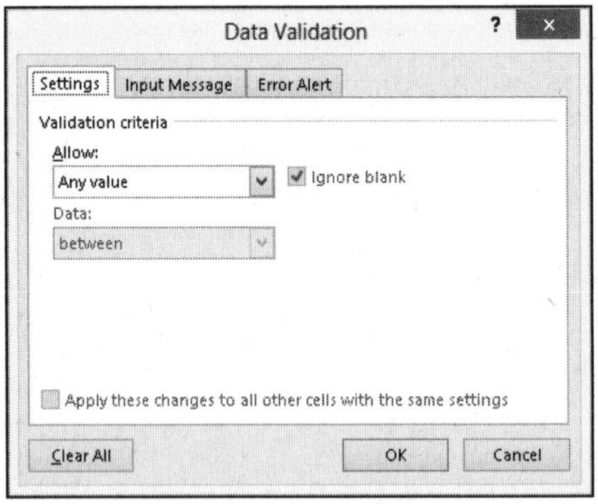

Data Validation

Settings | Input Message | Error Alert

Validation criteria

Allow:

Any value   ☑ Ignore blank

Data:

between

☐ Apply these changes to all other cells with the same settings

Clear All   OK   Cancel

Figure 9-11:
Define the
type and
range of
accept-
able data
allowed in
a cell.

4. **Click the Allow list box and choose one of the following:**

   • *Any Value:* The default value accepts anything the user types.

   • *Whole Number:* Accepts only whole numbers, such as 47 and 903.

   • *Decimal:* Accepts whole and decimal numbers, such as 48.01 or 1.00.

   • *List:* Allows you to define a list of valid data.

   • *Date:* Accepts only dates.

- *Time:* Accepts only times.

- *Text length:* Defines a minimum and maximum length for text.

- *Custom:* Allows you to define a formula to specify valid data.

Depending on the option you choose, you may need to define Minimum and Maximum values and whether you want the data to be equal to, less than, or greater than a defined limit.

5. Click the Input Message tab in the Data Validation dialog box, as shown in Figure 9-12.

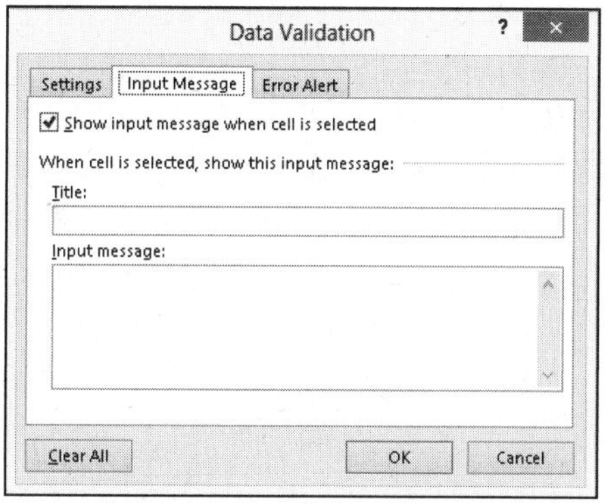

Figure 9-12:
The Input Message tab lets you display a message explaining the type of valid data a cell can hold.

6. Click in the Title text box and type a title.

7. Click in the Input Message text box and type a message you want to display when someone selects this particular cell.

8. Click the Error Alert tab in the Data Validation dialog box, as shown in Figure 9-13.

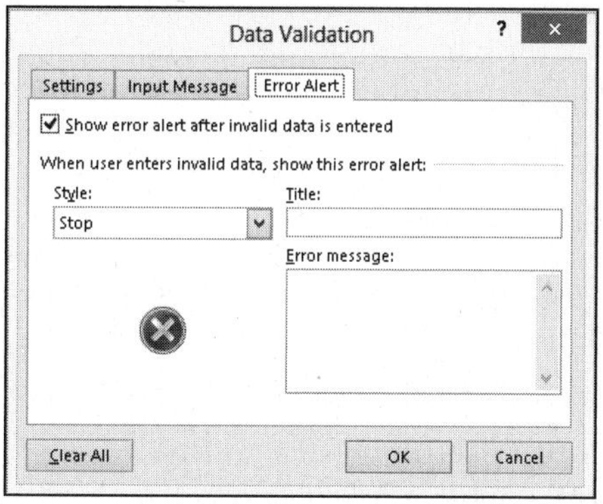

Figure 9-13:
Define an error message to show if the user types invalid data into the cell.

9. **Click the Style list box and choose an alert icon, such as Stop or Warning.**

10. **Click in the Title text box and type a title for your error message.**

11. **Click in the Error Message text box and type the message to appear if the user types invalid data into the cell.**

12. **Click OK.**

After you define data validation for a cell, you can always remove it later. To remove validation for a cell, follow these steps:

1. **Click in the cell that contains data validation.**

2. **Click the Data tab.**

3. **Click the top of the Data Validation icon in the Data Tools group.**

   The Data Validation dialog box appears (refer to Figure 9-11).

4. **Click the Clear All button and then click OK.**

   Excel clears all your data validation rules for your chosen cell.

Goal Seeking

When you create a formula, you can type in data to see how the formula calculates a new result. However, Excel also offers a feature known as *Goal Seeking.* With Goal Seeking, you specify the value you want a formula to calculate, and then Excel changes the data in the formula's cell references to tell you what values you need to achieve that goal.

For example, suppose you have a formula that calculates how much money you make every month by selling a product such as cars. Change the number of cars you sell, and Excel calculates your monthly commission. But if you use Goal Seeking, you can specify you want to earn $5,000 for your monthly commission, and Excel will work backward to tell you how many cars you need to sell. As its name implies, Goal Seeking lets you specify a goal and see what number, in a specific cell, needs to change to help you reach your goal.

To use Goal Seeking, follow these steps:

1. **Click in a cell that contains a formula.**

2. **Click the Data tab.**

3. **Click the What-If Analysis icon in the Data Tools group.**

   A pull-down menu appears, as shown in Figure 9-14.

Figure 9-14:
The What-If
Analysis
icon
displays the
Goal Seek
command.

4. **Click Goal Seek.**

   The Goal Seek dialog box appears, as shown in Figure 9-15.

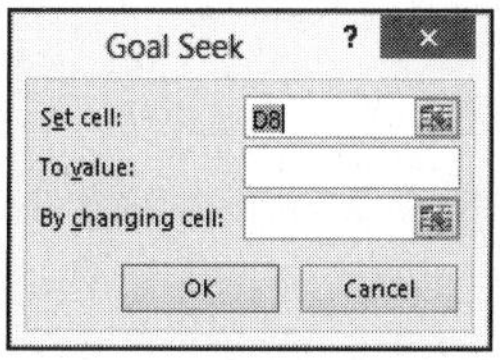

Figure 9-15:
Define your
goal in a cell
containing a
formula.

5. **Click in the To Value text box and type a number that you want to appear in the formula stored in the cell that you clicked in Step 1.**

6. **Click in the By Changing Cell text box and click one cell that contains data used by the formula you chose in Step 1.**

   Excel displays your cell reference, such as B5, in the Goal Seek dialog box.

7. **Click OK.**

   The Goal Seek Status dialog box changes the data in the cell you chose in Step 6, as shown in Figure 9-16.

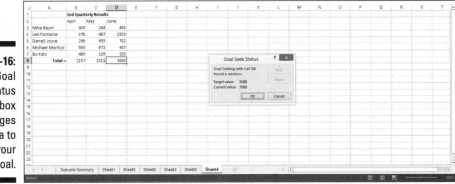

Figure 9-16:
The Goal
Seek Status
dialog box
changes
the data to
reach your
desired goal.

8. **Click OK (to keep the changes) or click Cancel (to display the original values your spreadsheet had before you chose the Goal Seek command).**

Creating Multiple Scenarios

Spreadsheets show you what happened in the past. However, you can also use a spreadsheet to help predict the future by typing in data that represents your best guess of what may happen.

When you use a spreadsheet as a prediction tool, you may create a best-case scenario (where customers flood you with orders) and a worst-case scenario (where hardly anybody buys anything). You can type in different data to represent multiple possibilities, but then you'd wipe out your old data. For a quick way to plug different data into the same spreadsheet, Excel offers scenarios.

A *scenario* lets you define different data for multiple cells, which creates multiple spreadsheets. That way, you can choose a scenario to plug in one set of data, and then switch back to your original data without retyping all your original data and formulas all over again.

Creating a scenario

Before you can create a scenario, you must first create a spreadsheet with data and formulas. Then you can create a scenario to define the data to plug into one or more cells.

To create a scenario, follow these steps:

1. **Click the Data tab.**

2. **Click the What-If Analysis icon in the Data Tools group.**

   A pull-down menu appears.

3. **Click Scenario Manager.**

   The Scenario Manager dialog box appears.

4. **Click Add.**

   The Add Scenario dialog box appears, as shown in Figure 9-17.

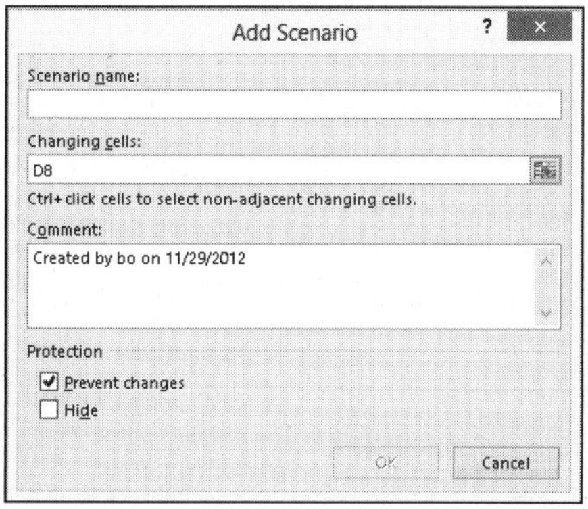

Figure 9-17: Define a scenario name, the cells you want to change, and any comments you want to include.

Add Scenario	?	X
Scenario name:		
Changing cells: D8		
Ctrl+click cells to select non-adjacent changing cells.		
Comment: Created by bo on 11/29/2012		
Protection ☑ Prevent changes ☐ Hide		
	OK	Cancel

5. **Click in the Scenario Name text box and type a descriptive name for your scenario, such as** Worst-case **or** Best-case.

6. **Click in the Changing Cells text box.**

7. **Click a cell in your spreadsheet that you want to display different data. If you want to choose multiple cells, hold down the Ctrl key and click multiple cells.**

8. **Click in the Comment text box and type any additional comments you want to add to your scenario, such as any assumptions your scenario made.**

9. **Click OK.**

   The Scenario Values dialog box appears, as shown in Figure 9-18.

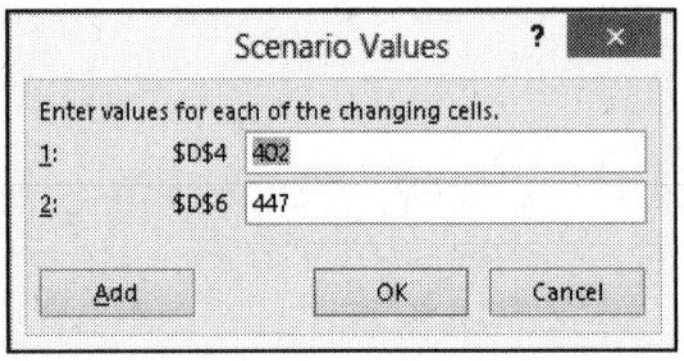

Figure 9-18:
Type in
new values
for your
selected
cells.

10. **Type a new value for each cell.**

11. **Click OK.**

    The Scenario Manager dialog box appears, as shown in Figure 9-19.

Figure 9-19:
The
Scenario
Manager
dialog box
lets you
view, edit, or
delete your
different
scenarios.

12. **Click Show.**

    Excel replaces any existing data with the data you typed in Step 10.

13. **Click Close.**

    The data from your scenario remains in the spreadsheet.

Viewing a scenario

After you create one or more scenarios, you can view them and see how they affect your data. To view a scenario, follow these steps:

1. **Click the Data tab.**

2. **Click the What-If Analysis icon in the Data Tools group.**

    A pull-down menu appears.

3. **Choose Scenario Manager.**

    The Scenario Manager dialog box appears (refer to Figure 9-19).

4. **Click the name of the scenario you want to view.**

5. **Click Show.**

    Excel shows the values in the cells defined by your chosen scenario.

6. **Click Close.**

Editing a scenario

After you create a scenario, you can always change it later by defining new data. To edit a scenario, follow these steps:

1. **Click the Data tab.**

2. **Click the What-If Analysis icon in the Data Tools group.**

    A pull-down menu appears.

3. **Choose Scenario Manager.**

    The Scenario Manager dialog box appears.

4. **Click the name of the scenario you want to edit and click Edit.**

    The Edit Scenario dialog box appears.

5. **(Optional) Edit the name of the scenario.**

6. **Click in the Changing Cells text box.**

    Excel displays dotted lines around all the cells that the scenario will change.

7. **Press Backspace to delete cells, or hold down the Ctrl key and click additional cells to include in your scenario.**

8. **Click OK.**

    The Scenario Values dialog box appears (refer to Figure 9-18).

9. **Type new values for your cells and click OK when you're done.**

    The Scenario Manager dialog box appears again.

10. **Click Show to view your scenario, or click Close to make the Scenario Manager dialog box disappear.**

Viewing a scenario summary

If you have multiple scenarios, it can be hard to switch back and forth between different scenarios and still understand which numbers are changing. To help you view the numbers that change in all your scenarios, you can create a scenario summary.

A *scenario summary* displays your original data, along with the data stored in each scenario, in a table. By viewing a scenario summary, you can see how the values of your spreadsheet can change depending on the scenario, as shown in Figure 9-20.

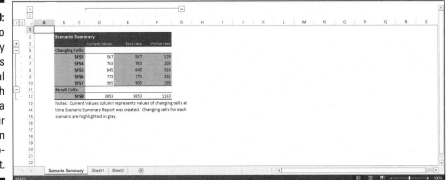

Figure 9-20: A scenario summary compares your original data with all the data from your scenarios in an easy-to-read chart.

To create a scenario summary on a separate sheet in your workbook, follow these steps:

1. **Click the Data tab.**

2. **Click the What-If Analysis icon in the Data Tools group.**

   A pull-down menu appears.

3. **Choose Scenario Manager.**

   The Scenario Manager dialog box appears.

4. **Click Summary.**

   The Scenario Summary dialog box appears, as shown in Figure 9-21.

5. **Select the Scenario Summary radio button.**

6. **Click in the Result Cells text box and then click in a cell that contains a formula that your scenario affects.**

7. **Click OK.**

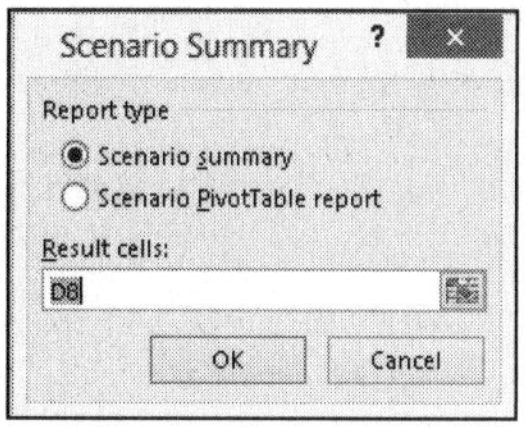

Figure 9-21:
Define the
type of
summary to
create.

Auditing Your Formulas

Your spreadsheet provides results that are only as good as the data you give it and the formulas you create. Feed a spreadsheet the wrong data, and it will (obviously) calculate the wrong result. More troublesome is when you feed a spreadsheet the right data but your formula is incorrect, which produces a misleading and incorrect result.

Even if Excel appears to be calculating your formulas correctly, recheck your calculations just to make sure. Some common errors that can mess up your formulas include

- ✔ **Missing data:** The formula isn't using all the data necessary to calculate the proper result.

- ✔ **Incorrect data:** The formula is getting data from the wrong cell (or wrong data from the right cell).

- ✔ **Incorrect calculation:** Your formula is incorrectly calculating a result.

If a formula is calculating data incorrectly, you probably didn't type the formula correctly. For example, you may want a formula to add two numbers, but you accidentally typed in the formula to multiply two numbers instead. To check whether a formula is calculating data incorrectly, give it data that you already know what the result should be. For example, if you typed the numbers 4 and 7 into a formula that should add two numbers, but it returns 28 instead, you know that it's not calculating correctly.

If your formula is correct but it's still not calculating the right result, chances are good that it's not getting the data it needs from the correct cells. To help you trace whether a formula is receiving all the data it needs, Excel offers auditing features that visually show you which cells supply data to which formulas. By using Excel's auditing features, you can

- ✔ Make sure that your formulas are using data from the correct cells.

- ✔ Find out instantly whether a formula can go haywire if you change a cell reference.

Finding where a formula gets its data

If a formula is retrieving data from the wrong cells, it's never going to calculate the right result. By tracing a formula, you can see all the cells that a formula uses to retrieve data.

Any cell that supplies data to a formula is a *precedent*.

To trace a formula, follow these steps:

1. **Click a cell that contains the formula you want to check.**

2. **Click the Formulas tab.**

3. **Click the Trace Precedents icon in the Formula Auditing group.**

   Excel draws arrows that show you all the cells that feed data into the formula you chose in Step 1, as shown in Figure 9-22.

Figure 9-22:
Excel draws arrows that trace the precedent cells that feed data into a formula.

	A	B	C	D	E
1		2nd Quarterly Results			
2		April	May	June	
3	Mike Baum	409	284	456	
4	Leo Fontaine	378	487	402	
5	Darrell Joyce	298	459	762	
6	Michael Montijo	583	872	447	
7	Bo Katz	489	109	392	
8	Total =	2157	2211	2459	

D8   =D3+D4+D5+D6+D7

4. **Click the Remove Arrows button to make the auditing arrows go away.**

Finding which formula(s) a cell can change

Sometimes you may be curious about how a particular cell may affect a formula stored in your worksheet. Although you can just type a new value in that cell and look for any changes, it's easier (and more accurate) to identify all formulas that are dependent on a particular cell.

Any formula that receives data is *a dependent*.

To find one or more formulas that a single cell may affect, follow these steps:

1. **Click any cell that contains data (not a formula).**

2. **Click the Formulas tab.**

3. **Click Trace Dependents.**

   Excel draws an arrow that points to a cell that contains a formula, as shown in Figure 9-23. This tells you that if you change the data in the cell you chose in Step 1, it will change the calculated result in the cell containing a formula.

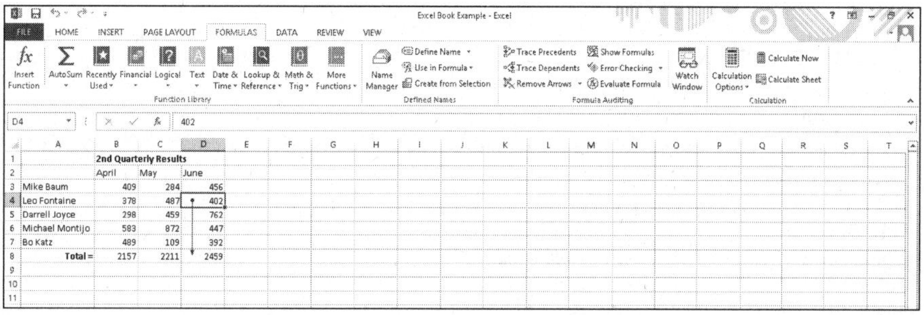

Figure 9-23: Excel can identify which formulas a particular cell can change.

4. **Click the Remove Arrows icon in the Formula Auditing group to make the arrows go away.**

Checking for Errors

If you create large worksheets with data and formulas filling rows and columns, it can be hard to check to make sure that there aren't any problems with your spreadsheet, such as a formula dividing a number with a nonexistent value in another cell.

Fortunately, you can get Excel to catch many types of errors by following these steps:

1. **Click the Formulas tab.**

2. **Click the left side of the Error Checking icon in the Formula Auditing group.**

   Excel displays a dialog box and highlights any errors, as shown in Figure 9-24.

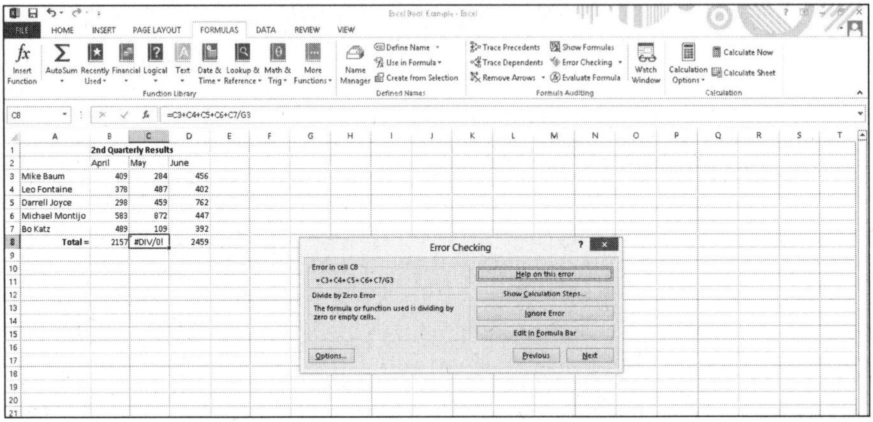

Figure 9-24:
Excel can
identify
many com-
mon errors
in a spread-
sheet.

3. **Click any of the options, such as Previous or Next, to see any additional errors.**

4. **Click the close box in the dialog box to make it go away when you're done using it.**

5. **Click in a cell that contains an error.**

6. **Click the downward-pointing arrow that appears to the right of the Error Checking icon.**

   A menu appears.

7. **Click Trace Error.**

   Excel displays arrows to show you the cells that are causing the problem for the error you chose in Step 5, as shown in Figure 9-25.

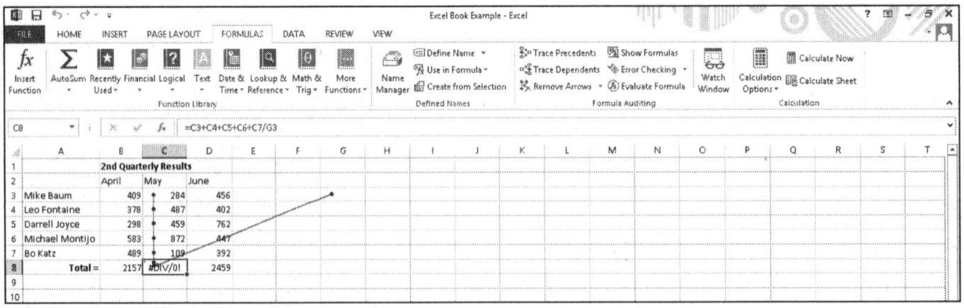

Figure 9-25:
Excel can
show you
where errors
are occur-
ring in your
spreadsheet.

8. **Click the Remove Arrows icon in the Formula Auditing group to make the arrows go away.**

Chapter 10

Charting and Analyzing Data

● ●

In This Chapter

▶ Understanding the parts of a chart

▶ Creating a chart

▶ Editing a chart

▶ Modifying the parts of a chart

▶ Playing with pivot tables

● ●

*L*ook at any Excel spreadsheet loaded with rows and columns of numbers and you may wonder, "What do all these numbers really mean?" Long lists of numbers can be intimidating and confusing, but fortunately, Excel has a solution.

To help you analyze and understand rows and columns of numbers quickly and easily, Excel can convert data into a variety of charts such as pie charts, bar charts, and line charts. By letting you visualize your data, Excel helps you quickly understand what your data means so you can spot trends and patterns.

Understanding the Parts of a Chart

To create charts that clarify your data (rather than confuse you even more), you need to understand the parts of a chart and their purposes, as shown in Figure 10-1:

✔ **Data Series:** The numeric data that Excel uses to create the chart

✔ **X-axis:** Defines the width of a chart

✔ **Y-axis:** Defines the height of a chart

✔ **Legend:** Provides text to explain what each visual part of a chart means

✔ **Chart Title:** Explains the purpose of the entire chart

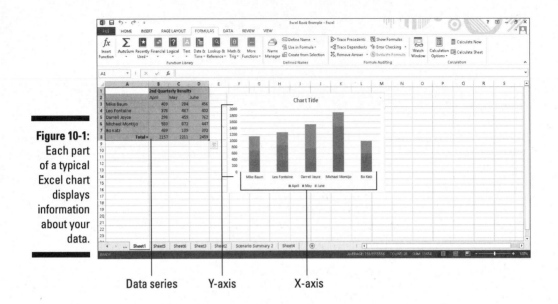

Figure 10-1:
Each part
of a typical
Excel chart
displays
information
about your
data.

Data series   Y-axis   X-axis

Charts typically use two data series to create a chart. For example, one data series may be sales made that month, while a second data series may be the products actually sold.

The X-axis of such a chart would list the names of different products while the Y-axis would list a range of numbers that represent amounts. The chart itself could display different colors that represent products sold in different months, and the legend would explain what each color represents.

By glancing at the column chart in Figure 10-1, you can quickly identify

- ✓ Which products sell best
- ✓ How each product sells in each month
- ✓ Whether sales of a particular product are improving (or getting worse)

All this data came from the spreadsheet in Figure 10-1. By looking at the numbers in this spreadsheet, identifying the information just mentioned is nearly impossible. However, by converting these numbers into a chart, identifying this type of information is so simple even your boss can do it.

Although Figure 10-1 shows a column chart, Excel can create a variety of other types of charts so you can look at your data in different ways, as shown in Figure 10-2. Some other types of charts Excel can create include

✔ **Column chart:** Displays quantities as vertical columns that "grow" upward. Useful for creating charts that compare two items, such as sales per month or sales per salesperson.

✔ **Line chart:** Displays quantities as lines. Essentially shows the tops of a column chart.

✔ **Area chart:** Identical to a line chart except that it shades the area underneath each line.

✔ **Bar chart:** Essentially a column chart turned on its side where bars "grow" from left to right.

✔ **Pie chart:** Compares multiple items in relation to a whole, such as which product sales make up a percentage of a company's overall profits.

Figure 10-2:
Common types of charts that Excel can create to help you visualize your data in different ways.

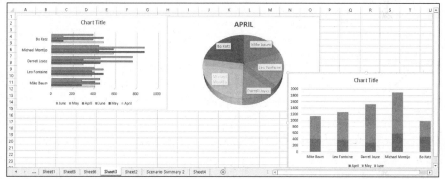

Excel can create both two- and three-dimensional charts. A 3-D chart can look neat, but sometimes the 3-D visual can obscure the true purpose of the chart, which is to simplify data and make it easy for you to understand in the first place.

Creating a Chart

Before you create a chart, you need to type in some numbers and identifying labels because Excel will use those labels to identify the parts of your chart. (You can always edit your chart later if you don't want Excel to display certain labels or numbers.)

To create a chart, follow these steps:

1. **Select the numbers and labels that you want to use to create a chart.**

2. **Click the Insert tab.**

   A list of chart type icons appears in the Charts group.

3. **Click a Chart icon, such as the Pie or Line icon.**

   A menu appears, displaying the different types of charts you can choose as shown in Figure 10-3.

Figure 10-3:
Clicking a chart icon displays different chart options.

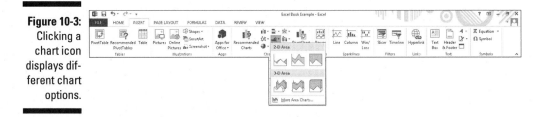

4. **Click a chart type.**

   Excel creates your chart and displays a Chart Tools Design/Format tab, as shown in Figure 10-4.

Figure 10-4:
The Chart Tools Design/ Format tab appears so you can modify a chart after you create it.

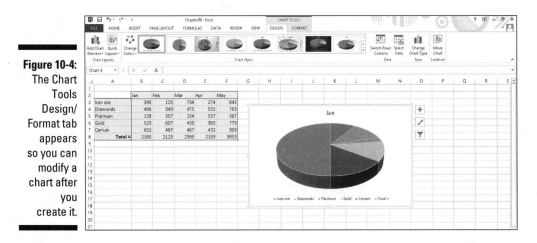

In case you aren't sure what type of chart would best display your data, click the Recommended Charts icon on the Insert tab. This displays an Insert Chart dialog box that lists the recommended chart types, as shown in Figure 10-5.

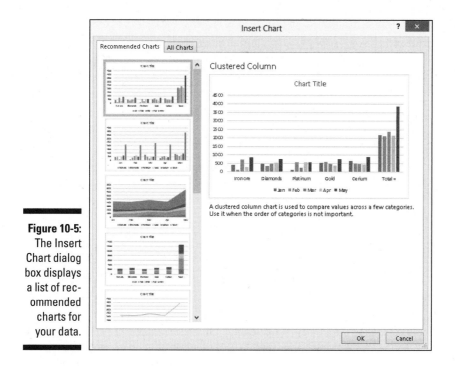

Figure 10-5:
The Insert
Chart dialog
box displays
a list of rec-
ommended
charts for
your data.

Editing a Chart

After you create a chart, you may want to edit it. Editing a chart can mean moving it to a new location, changing the data source (the numbers that Excel uses to create the chart), modifying parts of the chart itself (such as switching to a different chart type), or editing text (such as the chart title or legend).

Moving a chart on a worksheet

When you create a chart, Excel plops it right on your displayed spreadsheet, which may not be exactly where you want it to appear. Excel gives you the option of moving a chart to a different place on the current worksheet page or on a different worksheet page altogether.

To move a chart to a different location on the same worksheet, follow these steps:

1. **Move the mouse pointer over the border of the chart until the mouse pointer turns into a four-way pointing arrow.**

2. **Hold down the left mouse button and drag (move) the mouse.**

   The chart moves with the mouse.

3. **Move the chart where you want it to appear and release the left mouse button.**

Moving a chart to a new sheet

Rather than move a chart on the same sheet where it appears, you can also move the chart to another worksheet. That way your data can appear on one worksheet, and your chart can appear on another.

To move a chart to an entirely different sheet, follow these steps:

1. **Click the chart you want to move to another worksheet.**

   The Chart Tools tab appears.

2. **Click the Design tab.**

3. **Click the Move Chart icon in the Location group.**

   The Move Chart dialog box appears, as shown in Figure 10-6.

   As an alternative to Steps 1 through 3, you can right-click a chart; then when the pop-up menu appears, choose Move Chart.

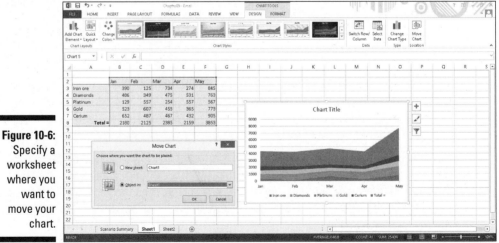

Figure 10-6: Specify a worksheet where you want to move your chart.

4. **Select one of the following radio buttons:**

   • *New Sheet:* Creates a new worksheet and lets you name it

   • *Object In:* Lets you choose the name of an existing worksheet

5. **Click OK.**

   Excel moves your chart.

Resizing a chart

You can always resize any chart to make it bigger or smaller. To resize a chart, follow these steps:

1. **Move the mouse pointer over any corner of the chart until the mouse pointer turns into a two-way pointing arrow.**

2. **Hold down the left mouse button and drag (move) the mouse to shrink or expand your chart.**

3. **Release the left mouse button when you're happy with the new size of your chart.**

Using the Chart Tools

As soon as you create a chart or click an existing chart, Excel displays the Chart Tools tabs (Design and Format). If you click the Design tab, you'll see tools organized into five categories:

✔ **Chart Layouts:** Lets you change the individual parts of a chart, such as the chart title, X- or Y-axis labels, or the placement of the chart legend (top, bottom, left, right).

✔ **Chart Styles:** Provides different ways to change the appearance of your chart.

✔ **Data:** Lets you change the source where the chart retrieves its data or switch the data from appearing along the X-axis to the Y-axis and vice versa.

✔ **Type:** Lets you change the chart type.

✔ **Location:** Lets you move a chart to another location.

Changing the chart type

After you create a chart, you can experiment with how your data may look when displayed as a different chart, such as switching your chart from a bar chart to a pie chart. To change chart types, follow these steps:

1. **Click the chart you want to change.**

   The Chart Tools tabs (Design and Format) appear.

2. **Click the Design tab under Chart Tools.**

3. **Click the Change Chart Type icon in the Type group.**

   The Change Chart Type dialog box appears, as shown in Figure 10-7.

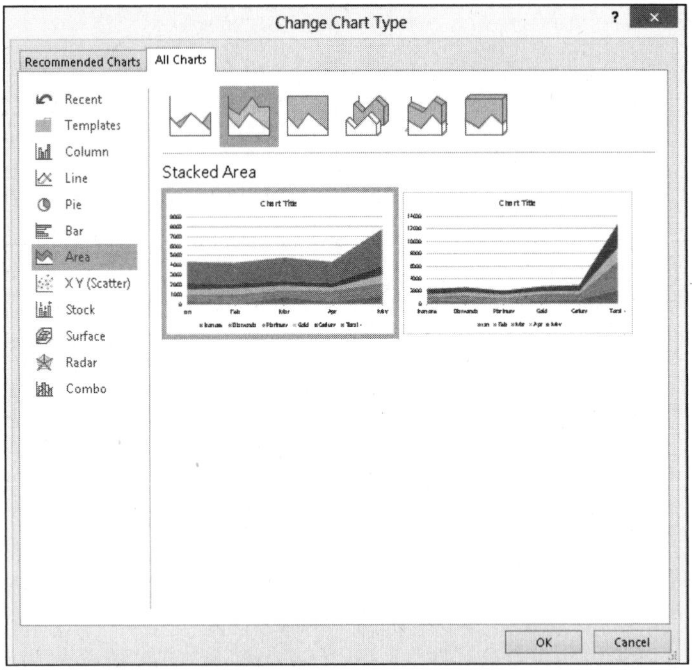

Figure 10-7:
The Change Chart Type dialog box lets you pick a different chart.

4. **Click a chart type, such as Pie or Column.**

   The dialog box displays a list of chart designs in the right panel of the dialog box.

5. **Click the chart design you want in the right panel.**

6. **Click OK.**

Excel displays your new chart.

If you don't like how your chart looks, just press Ctrl+Z to return your chart to its original design.

Changing the data source

Another way to change the appearance of a chart is to change its *data source* (the cells that contain the actual data that the chart uses). To change a chart's data source, follow these steps:

1. **Click the chart you want to change.**

   The Chart Tools tabs (Design and Format) appear.

2. **Click the Design tab under the Chart Tools category.**

3. **Click the Select Data icon in the Data group.**

   The Select Data Source dialog box appears, as shown in Figure 10-8.

4. **(Optional) Click the Shrink Dialog Box icon to shrink the Change Data Source dialog box so you can see more of your spreadsheet.**

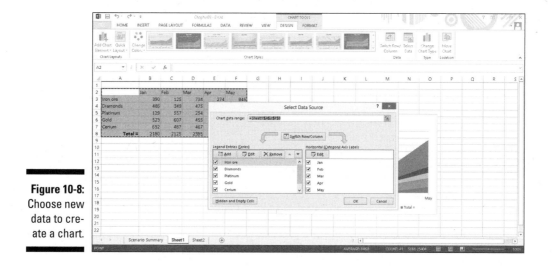

Figure 10-8: Choose new data to create a chart.

5. **Select all the cells that contain data to create a chart, including any cells that contain labels, numbers, and formulas.**

6. **Click OK.**

   Excel displays your chart, using the data you selected in Step 5.

Switching rows and columns

When Excel creates a chart, it displays your data's labels on the X- and Y-axes. However, you can switch these around, and Excel can show you how your chart may change.

To switch the rows and columns used to create a chart, follow these steps:

1. **Click the chart you want to change.**

   The Chart Tools tabs (Design and Format) appear.

2. **Click the Design tab under the Chart Tools category.**

3. **Click the Switch Row/Column icon in the Data group.**

   Excel switches the X-axis data to appear on the Y-axis and vice versa.

Changing the parts of a chart

To make your charts more informative, you can add additional text, such as

- ✔ A chart title
- ✔ A legend
- ✔ Data labels
- ✔ Axis labels
- ✔ Axes
- ✔ Gridlines

With each part of a chart, Excel can either hide it completely or move it to a different location. To modify any part of a chart, follow these steps:

1. **Click the chart you want to change.**

   The Chart Tools tabs (Design and Format) appear.

2. **Click the Design tab under the Chart Tools category.**

3. **Click the Add Chart Element icon.**

    A menu of different chart elements appears, as shown in Figure 10-9.

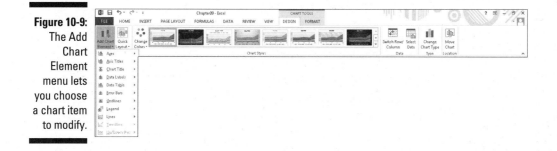

Figure 10-9: The Add Chart Element menu lets you choose a chart item to modify.

4. **Choose an option, such as Legend.**

    A submenu of options appears as shown in Figure 10-10.

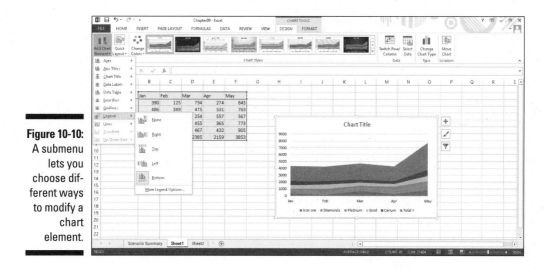

Figure 10-10: A submenu lets you choose different ways to modify a chart element.

5. **Choose an option.**

    As you move the mouse pointer over an option, Excel shows you how that option will change your chart. Now you no longer have to guess but can see exactly how each option will modify your chart.

Designing the layout of a chart

Although you can add and modify the individual parts of a chart yourself, such as the location of the chart title or legend, you may find it faster to choose a predefined layout for your chart. To choose a predefined chart layout, follow these steps:

1. **Click the chart you want to modify.**

   The Chart Tools tabs (Design and Format) appear.

2. **Click the Design tab under the Chart Tools category.**

3. **Click the Quick Layouts icon in the Chart Layouts group, as shown in Figure 10-11.**

   A pull-down menu appears. As you move the mouse pointer over each option, Excel shows you how that option will change the appearance of your chart.

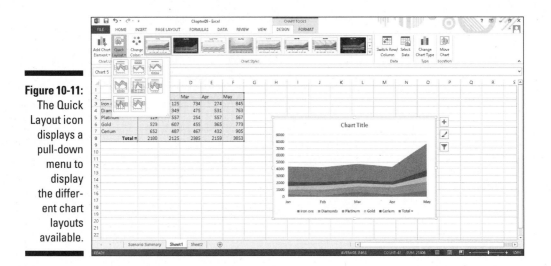

Figure 10-11:
The Quick Layout icon displays a pull-down menu to display the different chart layouts available.

4. **Click a chart layout.**

   Excel changes your chart.

Deleting a chart

Charts may be nice to look at, but eventually you may want to delete them. To delete a chart, follow these steps:

1. **Click the chart you want to delete.**

2. **Press Delete.**

You can also right-click a chart; then when the pop-up menu appears, choose Cut.

Using Sparklines

Creating a chart can help you visualize your data, but sometimes a massive chart with legends, titles, and X-/Y-axis can seem like too much trouble for just identifying trends in your data. For a much simpler tool, Excel offers Sparklines.

Sparklines allow you to see, at a glance, the relationship between values stored in multiple cells. Rather than look at a row or column of numbers to determine if the values are increasing or decreasing over time, you can create a Sparkline that condenses this information in a single cell that you can see at a glance. Excel offers three types of Sparklines, as shown in Figure 10-12:

✔ Line

✔ Column

✔ Win/Loss

Figure 10-12:
The three types of Sparklines you can create and display in one or more cells.

	A	B	C	D	E	F	G	H	I
1									
2									
3									
4							**Sparkline**		
5			Line	49.85	29.57	87.21			
6			Column	98.96	88.76	119.65			
7			Win/Loss	6.8	-8.53	6.83			
8									
9									
10									
11									

Secret Tax Evasion Data · Scenario Summary · Money Laundering Data · Sheet2

Creating a Sparkline

To create and display a Sparkline in a spreadsheet, follow these steps.

1. **Select the cells that contain the data you want to turn into a Sparkline.**

2. **Click the Insert tab.**

3. **Click the Line, Column, or Win/Loss icon in the Sparklines group.**

   The Create Sparklines dialog box appears, as shown in Figure 10-13.

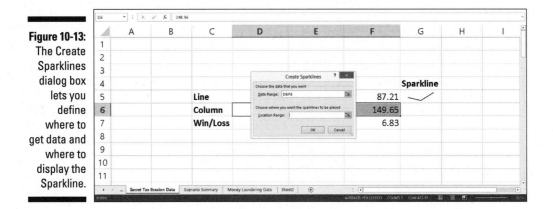

Figure 10-13:
The Create Sparklines dialog box lets you define where to get data and where to display the Sparkline.

4. **Click the cell where you want the Sparkline to appear. (You can select two or more cells.)**

   The Location Range text box displays the cell reference that you chose.

5. **Click OK.**

   Excel displays your chosen Sparkline in the cell that you selected.

Customizing a Sparkline

After you've created one or more Sparklines, you can modify their appearance. To modify a Sparkline, follow these steps:

1. **Click the cell that contains a Sparkline.**

   The Sparkline Tools Design tab appears.

2. **Click the Design tab.**

3. **Click a style in the Style group.**

   If you click the More button, you can view all the available styles.

4. **Click the Sparkline Color icon and click a color.**

5. Click the Marker Color icon.

A menu appears, as shown in Figure 10-14.

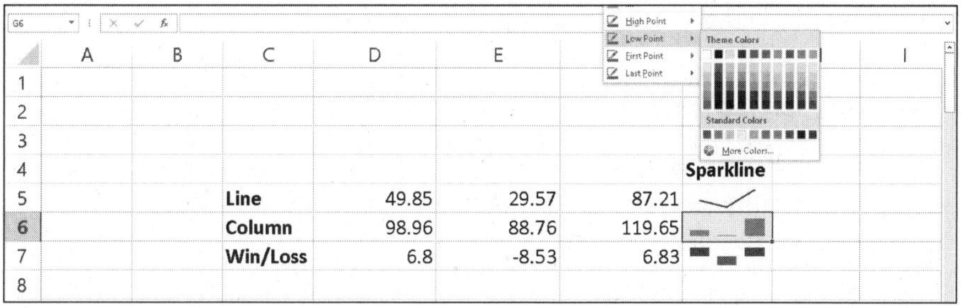

Figure 10-14:
The Marker
Color icon
lets you
define
different
colors for
parts of your
Sparkline.

	A	B	C	D	E		I
1							
2							
3							
4						Sparkline	
5			Line	49.85	29.57	87.21	
6			Column	98.96	88.76	119.65	
7			Win/Loss	6.8	-8.53	6.83	
8							

6. Move the mouse over an option, such as Low Point or First Point.

A color palette appears.

7. Click a color.

Your Sparkline appears with the changes you chose.

Deleting a Sparkline

After you've created one or more Sparklines, you may want to delete them. To delete a Sparkline, follow these steps:

1. Click the cell that contains a Sparkline.

2. Click the Design tab.

3. Click the Clear icon in the Group category.

Your chosen Sparkline disappears.

Organizing Lists in Pivot Tables

Ordinary spreadsheets let you compare two sets of data such as sales versus time or products sold versus the salesperson who sold them. Unfortunately, if you want to know how many products each salesperson sold in a certain month, deciphering this information from a spreadsheet may not be easy.

That's where pivot tables come in. A *pivot table* lets you yank data from your spreadsheet and organize it in different ways in a table. By rearranging (or *pivoting*) your data from a row to a column (and vice versa), pivot tables can help you spot trends that may not be easily identified trapped within the confines of an ordinary spreadsheet.

Creating a pivot table

Pivot tables use the column headings of a spreadsheet to organize data in a table. Ideally, each column in the spreadsheet should identify a different type of data, such as the name of each salesperson, the sales region he or she works in, and the total amount of sales made, as shown in Figure 10-15.

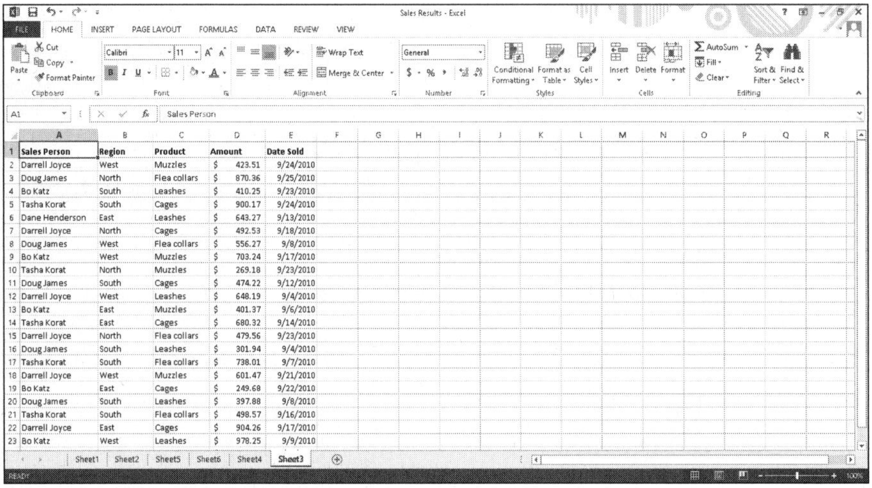

Figure 10-15:
Before you create a pivot table, you must create a spreadsheet where each column identifies a different set of data.

After you design a spreadsheet with multiple columns of data, follow these steps to create a pivot table:

1. **Select the cells (including column labels) that you want to include in your pivot table.**

2. **Click the Insert tab.**

3. **Click the PivotTable icon in the Tables group.**

   The Create PivotTable dialog box appears, as shown in Figure 10-16.

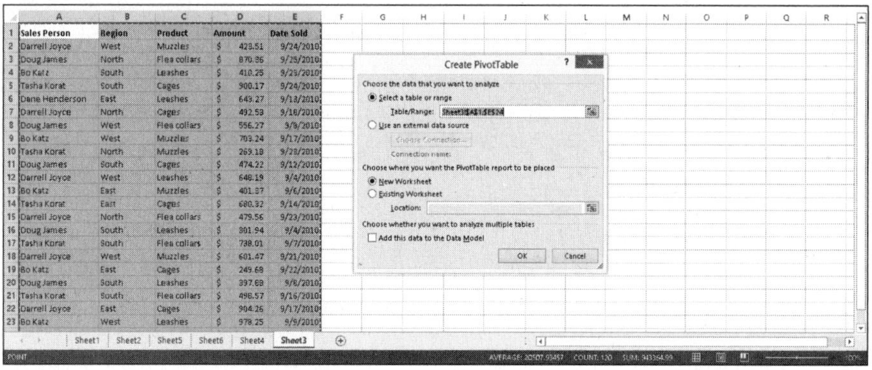

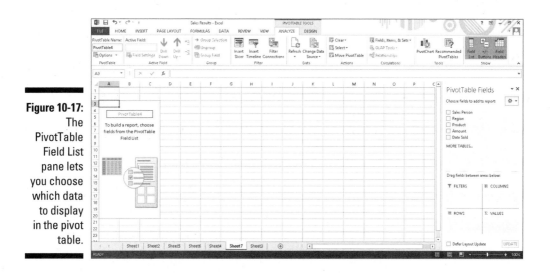

Figure 10-16:
Define the cells to use and a location to place your pivot table.

4. **(Optional) Select the cells that contain the data you want to use in your pivot table.**

   You need to follow Step 4 only if you didn't select any cells in Step 1, or if you change your mind and want to select different cells than the ones chosen in Step 1.

5. **Select one of the following radio buttons:**

   • *New Worksheet:* Puts the pivot table on a new worksheet.

   • *Existing Worksheet:* Puts the pivot table on an existing worksheet.

6. **Click OK.**

   Excel displays a PivotTable Field List pane, as shown in Figure 10-17.

Figure 10-17:
The PivotTable Field List pane lets you choose which data to display in the pivot table.

7. **Mark (select) one or more check boxes inside the PivotTable Field List pane.**

   Each time you select another check box, Excel modifies how data appears in your pivot table, as shown in Figure 10-18.

Figure 10-18: Adding column headings increases the information a pivot table displays.

Rearranging labels in a pivot table

A pivot table organizes data according to your spreadsheet's column headings (which appear in a pivot table row labels). The pivot table shown in Figure 10-18 shows sales divided by salesperson. Each salesperson's amounts are further divided by sales region, and the names of the products sold.

However, you may be more interested in seeing the sales organized by sales region. To do this, you can modify which column heading your pivot table uses to organize your data first. To rearrange column headings in a pivot table, follow these steps:

1. **Click the pivot table you want to rearrange.**

   The PivotTable Field pane appears. A group called Rows appears in the bottom-left corner of the PivotTable Field pane. This Rows box displays the names of your different PivotTable categories, such as Region, Product, and Sales Person.

2. **Click a label in the Row box.**

   A menu appears, as shown in Figure 10-19.

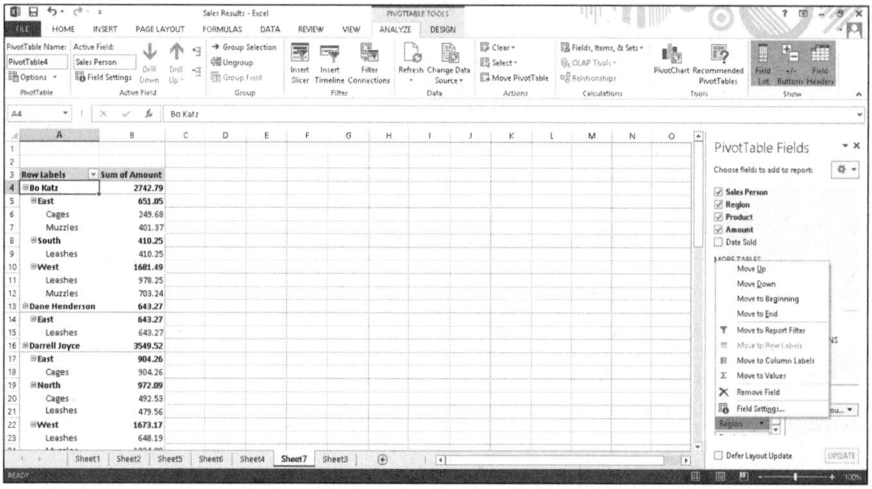

Figure 10-19:
The Rows
box lets you
rearrange a
pivot table
to view data
in different
ways.

Select one of the following:

- *Move Up:* Moves the label one level closer to the beginning

- *Move Down:* Moves the label one level down to the end

- *Move to Beginning:* Makes the label the dominant criteria for sorting data

- *Move to End:* Makes the label the last criteria for sorting data

Figure 10-20 shows different ways a pivot table can organize the same data.

Modifying a pivot table

Rows let you organize data according to different criteria, such as sales per region and then by product. For greater flexibility, you can also turn a row into a column heading. Figure 10-21 shows a pivot table where row labels are stacked on top of each other, and then the same pivot table where one row label (Products) is turned into a column heading.

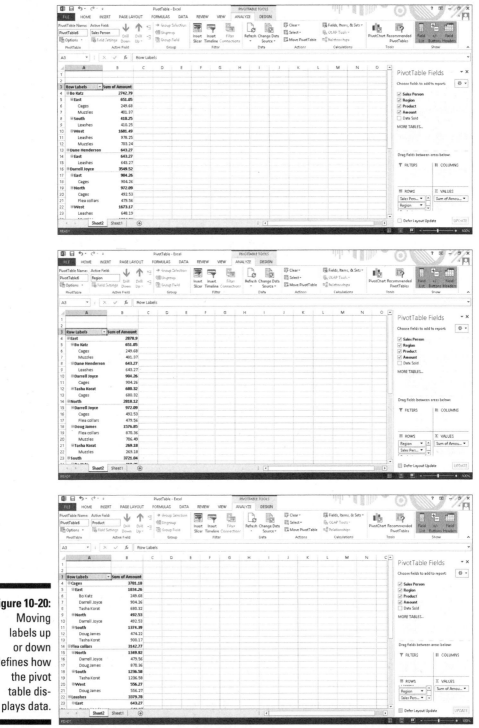

Figure 10-20: Moving labels up or down defines how the pivot table displays data.

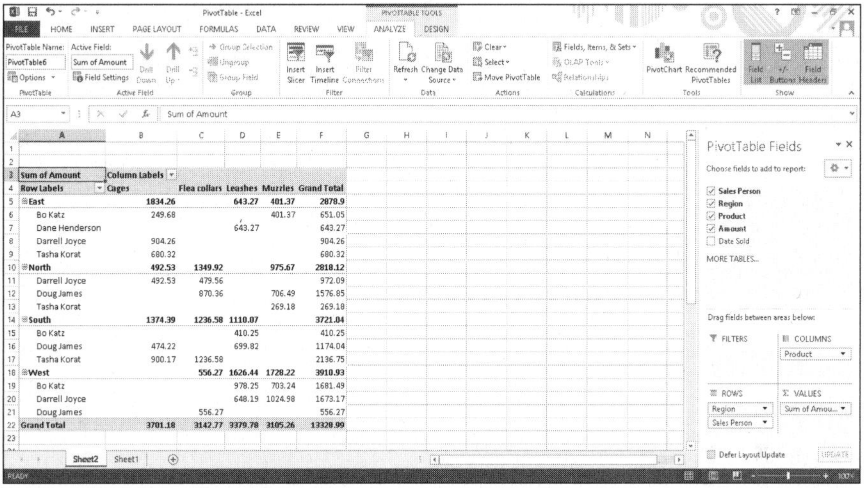

Figure 10-21:
Displaying
row labels
as column
headings
cancompare
spreadsheet
data in mul-
tiple ways.

To turn row labels into column headings in a pivot table (or vice versa),
follow these steps:

1. **Click the pivot table you want to modify.**

   The PivotTable Field List pane appears.

2. **Click a heading in the Rows box near the bottom-left corner of the
   PivotTable Field List pane.**

   A pop-up menu appears.

3. **Choose Move to Column Labels.**

   You can also drag headings from the Rows box to the Columns box and
   vice versa.

Filtering a pivot table

The more information your pivot table contains, the harder it can be to make
sense of any of the data. To help you out, Excel lets you filter your data to
view only certain information, such as sales made by each salesperson or
total sales within a region. To filter a pivot table, follow these steps:

1. **Click the pivot table you want to filter.**

   The PivotTable Fields pane appears.

2. **Click a heading in the Rows or Columns group in the PivotTable
   Fields pane.**

   A pop-up menu appears.

3. **Click Move to Report Filter.**

   Excel moves your chosen label into the Report Filter group in the PivotTable Field List pane, as shown in Figure 10-22.

Figure 10-22: A filtered pivot table displays only the information you want to see, such as only sales results for each salesperson regardless of the region where it was sold.

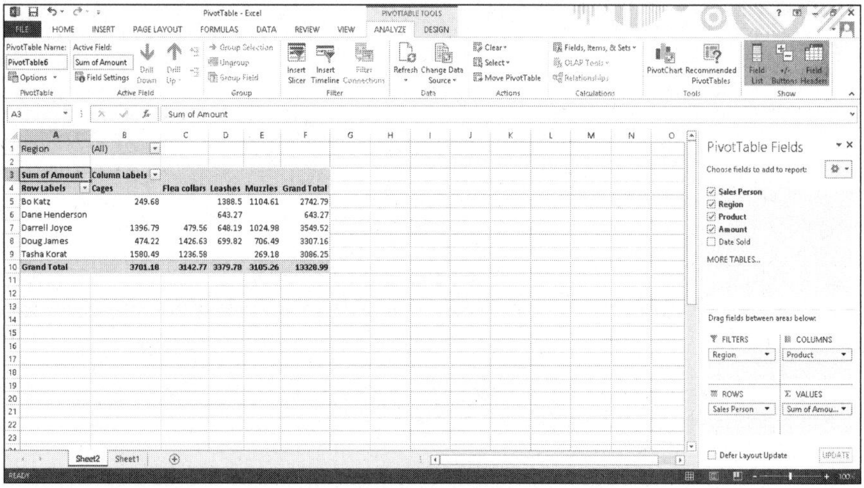

Summing a pivot table

A pivot table not only displays information, but it can also count the number of occurrences of information, such as the number of sales per sales region. To display a count of data, you need to move a heading in the Values group inside the PivotTable Field List pane by following these steps:

1. **Click the pivot table you want to modify.**

   The PivotTable Fields pane appears.

2. **Click a heading that you want to count in the PivotTable Field List pane.**

   A pop-up menu appears.

3. **Click Move to Values.**

   Excel moves your chosen heading to the Values group inside the PivotTable Field List pane and displays a count of items under your chosen heading, as shown in Figure 10-23.

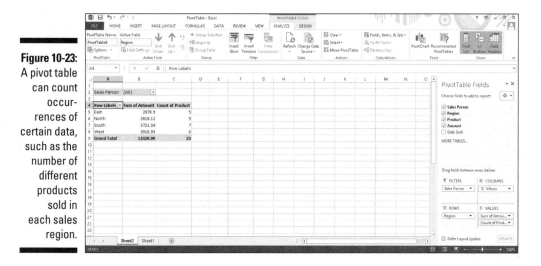

Figure 10-23:
A pivot table can count occur- rences of certain data, such as the number of different products sold in each sales region.

Slicing up a pivot table

If your pivot table contains large amounts of data, trying to decipher this information can be difficult. Rather than display all your pivot table's data, you can choose to slice the pivot table so it shows only the specific data you want to view.

To turn rows into columns in a pivot table (or vice versa), follow these steps:

1. **Click anywhere inside the pivot table you want to modify.**

   The PivotTable Tools tabs (Analyze and Design) appear.

2. **Click the Analyze tab, click the Insert Slicer icon in the Filter group, and choose Insert Slicer.**

   The Insert Slicers dialog box appears, as shown in Figure 10-24.

3. **Select one or more check boxes in the Insert Slicers dialog box and click OK.**

   Slicer panes appear, listing the types of data. For example, a Sales Person slicer pane would list the names of all the salespeople while a Product slicer pane would list the names of all products sold as shown in Figure 10-25.

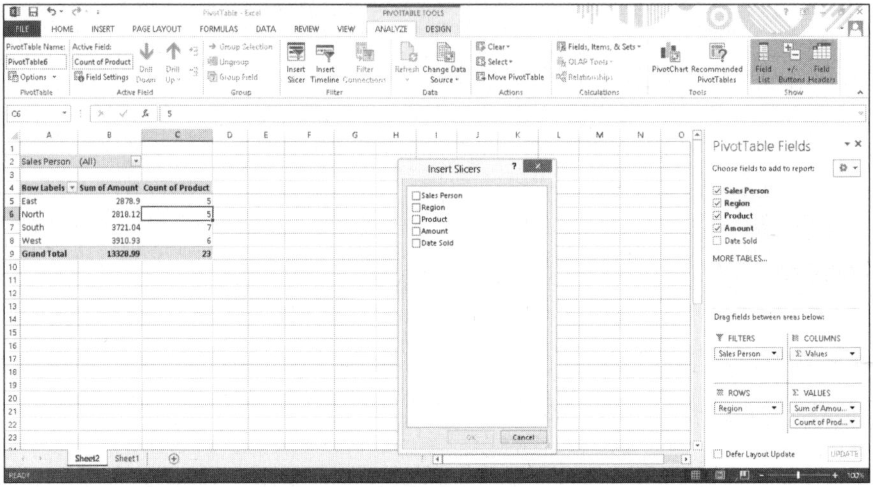

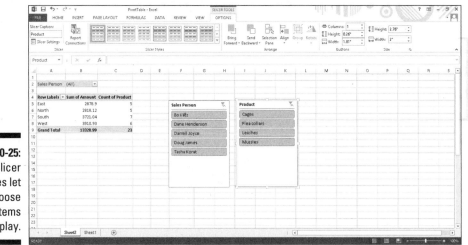

Figure 10-24:
The Insert Slicers dialog box lets you define the data you want to view.

4. **Click each slicer pane to select it, and then move the mouse pointer over the slicer pane border and drag the mouse to move the slicer pane to a more convenient location on the screen.**

Figure 10-25:
Slicer panes let you choose which items to display.

5. **Click the item inside each slicer pane to display that data in the pivot table. (Hold down the Ctrl key and click to choose multiple items.)**

If you want to view sales results from a single salesperson, select that salesperson's name and select all the products you want to examine to see how many sales that person made for each product, as shown in Figure 10-26.

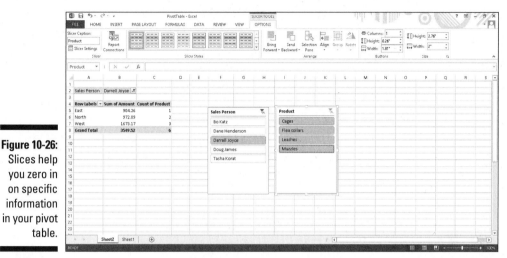

Figure 10-26:
Slices help
you zero in
on specific
information
in your pivot
table.

You can remove a slicer pane by right-clicking the slicer pane and, when a pop-up menu appears, choosing Remove.

Creating PivotCharts

Pivot tables can contain rows and columns of numbers that you may find easier to understand by converting them into a chart, called a PivotChart.

PivotCharts are like other types of charts except you can selectively display (or hide) different data. This lets you create a chart showing sales from all your salespeople, and then selectively hide all data except anything sold by a single salesperson, as shown in Figure 10-27.

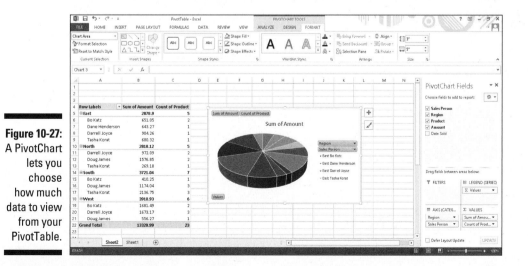

Figure 10-27:
A PivotChart
lets you
choose
how much
data to view
from your
PivotTable.

To create a PivotChart, follow these steps:

1. **Click the pivot table you want to turn into a chart.**

   The PivotTable Tools tabs (Analyze and Design) appear.

2. **Click the Analyze tab and click the PivotChart icon in the Tools group.**

   An Insert Chart dialog box appears.

3. **Click a chart type (such as Pie or Line), click a specific chart design, and click OK.**

   Your PivotChart appears, displaying your categories directly on the chart.

4. **Click the downward-pointing arrow of a category that appears on your PivotChart. A menu appears, as shown in Figure 10-28.**

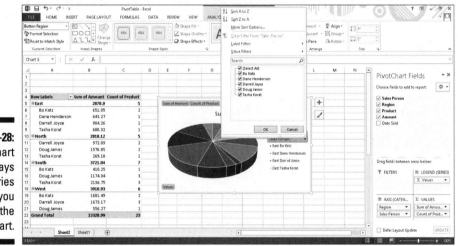

Figure 10-28: A PivotChart displays categories to let you modify the chart.

5. **Clear the check boxes next to the items that you don't want to display and select the check boxes next to the items that you do want to display.**

   Your PivotChart displays a chart that represents only your selected data, as shown in Figure 10-29.

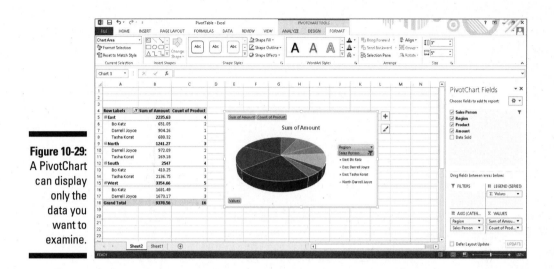

Figure 10-29:
A PivotChart
can display
only the
data you
want to
examine.

Part IV

Making Presentations with PowerPoint

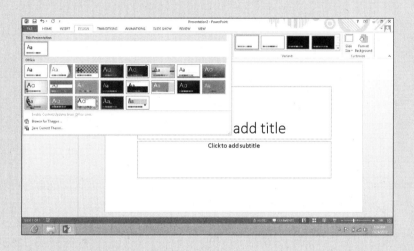

Visit www.dummies.com/extras/office2013 for great Dummies content online.

In this part . . .

- ✔ Creating a PowerPoint presentation
- ✔ Adding text
- ✔ Using themes
- ✔ Adding sound to a presentation
- ✔ Organizing slides
- ✔ Adding hyperlinks
- ✔ Visit www.dummies.com/extras/office2013 for great Dummies content online.

Chapter 11

Creating a PowerPoint Presentation

PowerPoint works as a visual aid for giving presentations. (If you never give presentations, you probably don't need PowerPoint.) Instead of fumbling around creating, organizing, and displaying transparencies with an overhead projector, you can use PowerPoint on your computer to create, organize, and display slides that organize information as text and graphics.

Besides displaying slides on the screen, PowerPoint also lets you add notes and turn your entire slide-show presentation into printed handouts so the audience can review your presentation with a printed copy of each slide. The next time you need to convince or inform an audience, use PowerPoint to create and deliver your presentation. (Just make sure that you never use PowerPoint to propose marriage, though.)

Defining the Purpose of Your Presentation

PowerPoint can make creating and delivering a presentation easy, but before you start creating fancy visuals with eye-popping graphics and colors, step away from your computer, put down your copy of PowerPoint, and place your hands in the open where anyone can see them.

Rushing into PowerPoint to create a presentation is likely to create a dazzling array of colors, fonts, and graphics that may look interesting but won't convey your message effectively. The best way to create an effective presentation is to take some time to think about the following:

- ✔ **What is your point?** Define the single most important idea of your presentation.

- ✔ **Who is the target audience?** A presentation given to engineers and scientists will look different from the same presentation given to CEOs and venture-capital executives.

- ✔ **What do you want the audience to do?** A speaker may present new ideas to a conference, while a politician may present ideas designed to sway the audience to take certain actions, such as voting a specific way.

After you understand the purpose of your presentation, your audience, and what you hope your presentation will do, you're ready to go through the physical steps of creating a presentation in PowerPoint.

Creating a PowerPoint Presentation

A PowerPoint *presentation* consists of one or more slides where each slide can display text and graphics. Creating a presentation means adding slides and typing text or pasting graphics on each slide.

If you've been working on another presentation in PowerPoint and you need to start a new, blank presentation from scratch, follow these steps:

1. **Click the File tab.**

2. **Click New.**

   PowerPoint displays different templates you can choose.

3. **Click Blank Presentation.**

   PowerPoint displays a blank slide with a title and subtitle box, as shown in Figure 11-1.

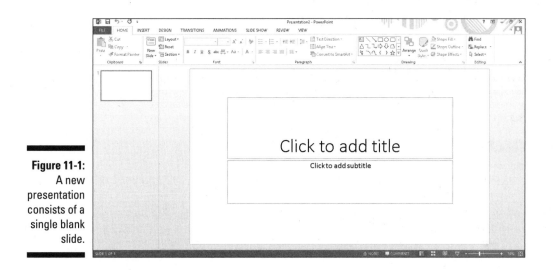

After you create a new presentation, you need to fill it with *content* (text and graphics). PowerPoint gives you two ways to view, edit, and design your presentation:

- ✔ Slide view
- ✔ Outline view

Both views let you add, delete, rearrange, and edit slides. The main difference is that *Slide view* lets you add graphics and modify the visual appearance of a slide. *Outline view* displays your entire presentation as an outline in which each slide appears as an outline heading, and additional text on each slide appears as a subheading. Outline view makes it easy to focus on the text of your presentation without the distraction of the visual appearance of your slides.

You can create an entire presentation in Slide view without ever using Outline view at all (or use Outline view without ever using Slide view at all). Outline view is most useful for creating and organizing a presentation. Slide view is most useful for viewing the appearance of multiple slides at once.

Designing a presentation with Slide view

Slide view shows your entire slide show as thumbnails in the left pane and the currently selected slide in full-size view in the right pane, as shown in Figure 11-2.

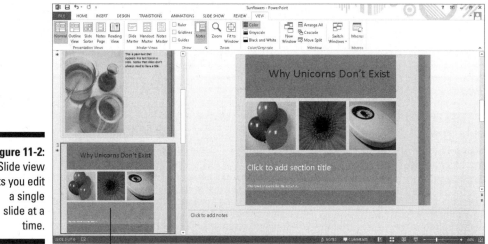

Figure 11-2:
Slide view
lets you edit
a single
slide at a
time.

Thumbnail pane

Creating a new slide

To create a new slide within Slide view, follow these steps:

1. **Click an existing slide in the thumbnail pane.**

2. **Click the Home tab.**

3. **Click the New Slide icon in the Slides group.**

   PowerPoint inserts your new slide after the slide you selected in Step 1.

If you click the top half of the New Slide icon, PowerPoint creates a blank slide based on the slide you selected in Step 1. If you click the bottom half of the New Slide icon, a menu appears, letting you choose from a variety of different slide designs (as shown in Figure 11-3).

Rearranging slides

You can rearrange the order of your slides by following these steps:

1. **In the thumbnail pane, click the slide that you want to move to a new position in your presentation.**

2. **Hold down the left mouse button and drag (move) the mouse up or down within the thumbnail pane.**

   PowerPoint displays a horizontal line between slides to show you where your slide will appear. If you drag the mouse to the top or bottom of the thumbnail pane, PowerPoint automatically scrolls up or down the list.

3. **Release the left mouse button when you're happy with the slide's new position.**

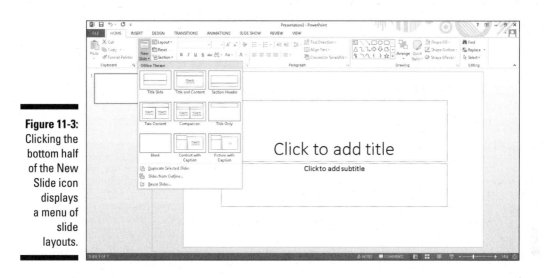

Click to add title

Click to add subtitle

Figure 11-3:
Clicking the
bottom half
of the New
Slide icon
displays
a menu of
slide
layouts.

Hiding or deleting a slide

If you have a slide that you no longer want in your presentation, you can either hide or delete it. Hiding a slide keeps the slide but doesn't display that slide when you give your presentation. You may want to hide a slide in case you need it later or so you can reference the information on this slide with the rest of your presentation.

To hide a slide, follow these steps:

1. **In the thumbnail pane, click the slide that you want to hide.**
2. **Click the Slide Show tab.**
3. **Click Hide Slide in the Set Up group.**

    PowerPoint dims your chosen slide and highlights the Hide Slide icon.

To unhide a slide, repeat the preceding steps.

If you're sure that you want to get rid of a slide, you can just delete it. To delete a slide, follow these steps:

1. **In the thumbnail pane, click the slide that you want to delete.**
2. **Press the Delete key.**

    PowerPoint deletes your chosen slide.

If you press Ctrl+Z or click the Undo icon right away, you can recover a deleted slide.

Designing a presentation with Outline view

In the Outline view, each slide appears with one or more of the following:

- ✔ A title (appears to the right of a slide icon)
- ✔ A subheading (appears to the right of a number in a small box)
- ✔ Text (appears without any icon next to it)

The Outline pane only displays the text on each slide. Clicking a slide in the Outline pane displays the entire slide, including graphics, as shown in Figure 11-4.

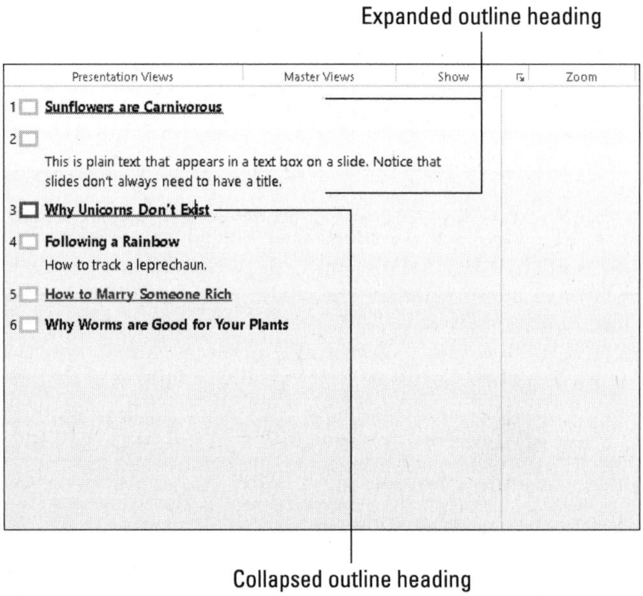

Expanded outline heading

Collapsed outline heading

Figure 11-4: Outline view lets you view just the titles and subtitles of your entire presentation.

The biggest advantage of Outline view is that it lets you rearrange and organize your slides by focusing on their content (title, subtitles, and text). To switch from Slide view to Outline view, click the View tab and then click the Outline View icon. To switch from Outline view to Slide view, click the View tab and then click the Normal icon.

Creating a new slide

In Outline view, each outline heading represents a slide. To create a new slide in Outline view, follow these steps:

1. **Click a slide title in the Outline pane.**

2. **Choose one of the following:**

    - *Press Home to move the cursor to the front of the outline heading.* This creates a new slide before the currently displayed slide.

    - *Press End to move the cursor to the end of the outline heading.* This creates a new slide after the currently displayed slide.

3. **Press Enter.**

    PowerPoint adds a new, blank slide to your presentation.

Creating subtitles on a slide

Outline view lets you create slides and add subtitles to each slide as well. To add a subtitle to a slide, follow these steps:

1. **Click a slide title and then press End to move the cursor to the end of the slide title.**

2. **Press Enter.**

    PowerPoint creates a blank slide title underneath.

3. **Press Tab.**

    PowerPoint indents your slide title and turns it into subtitle text under the preceding outline heading.

Collapsing and expanding subtitles

A large presentation consisting of multiple slides with subtitles can be hard to read. To simplify the appearance of your outline, PowerPoint lets you collapse or expand outline headings. To collapse or expand an outline heading, double-click the slide icon of a slide title in the Outline pane.

PowerPoint collapses any subtitles that appear under your chosen outline heading and displays a gray wavy line under your outline heading to let you know that its subtitle text is *collapsed* (hidden), as shown in Figure 11-5.

To expand a collapsed slide title, just double-click its slide icon.

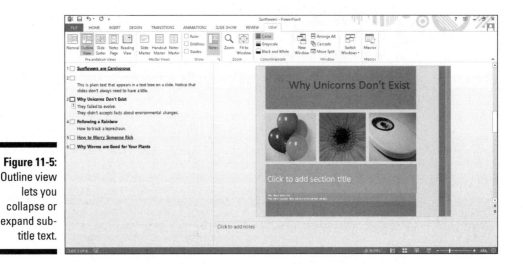

Figure 11-5:
Outline view
lets you
collapse or
expand sub-
title text.

Rearranging slides

Outline view makes it easy to rearrange slides just by moving slide titles up or down. To move a slide title, follow these steps:

1. **Move the mouse pointer over the slide icon that appears to the left of the slide title (or slide subtitle) that you want to move.**

    The mouse turns into a four-way-pointing arrow.

2. **Hold down the left mouse button and drag (move) the mouse up or down.**

    PowerPoint displays a horizontal gray line to show where the new position of the slide will appear in your presentation.

3. **Release the left mouse button.**

    PowerPoint moves your outline heading to its new position in your presentation.

Deleting a slide

To delete a slide in Outline view, follow these steps:

1. **Click the slide icon that appears to the left of the slide title (or subtitle) you want to delete.**

2. **Press Delete.**

Working with Text

Most slides contain exactly one title and one subtitle text box. The title text box typically defines the information that the slide presents, while the subtitle text box displays supporting information.

When you create a new slide, both the title and subtitle text boxes will be empty, although they'll both display the message Click to add title or Click to add subtitle. (This text won't appear on your slides if you don't type anything there.)

If you delete all the text inside a title or subtitle text box, PowerPoint automatically displays the Click to add title or Click to add subtitle text in the empty text boxes.

To add text inside a title or subtitle text box, follow these steps:

1. **Click in the title or subtitle text box, directly on the slide.**

   PowerPoint displays a cursor in your chosen text box.

2. **Type your text.**

You can also create title and subtitle text in Outline view, as explained in the earlier section, "Designing a presentation with Outline view."

Typing text in a text box

A typical PowerPoint slide lets you type text in the Title text box or the Subtitle text box. When you type text in the Title or Subtitle text box, the contents appear as slide titles and subheadings within Outline view.

However, PowerPoint also offers you a third option for displaying text on a slide: You can create your own text box and place it anywhere on the slide.

To create and place a text box on a slide, follow these steps:

1. **Click the Insert tab.**
2. **Click the Text Box icon in the Text group.**

   The mouse pointer turns into a downward-pointing arrow.

3. **Move the mouse pointer over the area on the slide where you want to create a text box.**
4. **Hold down the left mouse button and drag (move) the mouse to draw a text box on a slide.**

5. **Release the left mouse button.**

   PowerPoint displays a text box, as shown in Figure 11-6.

6. **Type your text inside the text box.**

Any text you type into a text box that you create will not appear in Outline view.

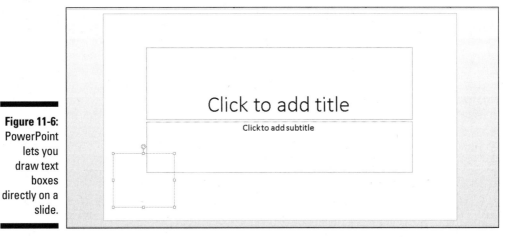

Click to add title

Click to add subtitle

Figure 11-6:
PowerPoint
lets you
draw text
boxes
directly on a
slide.

Formatting text

You can format text that you type on a slide by choosing different fonts, font sizes, and colors. To change the appearance of text, follow these steps:

1. **Click the Home tab.**

2. **Click in a text box and select the text you want to format.**

3. **Click one of the following font tools, as shown in Figure 11-7:**

   - Font list box
   - Font Size list box
   - Increase Font Size
   - Decrease Font Size
   - Clear All Formatting
   - Bold
   - Italic
   - Underline
   - Shadow

- Strikethrough
- Character Spacing
- Change Case
- Font Color

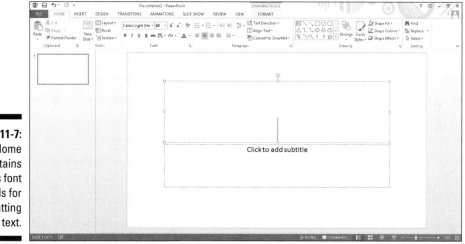

Figure 11-7:
The Home
tab contains
various font
tools for
formatting
text.

Aligning text

PowerPoint can align text both horizontally and vertically inside a text box.
To align text, follow these steps:

1. **Click the Home tab.**
2. **Click in a text box and select the text you want to align.**
3. **Click one of the following text-alignment tools in the Paragraph group:**
   - Align Left
   - Center
   - Align Right
   - Justify
   - Align Text (Top, Middle, Bottom, Top Centered, Middle Centered, Bottom Centered)
4. **Click the Align Text icon in the Paragraph group.**

   A pop-up menu appears, as shown in Figure 11-8.
5. **Click a vertical alignment option, such as Top or Middle.**

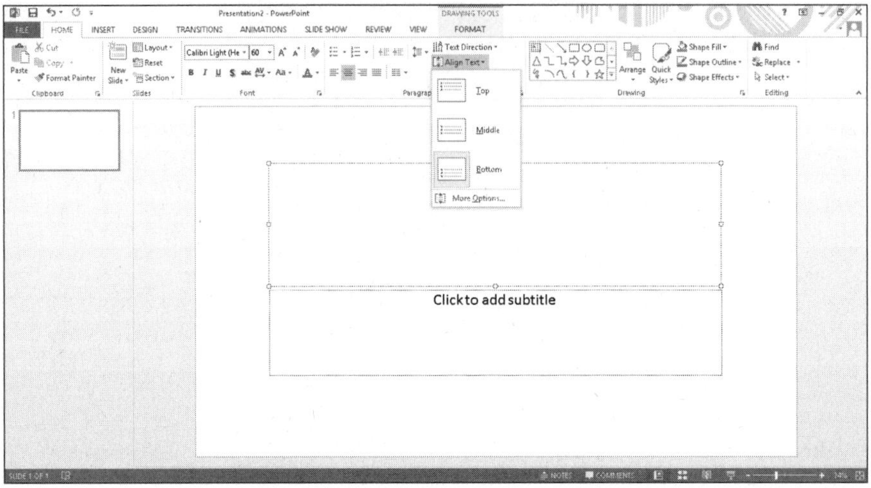

Figure 11-8:
The Align
Text icon
displays
different
ways to
align text
vertically
within a
text box.

Adjusting line spacing

Line spacing defines the space that appears between each line in a text box. To define the line space in a text box, follow these steps:

1. **Click the text box that contains text.**
2. **Click the Home tab.**
3. **Click the Line Spacing icon in the Paragraph group.**

   A pull-down menu appears, as shown in Figure 11-9.

4. **Select a line spacing value, such as 1.5 or 2.**

   PowerPoint adjusts line spacing in your chosen text box.

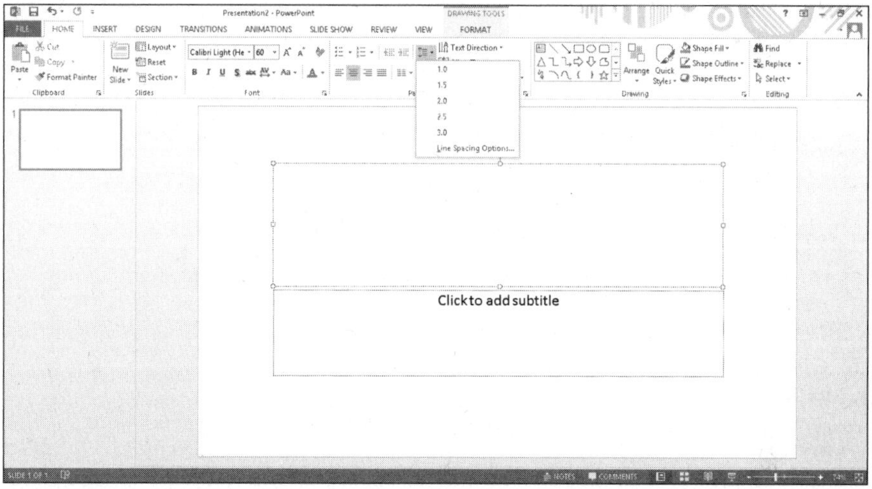

Figure 11-9:
The Line
Spacing
icon
displays
different
line spacing
options.

Making numbered and bulleted lists

PowerPoint can display text as bulleted or numbered lists. The two ways to create such a list are before you type any text or after you've already typed some text.

To create a bulleted or numbered list as you type new text, follow these steps:

1. **Click in a text box.**

2. **Click the Home tab.**

3. **Click the Bullets or Numbering icon in the Paragraph group.**

   A pull-down menu appears, as shown in Figure 11-10.

4. **Click a bullet or numbering option.**

   PowerPoint displays a bullet or number.

5. **Type any text and press Enter.**

   As soon as you press Enter, PowerPoint displays a new bullet or number.

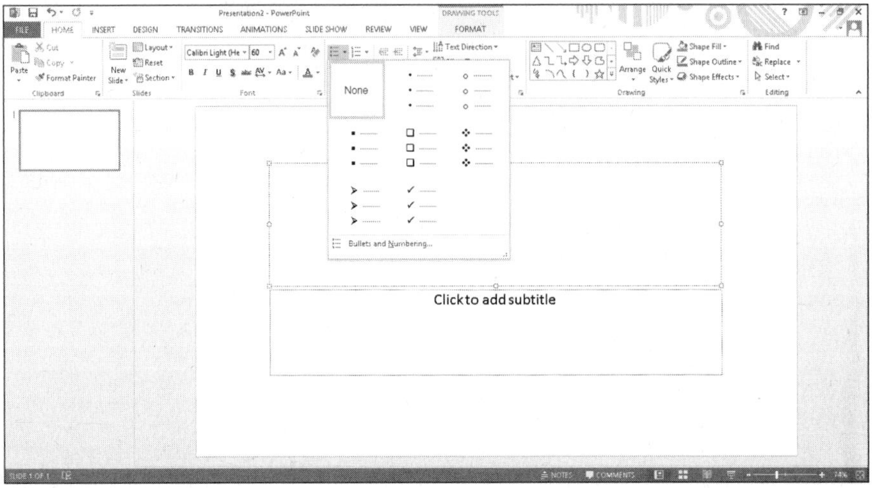

Figure 11-10:
The
Bullets and
Numbering
icons let you
create lists
as you type.

If you have existing text, you can convert it to a bulleted or numbered list. To convert existing text into a list, follow these steps:

1. **Click in the text box that contains the text you want to convert into a bulleted or numbered list.**

2. **Select the text you want to convert into a list.**

3. **Click the Home tab.**

4. **Click the Bullets or Numbering icon in the Paragraph group.**

   PowerPoint converts your text into a list.

PowerPoint displays each paragraph as a separate item in a bulleted or numbered list. A *paragraph* is any amount of text that ends with a paragraph mark (¶), which is an invisible character that you create when you press the Enter key.

Making columns

You can divide a text box into multiple columns, which can be especially useful if you need to display large lists on a slide. To divide a text box into columns, follow these steps:

1. **Click the text box that you want to divide into columns.**

2. **Click the Home tab.**

3. **Click the Columns icon in the Paragraph group.**

   A menu appears, as shown in Figure 11-11.

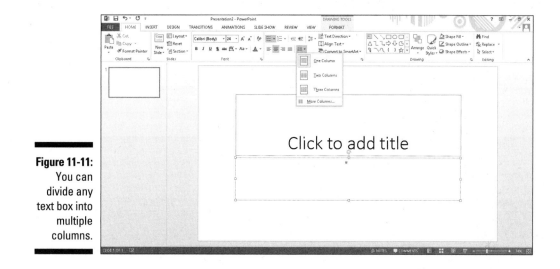

Figure 11-11:
You can
divide any
text box into
multiple
columns.

4. **Click a column option, such as Two Columns or Three Columns.**

   PowerPoint divides your text box into columns.

Moving and resizing a text box

PowerPoint lets you move text boxes anywhere on the slide. To move a text box, follow these steps:

1. **Move the mouse pointer over the edge of the text box that you want to move.**

   The mouse turns into a four-way-pointing arrow.

2. **Hold down the left mouse button and drag (move) the mouse to move the text box.**

3. **Release the left mouse button when you're happy with the new location of the text box.**

To resize a text box, follow these steps:

1. **Click the text box you want to resize.**

   PowerPoint displays handles around your chosen text box, as shown in Figure 11-12.

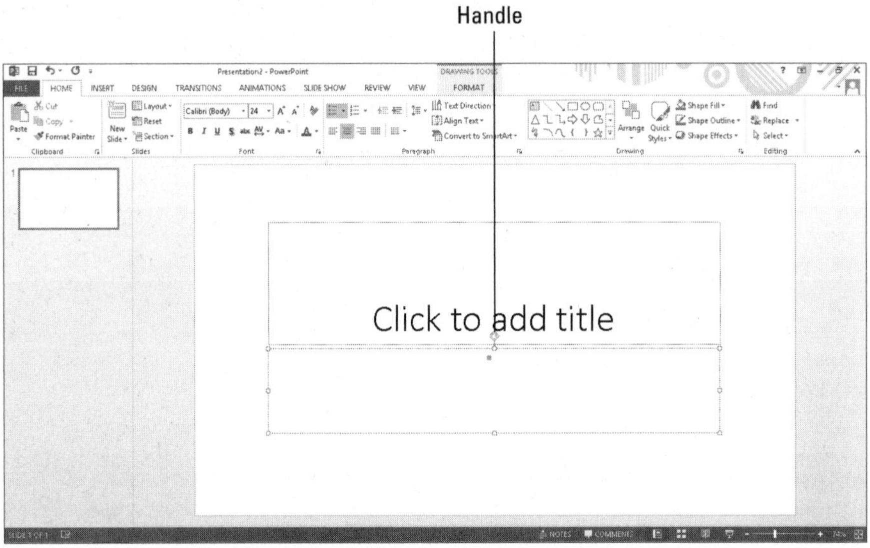

Handle

Click to add title

2. **Move the mouse pointer over a handle.**

   The mouse pointer turns into a two-way-pointing arrow.

3. **Hold down the left mouse button and drag (move) the mouse.**

   PowerPoint resizes your text box in the direction you move the mouse.

4. **Release the left mouse button when you're happy with the size of the text box.**

Rotating a text box

After you type text in a title or subtitle text box, you can rotate the text box on your slide. To rotate a text box, follow these steps:

1. **Click the text box you want to rotate.**

   PowerPoint displays a rotate handle at the top of your text box, as shown in Figure 11-13.

2. **Move the mouse pointer over the rotate handle.**

   The mouse pointer turns into a circular arrow.

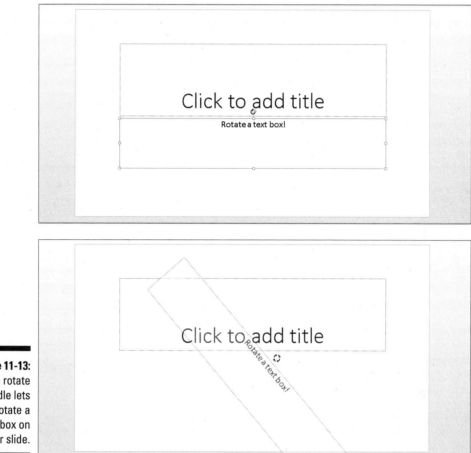

Figure 11-13:
The rotate
handle lets
you rotate a
text box on
your slide.

3. **Hold down the left mouse button and drag (move) the mouse to rotate your text box.**

   If you hold down the Shift key while dragging the mouse, you can rotate the text box in 15-degree increments.

4. **Release the left mouse button when you're happy with the rotated position of your text box (or press Esc to cancel the rotation).**

You can still edit and format text in a text box that appears rotated.

Chapter 12

Adding Color and Pictures to a Presentation

. . . .

In This Chapter

▶ Using themes

▶ Changing a background

▶ Adding graphics

▶ Showing movies on a slide

▶ Adding sound to a presentation

. . . .

*T*o make your presentations look more visually appealing, PowerPoint lets you add color and graphics to your slides. Color and graphics can't turn a worthless presentation into an informative one, but they can enhance an informative presentation and make it easier for people to watch.

For additional appeal, PowerPoint lets you add audio and video to a presentation. That way, you can make your presentation more interesting by letting people read, hear, and see information.

Applying a Theme

By default, PowerPoint displays each slide with a white background. Although you can change the colors and appearance of each slide individually, it's much easier to change every slide in your presentation by using a theme. A *theme* provides predesigned colors and designs that are applied to each slide to give your presentation a uniform and professional look.

To define a theme for a presentation, follow these steps:

1. Click the Design tab.

If you click a slide in the thumbnail view and hold down the Ctrl key, you can select which slides you'll change. If you don't select any slide, PowerPoint will change all your slides.

2. **Click the More button under the Themes group.**

A menu appears, as shown in Figure 12-1.

If you move the mouse pointer over a theme, PowerPoint shows how your presentation will look.

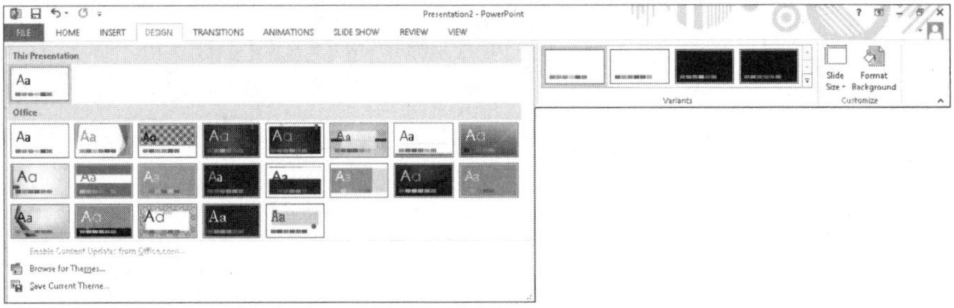

Figure 12-1:
Themes provide predesigned backgrounds for your presentation.

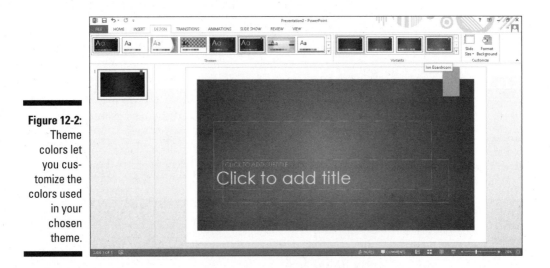

3. **Click a theme.**

PowerPoint displays your chosen theme on your slides.

4. **Move the mouse pointer over a theme displayed in the Variants group.**

PowerPoint shows how the theme will change the appearance of your slides, as shown in Figure 12-2.

5. **Click a theme.**

PowerPoint displays your new theme colors.

Figure 12-2:
Theme colors let you customize the colors used in your chosen theme.

Changing the Background

PowerPoint often creates presentations with a plain white background. While this may be fine in some cases, you may still want to spice up your slide backgrounds so they look a prettier. PowerPoint offers four ways to change the background:

- ✔ **Solid fill:** Creates a solid background color
- ✔ **Gradient fill:** Mixes two colors that gradually fade into one another
- ✔ **Picture or texture fill:** Lets you choose a picture stored on your computer
- ✔ **Pattern fill:** Creates a background pattern of lines or zigzags

Choosing a solid color background

Solid colors can provide contrast to your slides, but you have to make sure that any text or graphics that appear on your slides can still be seen. For example, if you choose a dark red background, any text or graphics on your slides should appear in light colors to make them visible against the dark red background.

To make sure that solid background colors don't obscure your text and graphics, you can also adjust its transparency to make the color appear darker or lighter.

To change the background to a solid color, follow these steps:

1. **Click the Design tab.**

   If you click a slide in the thumbnail view and hold down the Ctrl key, you can select which slides you'll change. If you don't select any slide, PowerPoint will change all your slides.

2. **Click the Format Background icon in the Customize group.**

   The Format Background pane appears, as shown in Figure 12-3.

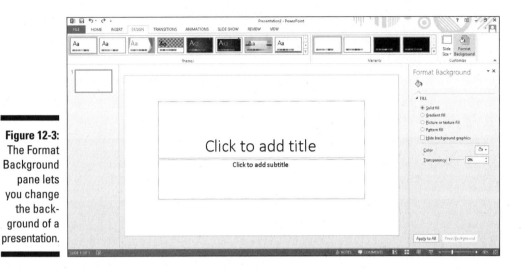

Figure 12-3:
The Format
Background
pane lets
you change
the back-
ground of a
presentation.

3. **Select the Solid Fill radio button.**

4. **Click the Color icon.**

   A pull-down menu appears, listing a palette of colors.

5. **Click a color.**

   PowerPoint fills your slide background with your chosen color.

6. **(Optional) Drag the Transparency slider left (0%) or right (100%).**

   The higher the transparency value, the lighter the background color appears.

7. **(Optional) Click Apply to All to change the background of every slide in your presentation.**

   If you don't click the Apply to All button, PowerPoint changes only the background of the currently selected slide.

   If you click the Reset All Background button, you can remove any back-ground changes you made.

8. **Click the Close button in the Format Background pane.**

Choosing a gradient background

A gradient displays one color that gradually fades into another color, such as green to orange. To define a gradient, you can define one or more stops, transparency, and the gradient direction. *Stops* define where the colors in the gradient start and end. *Transparency* defines how opaque a color appears. The *gradient direction* defines how the gradient appears, such as vertically or diagonally.

To define a gradient background, follow these steps:

1. **Click the Design tab.**

   If you click a slide in the thumbnail view and hold down the Ctrl key, you can select which slides you'll change. If you don't select any slide, PowerPoint will change all your slides.

2. **Click the Format Background icon in the Customize group.**

   The Format Background pane appears (refer to Figure 12-3).

3. **Select the Gradient Fill radio button.**

   The Format Background pane displays additional options for defining a gradient, as shown in Figure 12-4.

   If you click the Preset gradients icon, you can choose from a variety of predefined gradients.

4. **Click in the Type list box and choose an option such as Linear or Rectangular.**

5. **Click in the Direction list box and choose a direction for the gradient.**

6. **Click the up/down arrows in the Angle box to increase or decrease the angle.**

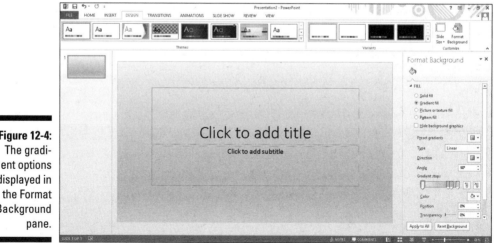

Figure 12-4: The gradient options displayed in the Format Background pane.

7. **Drag the Gradient stops sliders left or right.**

   The far-left and far-right positions of the stop-position slider define where the gradient begins and ends on the slide.

8. **Click the Color icon.**

   A color palette appears.

9. **Click a color.**

   PowerPoint displays your chosen color as a gradient on the current slide.

10. **Click the up/down arrows in the Position text box to change the position of the gradients.**

11. **Drag the Transparency slider left or right.**

    The far-left position (0%) displays your chosen color in full strength, and the far-right position (100%) displays your chosen color to the point where it disappears from view completely (100% transparency).

12. **(Optional) Click Apply to All if you want your gradient to apply to every slide in your presentation.**

    If you don't click the Apply to All button, PowerPoint displays only the background of the currently selected slide.

13. **Click the Close button in the Format Background pane.**

Choosing a picture background

A picture, such as clip art or a photograph captured with a digital camera, can appear in your background. After you use a picture for the background, you can also adjust its transparency so that you can read any title or subtitle text that appears on each slide.

To add a picture background to slides, follow these steps:

1. **Click the Design tab.**

2. **Click the Format Background icon in the Customize group.**

   The Format Background pane appears (refer to Figure 12-3).

3. **Select the Picture or texture fill radio button.**

   The Format Background pane displays options for adding a picture to your background.

4. **Click one of the following buttons:**

   - *File:* Retrieves a graphic image stored on your computer, such as a digital photo. When the Insert Picture dialog box appears, click the picture you want to use and then click Open.

   - *Clipboard:* Pastes a previously cut or copied graphic image from another program, such as Photoshop.

   - *Online:* Displays a library of clip-art images you can choose. Just type a description of the picture you want and when clip art images appear, click the one you want to use and then click Insert.

5. **Drag the Transparency slider to the left or right until you're happy with the way the picture appears.**

6. **(Optional) Click in the up/down arrows of the Offset left/right/top/bottom text boxes to change the position of your picture.**

7. **(Optional) Click Apply to All if you want to apply your picture to every slide in your presentation.**

   If you don't click the Apply to All button, PowerPoint displays only the background of the currently selected slide.

8. **Click the Close button in the Format Background pane.**

Adding Graphics to a Slide

Another way to spice up the appearance of your presentation is to include graphics on one or more slides. Such graphics can be informative, such as a chart that displays sales results; or they can be decorative, such as a cartoon smiley face that emphasizes the presentation's good news.

Three common types of graphics you can add to a PowerPoint slide include

- ✔ **Picture files:** Includes clip art images as well as images you may have stored on your hard drive, such as photographs from your digital camera
- ✔ **Charts:** Displays bar, column, line, pie, and other types of charts
- ✔ **WordArt:** Displays text as colorful text

Placing picture files on a slide

To liven up a presentation, you can add pictures you may have already stored on your computer. To add a picture to a slide, follow these steps.

1. **Click a slide (in either Slide or Outline view) to which you want to add a picture.**

2. **Click the Insert tab.**

3. **Click the Picture icon in the Images group.**

   The Insert Picture dialog box appears. You may need to change folders or drives to find the picture file you want.

4. **Choose the picture file you want and then click Open.**

   PowerPoint displays your chosen picture on the currently displayed slide. You may need to resize or move your picture.

Placing clip art on a slide

Clip art consists of drawings that come with PowerPoint. To add a clip art image to a slide, follow these steps:

1. **Click a slide (in either Slide or Outline view) to which you want to add a picture.**

2. **Click the Insert tab.**

3. **Click the Online Pictures icon in the Images group.**

   An Insert Pictures window appears, giving you a choice of typing a picture description to look for clip art, either on Office.com or through the Bing image-search engine, as shown in Figure 12-5.

   You need an Internet connection to search for clip art.

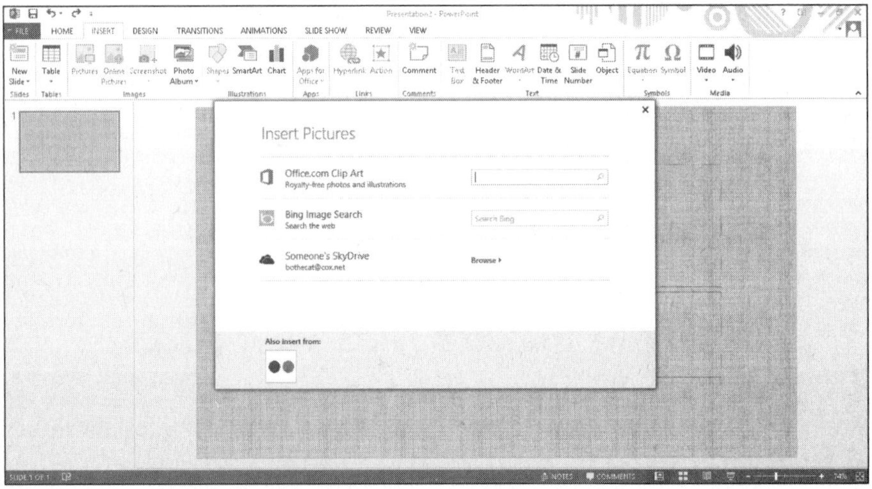

Figure 12-5:
The Insert
Pictures
window lets
you search
for clip art.

4. **Click in the Office.com Clip Art or Bing Image Search text box and type a word that describes the type of image you want to find.**

5. **Press Enter.**

   The window displays all the clip art images it can find that match the descriptive word you typed in Step 4.

6. **Choose the clip art image you want to use and click the Insert button.**

   PowerPoint displays your chosen image on the current slide. (You may need to move or resize the image.)

Creating WordArt

WordArt provides another way to display text. Unlike ordinary text that you can format, WordArt lets you create graphically oriented text to use as headlines for added emphasis. To create WordArt, follow these steps:

1. **Click the slide (in either Slide or Outline view) to which you want to add WordArt.**

2. **Click the Insert tab.**

3. **Click the WordArt icon in the Text group.**

   A WordArt menu appears.

4. **Click a WordArt style to use.**

   PowerPoint displays a WordArt text box on the current slide.

5. **Click in the WordArt text box and type text.**

Capturing screenshots

Sometimes you may want to show an image of an actual computer screen to show how a program works, or to show what a competitor's website looks like. If you need a screenshot, PowerPoint can import all or part of a screen.

To capture a screenshot, follow these steps:

1. **Click the slide (in either Slide or Outline view) to which you want to add a screenshot.**

2. **Click the Insert tab.**

3. **Click the Screenshot icon in the Images group.**

   A menu appears, showing all currently open windows, as in Figure 12-6.

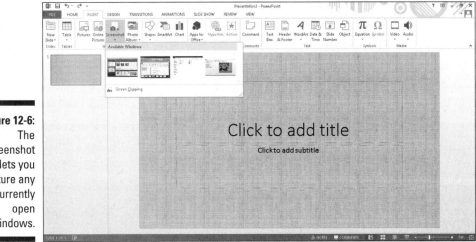

Figure 12-6:
The Screenshot icon lets you capture any currently open windows.

4. **Click a screenshot that you want to capture.**

   PowerPoint displays the screenshot on the current slide.

   If you choose Screen Clipping from the bottom of the menu, you can drag the mouse to select just a portion of a screen to capture and store on your slide.

Resizing, moving, and deleting graphic images

When you add graphics to a slide, you may need to resize or move them to another location. To resize a graphic image, follow these steps:

1. **Click the graphic (picture, clip art, screenshot, or WordArt) that you want to resize.**

   PowerPoint displays handles around your chosen object.

2. **Move the mouse pointer over a handle.**

   The mouse pointer turns into a two-way-pointing arrow.

3. **Hold down the left mouse button and drag (move) the mouse.**

   PowerPoint resizes your chosen graphic image.

4. **Release the left mouse button when you're happy with the new size of your graphic image.**

To move a graphic image, follow these steps:

1. **Move the mouse pointer over the edge of the graphic image you want to move.**

   The mouse turns into a four-way-pointing arrow.

2. **Hold down the left mouse button and drag (move) the mouse.**

   PowerPoint moves your graphic image.

3. **Release the left mouse button when you're happy with the new position of your graphic image.**

After you add a graphic image to a slide, you may later decide to delete it. To delete a graphic image, follow these steps:

1. **Click the graphic image you want to delete.**

   PowerPoint displays handles around your chosen graphic image.

2. **Press Delete.**

   PowerPoint deletes your chosen graphic image.

Rotating graphics

You may want to rotate graphic images for added visual effects. To rotate images or to flip them vertically or horizontally, follow these steps:

1. **Click the graphic image you want to rotate.**

   PowerPoint displays handles around your image along with a green rotate handle.

2. **Move the mouse pointer over the rotate handle.**

   The mouse pointer turns into a circular arrow.

3. **Hold down the left mouse button and move (drag) the mouse.**

   PowerPoint rotates your graphic image.

   If you hold down the Shift key while dragging the mouse, you can rotate an image at 15-degree increments.

4. **Release the left mouse button when you're happy with the rotation of the image.**

Layering objects

PowerPoint treats graphics and text boxes (see Chapter 11) as objects that you can move around on a slide. If you move one object over another, it may block part of another object, as shown in Figure 12-7.

When one object covers another one, PowerPoint considers the first object to be on top and the other object (the one being obscured) to be on the bottom. By moving objects from top to bottom (or vice versa), you can create unique visual effects (or just cover up parts of other objects by mistake).

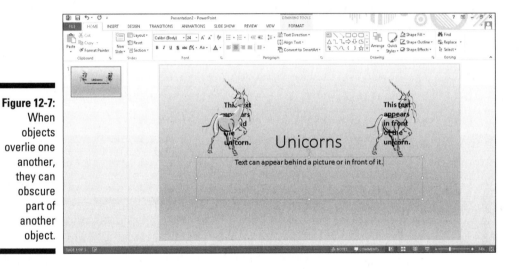

Figure 12-7: When objects overlie one another, they can obscure part of another object.

To move a graphic image to the top or bottom when layered over another object, follow these steps:

1. **Click the graphic image you want to move.**

   The Picture Tools Format tab appears.

2. **Click the Format tab.**

3. **Click the Bring Forward or Send Backward icon in the Arrange group.**

   PowerPoint rearranges the layering of your graphic images.

   You can also right-click an object and choose the Bring Forward or Send Backward command.

Adding Movies to a Slide

Besides adding static graphic images, you can also add movies to a slide so that they play as part of your presentation. To get a video, you can either search for one over the Internet or look for one stored on your computer.

Searching for a video on the Internet

PowerPoint can access a library of videos over the Internet. Make sure you have an Internet connection and then follow these steps:

1. **Click the slide (in either Slide or Outline view) to which you want to add a video.**

2. **Click the Insert tab.**

3. **Click the Video icon in the Media group.**

   A menu appears as shown in Figure 12-8.

4. **Choose Online Videos.**

   An Insert Video window appears, as shown in Figure 12-9.

5. **Click in a text box (such as the Bing Video Search) and type a description of the video you want such as "dogs," and then press Enter.**

   A list of videos appears.

Figure 12-8: The Video menu lets you choose a video on your hard drive or on the Internet.

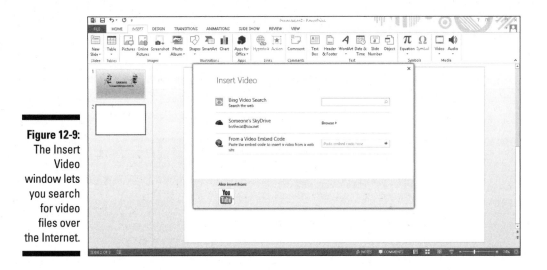

Figure 12-9:
The Insert Video window lets you search for video files over the Internet.

6. Click the video you want to place on your slide and click the Insert button.

PowerPoint displays the video on your slide. You may need to move or resize it.

You won't see the video in action until you view your presentation by pressing F5 or (if you click the video) you click the Playback tab and then click the Play icon.

Searching for video on your computer

If you've captured video through your computer's web cam or through a mobile phone that you've stored on your computer, you may want to search for that video instead of searching for one over the Internet.

PowerPoint can use movies stored in common video formats such as AVI, MPEG, ASF (streaming video), QuickTime, Flash, and WMV files. If your movie is stored in a different file format, such as Real Video, you must convert the file before you add it to a PowerPoint presentation.

To add a movie stored on your computer, follow these steps:

1. Click the slide (in either Slide or Outline view) to which you want to add a movie.

2. Click the Insert tab.

3. Click the Video icon in the Media group.

A menu appears.

4. **Choose Videos on My PC.**

   An Insert Video dialog box appears.

5. **Click the movie file you want to add and then click the Insert button.**

   PowerPoint displays your video on the slide.

   If you click the Play button on the Format or Playback tab, you can view your video.

Trimming a video

Before you add a video to your PowerPoint presentation, take a moment to edit it by using a video-editing program. However, you may still add a video to your presentation and suddenly realize that the video is too long. To fix this problem, PowerPoint lets you trim a video from the beginning or end.

You can trim only those videos retrieved from your computer, not videos retrieved off the Internet.

To trim a video, follow these steps:

1. **Click the slide (in either Slide or Outline view) that contains the video you want to trim.**

2. **Click the video.**

   The Video Tools Format and Playback tabs appear.

3. **Click the Playback tab and then click the Trim Video icon.**

   The Trim Video dialog box appears, as shown in Figure 12-10.

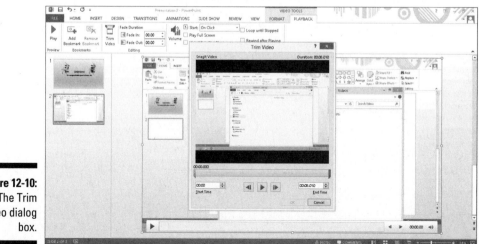

Figure 12-10:
The Trim Video dialog box.

4. **To trim the beginning of the video, drag the Beginning Marker to the right or click the Up/Down arrows in the Start Time box.**

5. **To trim the end of the video, drag the Ending Marker to the right or click the Up/Down arrows in the End Time box.**

6. **Click the OK button.**

   PowerPoint displays your trimmed video on the slide.

Coloring a video

To spice up the appearance of a video, you can modify its brightness, contrast, or color. Modifying one or more of these options can correct flaws in a video or just create unique visual effects that may make your video more memorable.

To change the color of a video, follow these steps:

1. **Click the slide (in either Slide or Outline view) that contains the video you want to trim.**

2. **Click the video that you want to format.**

   The Video Tools Format and Playback tabs appear.

3. **Click the Format tab.**

4. **Click the Corrections icon in the Adjust group.**

   A menu appears, letting you choose different brightness and contrast settings as shown in Figure 12-11.

5. **Click a brightness and contrast option.**

6. **Click the Color icon in the Adjust group.**

   A menu appears, letting you choose different color settings.

Figure 12-11:
You can
adjust the
brightness
and contrast
of a video.

Formatting the shape of a video

To make your video appear even more visually interesting, PowerPoint lets you modify the shape of the video. Instead of appearing as a boring rectangle, your video can now appear with shadows, in shapes like a triangle or arrow, or with a frame around it.

To format the shape of a video, follow these steps:

1. **Click the slide (in either Slide or Outline view) that contains the video you want to trim.**

2. **Click the video that you want to format.**

    The Video Tools Format and Playback tabs appear.

3. **Click the Format tab.**

4. **Click the Video Shape icon in the Video Styles group.**

    A menu appears, letting you choose a shape to format your video, as shown in Figure 12-12.

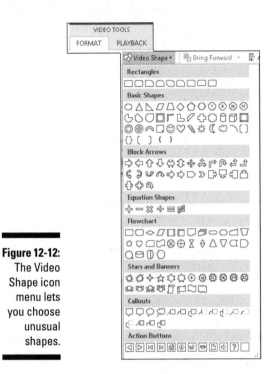

Figure 12-12:
The Video Shape icon menu lets you choose unusual shapes.

5. **Click the Video Border icon in the Video Styles group.**

   A color palette appears, letting you choose a color for your border. If you click the Weight or Dashes option from this color palette, you can choose a border thickness and style, such as a dotted line.

6. **Click the Video Effects icon in the Video Styles group.**

   A menu appears, letting you choose from different effects such as Shadow or Rotation, as shown in Figure 12-13.

   If you click a style in the Video Styles group, you can choose a pre-defined appearance for your video.

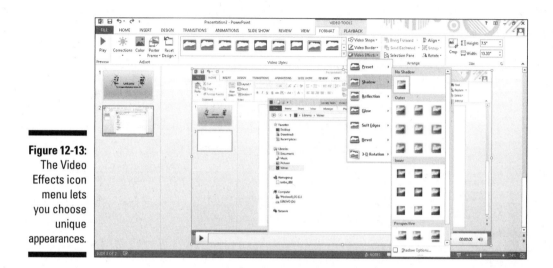

Figure 12-13:
The Video
Effects icon
menu lets
you choose
unique
appearances.

Adding Sound to a Slide

Sound can be as simple as a sound effect (like a gun firing to wake up your audience in the middle of your presentation) or a recorded speech from the CEO, explaining who has to take a 25-percent pay cut and who gets a golden parachute for life.

PowerPoint can use audio files stored in common formats such as AIFF, MIDI, MP3, and WAV files. If your audio file is stored in a different file format, such as Real Audio, you have to convert the file before you add it to a PowerPoint presentation.

Adding an audio file off the Internet

Microsoft provides plenty of audio clips stored on the Internet that you can download and use in your PowerPoint presentation.

To add an audio file off the Internet, make sure you have an Internet connection and then follow these steps:

1. **Click the slide (in either Slide or Outline view) to which you want to add an audio file.**

2. **Click the Insert tab.**

3. **Click the Audio icon in the Media group.**

   A menu appears.

4. **Choose Online Audio.**

   An Insert Audio window appears.

5. **Click in the Office.com Clip Art text box and type a description of the audio you want such as "barking," and then press Enter.**

   A list of audio clips appears.

6. **Click the audio clip you want to place on your slide and click the Insert button.**

   PowerPoint displays your audio clip as an audio icon that won't appear during your presentation.

   You may want to move the audio icon on your slide so you can edit and view the rest of your slide.

Adding audio from a file

If you already have music, sound effects, or a speech stored as a file, such as an MP3 file, you can add it to your presentation. To add an audio file stored on your computer, follow these steps:

1. **Click the slide (in either Slide or Outline view) to which you want to add an audio file.**

2. **Click the Insert tab.**

   A menu appears.

3. **Choose Audio on My PC.**

   An Insert Audio dialog box appears.

4. **Click the audio clip you want to place on your slide and click the Insert button.**

   PowerPoint displays your audio clip as an audio icon that won't appear during your presentation. However, you may want to move the audio icon on your slide so you can edit and view the rest of your slide.

To hear your audio file, click the audio file to display a Play button underneath. Then click the Play button.

Recording audio

For greater flexibility, PowerPoint lets you record audio directly from your computer's microphone (if you have one, of course). Recorded audio lets you or someone else (such as the CEO) make comments that you can insert and play into your presentation.

To record audio for your presentation, follow these steps:

1. **Click the slide (in either Slide or Outline view) to which you want to add an audio file.**

2. **Click the Insert tab.**

3. **Click the Audio icon in the Media group.**

    A menu appears.

4. **Choose Record Audio.**

    The Record Sound dialog box appears, as shown in Figure 12-14.

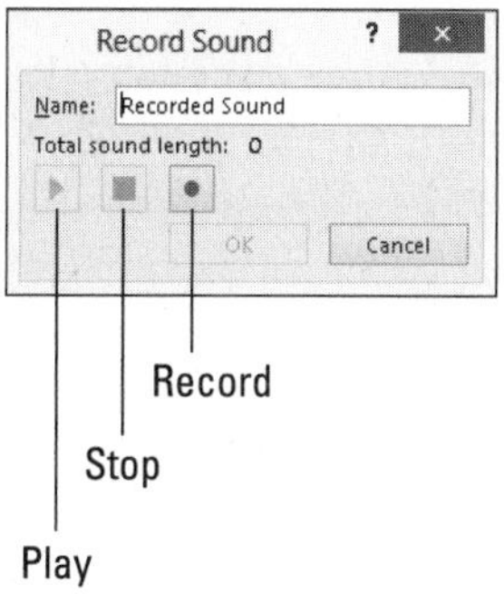

Figure 12-14:
The Record
Sound
dialog box.

Record Sound   ? ✕

Name: | Recorded Sound |
Total sound length: 0

▶ ■ ●

OK   Cancel

Record

Stop

Play

5. **Click in the Name text box and type a description for your recording.**

6. **Click the Record button and start talking.**

7. **Click the Stop button and click OK.**

    PowerPoint displays your recording as a horn icon on the slide. You may want to move this audio icon to keep it from obscuring part of your slide.

The audio icon that represents an audio file won't appear when you show off your presentation.

Chapter 13

Showing Off a Presentation

- -

In This Chapter

▶ Spell-checking a presentation

▶ Organizing slides

▶ Adding visual transitions

▶ Adding hyperlinks on a slide

▶ Viewing a presentation

▶ Printing handouts

- -

*T*he whole point of creating a PowerPoint presentation is to show it off to an audience. To help you keep an audience's attention, PowerPoint provides Hollywood-style special effects to make your presentation look more interesting.

PowerPoint also provides features for creating handouts for your audience. Because people often want to take notes during an interesting presentation (or just doodle during a really boring presentation), PowerPoint can create handouts that you can print and distribute.

Spell-Checking Your Presentation

You can have the best presentation in the world, but it will look like the worst presentation in the world if you have misspellings and typos on your slides for everyone to snicker at. To prevent this problem from occurring, PowerPoint can spell-check your entire presentation.

PowerPoint automatically underlines all misspelled words with a red squiggly line. If you right-click any word underlined with a red squiggly line, a pop-up menu appears with a list of correctly spelled alternatives that you can choose.

To spell-check your entire presentation, follow these steps:

1. **Click the Review tab.**

2. **Click the Spelling icon in the Proofing group.**

    PowerPoint displays the Spelling pane when it finds a misspelled word, as shown in Figure 13-1.

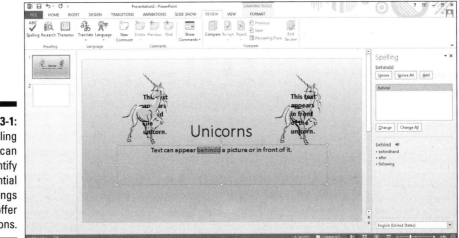

Figure 13-1:
The Spelling pane can identify potential misspellings and offer corrections.

3. **Choose one of the following for each word that PowerPoint highlights as misspelled:**

    • *Change:* Click the correct spelling of the word and then click Change. (Click Change All to change all identical misspellings throughout your presentation.)

    • *Ignore:* Click Ignore to ignore this one instance of that word throughout your presentation.

    • *Ignore All:* Click Ignore All to ignore all instances of that word throughout your presentation.

    • *Add:* Click Add to add the word to the PowerPoint dictionary so it won't flag the word as misspelled again.

4. **Click the Close icon in the Spelling pane to stop spell-checking.**

PowerPoint won't recognize technical terms, proper names, or correctly spelled words used incorrectly, such as using the word *there* instead of *their*, so it's important to also proofread your presentation yourself.

Organizing Slides in Sections

PowerPoint displays all the slides of your presentation in the Slides or Outline view. While this makes it easy to see all the slides that make up your presentation, such a long list of slides can make it hard for you to find any particular slide.

To help you avoid searching for a single slide among a huge list, PowerPoint gives you the option of organizing in groups called *sections*. You may group the first slides in one section (labeled "Problems"), the next 7 slides in a second section (labeled "Consequences"), and the last 13 slides in a third section (labeled "My Solutions").

After grouping slides into sections, you can selectively hide or display all slides in a section. Sections simply help you organize a large presentation of slides so you can find and edit particular slides at any given time.

Adding a section

By default, presentations don't contain any sections. When you add a section, PowerPoint groups all slides in that section, starting with the first slide you picked all the way to the end of your presentation or the next section heading, whichever comes first.

To add a section to a presentation, follow these steps:

1. **Click the slide that you want to define the beginning of a section.**

2. **Click the Home tab and click the Section icon under the Slides group.**

   A pull-down menu appears, as shown in Figure 13-2.

3. **Choose Add Section.**

   PowerPoint displays a section heading (named Untitled Section) above the slide you selected in Step 1.

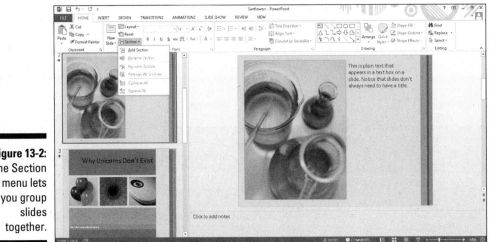

Figure 13-2:
The Section
menu lets
you group
slides
together.

4. **Click the selection heading, click the Section icon in the Slides group, and choose Rename Section.**

   The Rename Section dialog box appears, as shown in Figure 13-3.

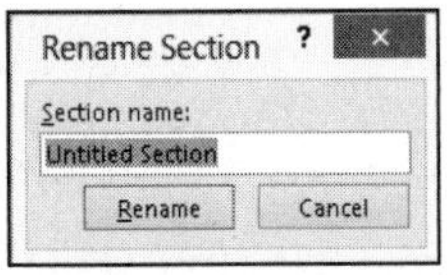

Figure 13-3:
The Rename
Section
dialog box.

5. **Click in the Section Name text box and type a descriptive name for your section. Then click Rename.**

   PowerPoint renames your chosen section.

When you add a section to a presentation, PowerPoint automatically creates a Default Section that contains the first slide and all additional slides up to the section heading you just created.

Expanding and collapsing a section

After you've created at least one section, you can collapse and expand it. Collapsing a section temporarily hides those slides in that section from view so you can focus on the rest of your slides. Expanding a section makes the slides in that section appear again.

To expand and collapse a section, follow these steps:

1. **Click the Collapse Section arrow that appears to the left of the section name, as shown in Figure 13-4.**

   PowerPoint collapses your chosen section and displays the number of slides (in parentheses) hidden in that collapsed section, as shown in Figure 13-5.

2. **Click the Expand Section arrow that appears to the left of the collapsed section name.**

   The section expands, displaying all slides within that section.

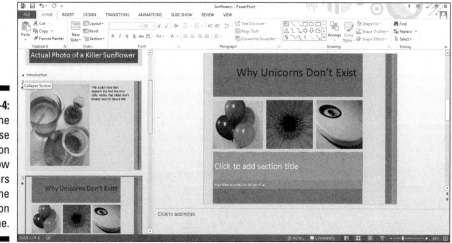

Figure 13-4: The Collapse Section arrow appears next to the section name.

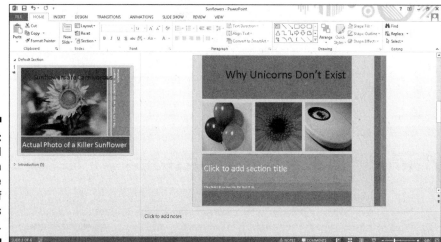

Figure 13-5: A collapsed section displays the number of slides hidden.

Deleting a section

Sections can help divide a large presentation into more manageable chunks, but you may eventually decide you don't need a section anymore. When you delete a section, you have the option of just deleting the section (and leaving the slides intact) or deleting both the section and all slides inside that section.

To delete a section, follow these steps:

1. **Right-click the section name that you want to delete.**

   PowerPoint displays a pop-up menu, as shown in Figure 13-6.

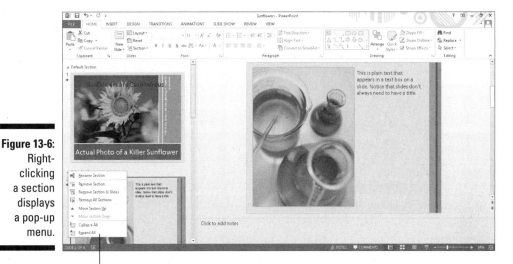

Figure 13-6: Right-clicking a section displays a pop-up menu.

Pop-up menu

2. **Choose Remove Section (to remove your chosen section), Remove All Sections (to remove all sections), or Remove Section & Slides (to remove your chosen section and all the slides in that section).**

   PowerPoint deletes your section (or sections).

Adding Visual Transitions

Transitions define how slides or part of a slide (text or graphics) appear during your presentation. By default, slides appear one at a time with all the text and graphics displayed at once, which can get monotonous.

To spice up your presentation, PowerPoint offers two types of transitions:

- ✔ Slide transitions (these occur between two different slides)
- ✔ Text and picture animations (these occur on a single slide)

Use transitions sparingly. Transitions may be visually interesting, but too many transitions can be distracting.

Adding slide transitions

Slide transitions can make a slide appear to melt or break into multiple pieces that slip away, revealing the next slide underneath.

When creating a transition, you need to define the following:

- ✔ The actual visual appearance of the transition
- ✔ The speed of the transition (Slow, Medium, or Fast)
- ✔ Any sound effects you want to play during the transition (these can get really annoying, so use them sparingly)
- ✔ When to display the transition (after a certain time period or when you click the mouse)

To create a slide transition, follow these steps:

1. **Click a slide (in the Slide or Outline view pane).**

   Any transition you choose will end by displaying the slide you choose in this step.

2. **Click the Transitions tab.**

   PowerPoint displays the different animation (transition) tools, as shown in Figure 13-7.

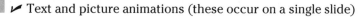

3. **Click the More button of the Transition To This Slide group.**

   A pull-down menu appears, listing all the different transitions available as shown in Figure 13-8.

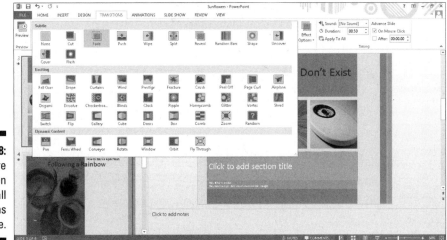

Figure 13-8:
The More
button
displays all
transitions
available.

4. **Click the transition you want.**

   PowerPoint shows you how your transition will look.

5. **(Optional) Click in the Sound list box in the Timing group.**

   A pull-down menu appears, listing all the sound effects you can choose, as shown in Figure 13-9.

6. **(Optional) Select the On Mouse Click or After check box in the Timing group of the Transitions tab.**

   If you select the After check box, you have to specify a time to wait before running the transition.

   You can select both the On Mouse Click and Automatically After check boxes, so the slide transition waits until you click the mouse or until a specified amount of time passes.

7. **(Optional) Click Apply to All to apply your transitions to every slide in your presentation.**

Applying the same transition throughout your presentation can give your slide show a consistent look, but it's best for only simple, visual transitions and not for transitions that involve noisy sound effects that get tedious after awhile.

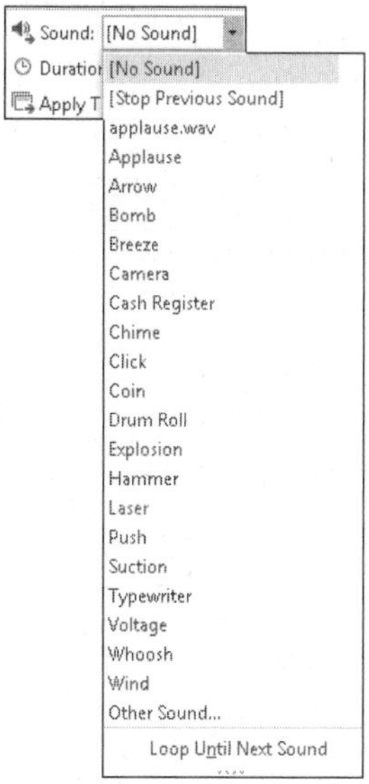

Sound: [No Sound]
Duratio [No Sound]
Apply T [Stop Previous Sound]
applause.wav
Applause
Arrow
Bomb
Breeze
Camera
Cash Register
Chime
Click
Coin
Drum Roll
Explosion
Hammer
Laser
Push
Suction
Typewriter
Voltage
Whoosh
Wind
Other Sound...
Loop Until Next Sound

Figure 13-9:
The Sound
list box
shows avail-
able sound
effects.

Text and graphic transitions

Besides animating how your slides appear and disappear, you can also add
transitions to your text boxes or graphics so they fly or drop into place
across a slide.

Use text and graphic transitions sparingly. Transitions can get distracting when
people just want to read your presentation without having to watch letters
zoom around the screen.

To create a simple text or graphic transition, follow these steps:

1. **Click a text box or picture on a slide.**

   PowerPoint displays handles around your chosen item.

2. **Click the Animations tab.**

3. **Click the More button in the Animations group to display a menu of
   options, as shown in Figure 13-10.**

4. **Click an animation, such as Fly In or Wipe.**

   PowerPoint displays a number near your chosen item. These numbers
   define the order that your transitions will appear.

5. **Click the Preview icon to see how your animation will look.**

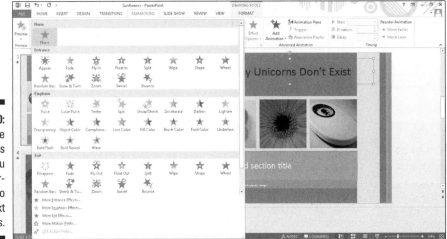

Figure 13-10:
The
Animations
menu
displays var-
ious ways to
animate text
or graphics.

To remove an animation, just select that text box or graphic, click the Animations tab, and choose None from the Animation group.

Using the Animation Painter

If you create an animation that you want to apply to other text boxes or graphic objects, you can tediously re-create that transition all over again. However, it's much simpler to use the Animation Painter, which lets you copy animations from one object to another.

To use the Animation Painter, follow these steps:

1. **Click a text box or picture that contains the animation you want to copy.**

   PowerPoint displays handles around your chosen item.

2. **Click the Animations tab.**

3. **Click the Animation Painter icon under the Advanced Animation group.**

4. **Click a text box or picture.**

   PowerPoint applies the transition, from the object you selected in Step 1, to the object you selected in Step 4.

Adding Hyperlinks

For greater flexibility in presenting information, PowerPoint lets you add hyperlinks to your slides. Hyperlinks let you open a web page (provided you have an Internet connection) or a file (such as a Word document). By adding hyperlinks to your slides, you can display additional information stored outside of your PowerPoint presentation.

Creating web page hyperlinks

A web-page hyperlink lets you convert text into a hyperlink that can load your default browser and display any website. When you exit the browser (or just switch back to PowerPoint), you can see your slide again and continue with your presentation.

By accessing a website, you can avoid copying data and pasting it on a slide. For example, if you're giving a presentation about advertising, you can create web page hyperlinks to show how your competitors use the Internet to advertise and sell their products.

To create a web page hyperlink, follow these steps:

1. **Highlight the text in a title or subtitle text box that you want to turn into a web page hyperlink.**

2. **Click the Insert tab.**

3. **Click the Hyperlink icon in the Links group.**

   The Insert Hyperlink dialog box appears, as shown in Figure 13-11.

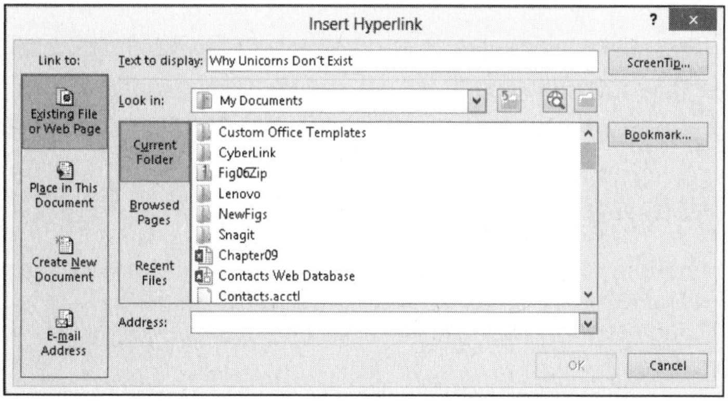

Figure 13-11: The Insert Hyperlink dialog box lets you type in a website address.

4. **Click in the Address text box and type a website address, such as** www.dummies.com.

5. **Click OK.**

    PowerPoint underlines the text you selected in Step 1. When you view your presentation, PowerPoint turns the mouse pointer into a hand icon when you move the pointer over the hyperlink. Clicking your hyperlink loads the default browser.

Creating hyperlinks to external files

You may have data stored in another file that you want to include in your PowerPoint presentation. Rather than copy the data and paste it in your presentation, it may be easier just to display the file itself. That way you can update the file, and PowerPoint will always link to the updated file.

When you create a hyperlink to a file, PowerPoint opens that file by loading the program that created it. For example, if you want to view a Microsoft Word file, make sure that you have a copy of Microsoft Word installed on your computer.

To create a hyperlink that opens an external file, follow these steps:

1. **Highlight the text in a title or subtitle text box that you want to turn into an external file hyperlink.**

2. **Click the Insert tab.**

3. **Click the Hyperlink icon in the Links group.**

    The Insert Hyperlink dialog box appears (refer to Figure 13-11).

4. **Click in the Look In list box and choose a drive and folder that holds the file you want to use.**

    You may need to click through several folders to find the file you want.

5. **Click the file you want to use and then click OK.**

Running a program through a hyperlink

A PowerPoint hyperlink can also run any program from within a presentation. For example, you can create a presentation that explains how to market a new computer program, and then create a hyperlink to that same program so you can demonstrate how that program actually works. When you exit that program, you return to your PowerPoint presentation again.

Make sure that your computer has enough memory to run both PowerPoint and any other program you want to run.

To create a hyperlink that runs a program, follow these steps:

1. **Highlight the text in a text box that you want to turn into a program hyperlink.**

2. **Click the Insert tab.**

3. **Click the Action icon in the Links group.**

   The Action Settings dialog box appears.

4. **Select the Run Program radio button.**

5. **Click Browse.**

   The Select a Program to Run dialog box appears.

6. **Click the program you want to run.**

   You may have to open multiple folders to find the program you want to run.

7. **Click the program you want to run and then click OK.**

   The Action Settings dialog box appears again.

8. **Click OK.**

When you run your presentation and click your link to run an external program, PowerPoint displays a Security Notice dialog box as shown in Figure 13-12. This dialog box gives you the option of letting any presentation run external programs (Enable All), just letting the current presentation run an external program (Enable), or blocking all external programs from running at all (Disable).

Figure 13-12:
When you run your presentation, PowerPoint gives you several options for running external programs within a slide show.

Microsoft PowerPoint Security Notice   ?   ×

🛡 **Microsoft Office has identified a potential security concern.**

File Path: C:\Users\bothe_000\Documents\Sunflowers.pptx

To help protect your security, Microsoft Office has blocked the ability to run an external program automatically. If you choose to enable the external programs, your document and computer may no longer be secure.

If you wish to run external programs in Action Settings, click Enable. If you wish for external programs in Action settings to run automatically, click Enable All, but note that this may be a security risk. Otherwise, click Disable to continue.

[Enable All (not recommended)]   [Enable]   [Disable]

Viewing a Presentation

After you finish arranging your slides, adding transitions, and adding hyperlinks, you're ready to test how your entire presentation looks. To view your entire presentation, follow these steps:

1. **Click the Slide Show tab.**

2. **Click the From Beginning icon in the Start Slide Show group, as shown in Figure 13-13.**

   PowerPoint displays the first slide of your presentation.

   You can also choose the From Beginning command by pressing F5.

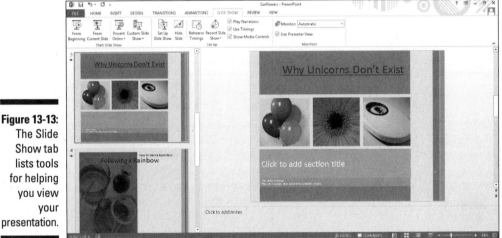

Figure 13-13:
The Slide Show tab lists tools for helping you view your presentation.

3. **Choose one of the following:**

   • Click the mouse or press the spacebar to view the next slide.

   • Press Esc to exit your presentation.

If you have a large presentation consisting of 300 slides, you may not want to view the first 290 slides just to test how your last 10 slides look. To avoid this problem, click the slide you want to view and then click the From Current Slide icon in Step 2.

Creating a custom slide show

You may have a presentation organized for one audience (engineers and scientists) but need to give the same presentation to a different audience (sales executives). Although you can copy your original presentation and then modify it, now you'll be stuck with two copies of the same information. And, if you modify the information in one presentation, you have to modify the same information in the second (or third or fourth) presentation.

To avoid this problem, PowerPoint lets you create custom slide shows based on an existing presentation. Such a custom slide show can selectively show slides in a different order. To create a custom slide show, you need to define the order you want to display the slides.

To arrange the order of a custom slide show, follow these steps:

1. **Click the Slide Show tab.**

2. **Click the Custom Slide Show icon in the Start Slide Show group.**

   A pull-down menu appears.

3. **Choose Custom Shows.**

   The Custom Shows dialog box appears, as shown in Figure 13-14.

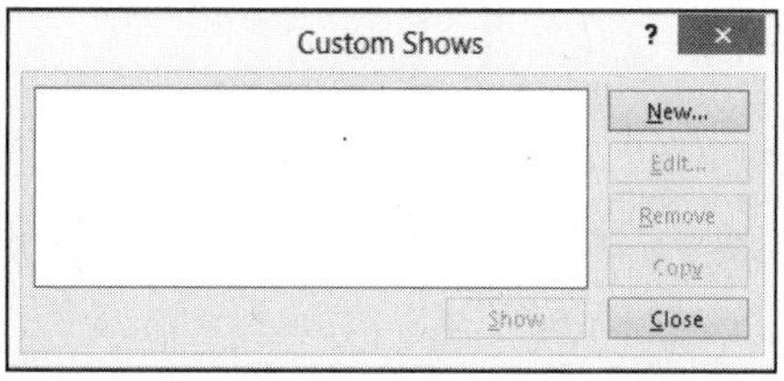

Figure 13-14: The Custom Shows dialog box lets you define a name for your custom slide show.

4. **Click New.**

   The Define Custom Show dialog box appears, as shown in Figure 13-15.

5. **Click in the Slide Show Name text box and type a name for your custom slide show.**

6. **Click in the check box for a slide in the Slides In Presentation list box and then click the Add button.**

This tells PowerPoint which existing slides you want to use in your custom slide show.

7. Repeat Step 6 for each slide you want to include in your custom slide show.

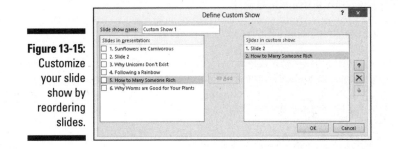

Figure 13-15:
Customize
your slide
show by
reordering
slides.

8. (Optional) Click a slide in the Slides In Custom Show list box and click the Up or Down arrow button to rearrange their order.

9. Repeat Step 8 for each slide you want to rearrange in your custom slide show.

10. Click OK.

The Custom Shows dialog box appears again.

11. Click the name of your custom slide show and then click Close.

To present a custom slide show, follow these steps:

1. Click the Slide Show tab.

2. Click the Custom Slide Show icon in the Start Slide Show group.

A pull-down menu appears that lists the names of all the custom slide shows you've created.

3. Click the name of the custom slide show you want to view.

4. Choose one of the following:

- Click the mouse or press the spacebar to view the next slide.

- Press Esc to exit your presentation.

Eventually you may need to delete a custom slide show. When you delete a custom slide show, you don't delete any slides used in your original presentation.

To delete a custom slide show, follow these steps:

1. **Click the Slide Show tab.**
2. **Click the Custom Slide Show icon in the Start Slide Show group.**

   A pull-down menu appears, listing the names of all the custom slide shows you've created.
3. **Click Custom Shows.**

   The Custom Shows dialog box appears.
4. **Click the name of the custom slide show you want to delete and click the Remove button.**
5. **Click the Close button.**

Hiding a slide

PowerPoint can hide a slide, which lets you keep your slide but not display it during a presentation. Hiding a slide can be especially handy when you need to create a custom slide show and need a slide to appear only in the custom slide show but not the original presentation (or vice versa).

To hide a slide, follow these steps:

1. **Click the slide that you want to hide (in Slide or Outline view).**
2. **Click the Slide Show tab.**
3. **Click the Hide Slide icon in the Set Up group.**

   PowerPoint dims your selected slide.

To unhide a slide, just repeat the preceding three steps.

Organizing with Slide Sorter view

After you view your presentation, you may want to rearrange slides. To help you organize your presentation, switch to Slide Sorter view, which numbers each slide to show you the order that they appear, as shown in Figure 13-16.

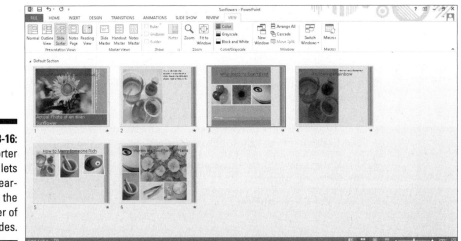

Figure 13-16:
Slide Sorter
view lets
you rear-
range the
order of
your slides.

To use Slide Sorter view, follow these steps:

1. **Click the View tab.**

2. **Click the Slide Sorter view icon in the Presentation Views group.**

   You can also click the Slide Sorter icon in the bottom-right corner of the PowerPoint window.

3. **(Optional) To delete a slide, click a slide and press Delete.**

4. **(Optional) To hide a slide, click a slide, click the Slide Show tab, and click Hide Slide.**

5. **(Optional) To move a slide**

   a. *Move the mouse pointer over a slide.*

   b. *Hold down the left mouse button and move (drag) the mouse.*

   PowerPoint displays a vertical line where it will place your slide.

   c. *Release the left mouse button.*

6. **Click the Normal icon on the View tab to switch out of Slide Sorter view.**

Creating Handouts

When people view a particularly interesting presentation, they often want copies of that presentation so they can review the information later or have a place to jot down notes during the presentation itself. For that reason, PowerPoint lets you create handouts from your presentation.

Handouts typically contain a thumbnail of each slide along with blank space for jotting down notes about the information presented by that slide. To create a handout, follow these steps:

1. **Click the File tab.**

2. **Choose Print.**

   The middle pane displays a variety of print options, as shown in Figure 13-17.

Figure 13-17: The middle pane displays print settings.

3. **Click the Full Page Slides button in the middle pane under the Settings heading.**

   A menu appears, showing different ways to print slides (as shown in Figure 13-18).

4. **Choose the print option you want, and then click the Print button in the top of the middle pane when you're ready to start printing.**

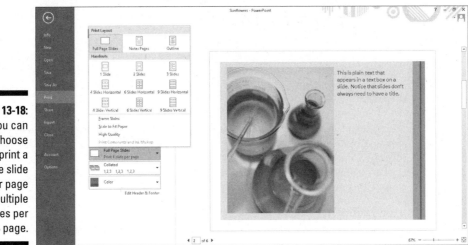

Figure 13-18:
You can
choose
to print a
single slide
per page
or multiple
slides per
page.

Part V

Getting Organized with Outlook

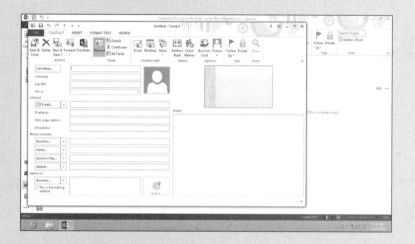

Visit www.dummies.com/extras/office2013 for great Dummies content online.

In this part . . .

- ✔ Configuring e-mail account settings
- ✔ Adding file attachments
- ✔ Setting an appointment
- ✔ Tracking your tasks
- ✔ Visit www.dummies.com/extras/office2013 for great Dummies content online.

Chapter 14

Managing E-Mail with Outlook

• •

• •

Microsoft Outlook is the personal organizer portion of Office 2013 for tracking appointments, storing names and addresses of important people, and keeping a list of to-do tasks. However, the most popular uses for Outlook are reading, writing, and organizing your e-mail.

Configuring E-Mail Settings

The first time you run Outlook, you need to configure your e-mail account information. To retrieve e-mail from your account within Outlook, you may need to know the following:

✔ Your name

✔ The username of your e-mail account, which may be JSmith (for Joe Smith)

✔ Your e-mail address (such as `JSmith@microsoft.com`)

✔ Your e-mail account password

✔ Your e-mail account type (such as POP3 or IMAP)

✔ Your incoming mail server name (such as `pop.microsoft.com`)

✔ Your outgoing mail server name (such as `smtp.microsoft.com`)

Outlook can often recognize many popular e-mail accounts such as Yahoo! Mail, but if Outlook can't set up your e-mail account automatically, you will need to ask your Internet service provider (ISP) for all these details.

Before you can use Outlook to manage your e-mail, you must add your e-mail account. The first time you run Outlook, the program will try to set up an e-mail account to use.

If you want to add a new e-mail account later, follow these steps:

1. **Load Outlook and click the File tab.**

2. **Click Info and then click the Add Account button.**

    An Add Account dialog box appears, as shown in Figure 14-1.

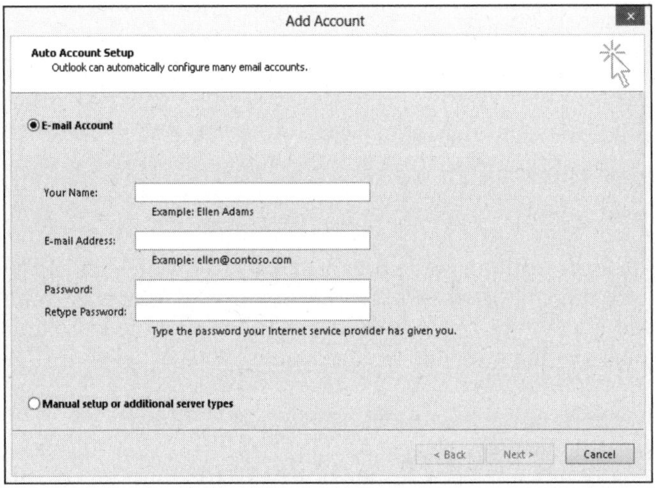

Figure 14-1:
The Add
Account
dialog box
lets you
create
an e-mail
account to
work with
Outlook.

> **Add Account**   ✕
>
> **Auto Account Setup**
> Outlook can automatically configure many email accounts.
>
> ● **E-mail Account**
>
> Your Name: [_____]
>   Example: Ellen Adams
>
> E-mail Address: [_____]
>   Example: ellen@contoso.com
>
> Password: [_____]
> Retype Password: [_____]
>   Type the password your Internet service provider has given you.
>
> ○ **Manual setup or additional server types**
>
>   [< Back] [Next >] [Cancel]

3. **Type in the appropriate information and click Next.**

    You may need to wade through several sets of questions before Outlook can properly configure your e-mail account.

To delete an e-mail account, click the File tab, click Info, click Account Settings, and when a pop-up menu appears, choose Account Settings. When an Account Settings dialog box appears, click the e-mail account you want to delete, and then click the Remove icon.

Creating E-Mail

After you set up an e-mail account, you can start sending e-mail. The three ways to create and send e-mail are

- ✔ **Create a message and type the recipient's e-mail address manually.**
- ✔ **Reply to a previously received message.** Outlook then adds the recipient's e-mail address automatically.
- ✔ **Create a message and use a previously stored e-mail address.** Outlook adds the e-mail address automatically.

Creating a new e-mail message

The most straightforward way to send a message is to type the recipient's e-mail address and then type your message. To create a new e-mail message and type the e-mail address, follow these steps:

1. **Click the Mail icon in the bottom-left corner of the Outlook window.**

2. **Click the Home tab and then click the New Email icon.**

   Outlook displays a message window, as shown in Figure 14-2. Notice that the message window displays a Ribbon with File, Message, Insert, Options, Format Text, and Review tabs.

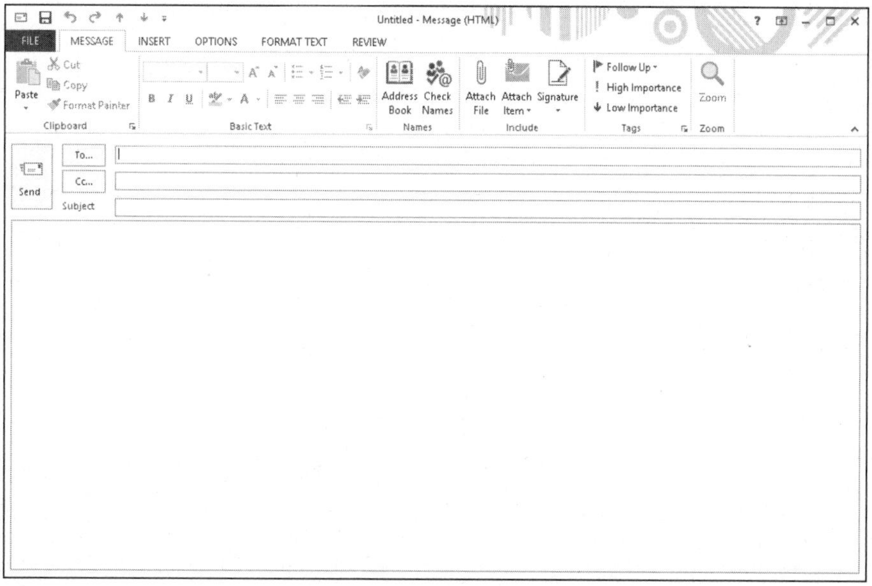

Figure 14-2:
The message window lets you type and format a message.

3. **Click in the To text box and type the e-mail address of the person you want to receive your message.**

   Make sure that you type the e-mail address correctly. One incorrect character, and your message won't go to your intended recipient.

4. **(Optional) Click in the Cc text box and type another e-mail address to send the message to more than one person.**

5. **Click in the Subject text box and type a brief description of your message.**

   Many people use spam filters that examine the Subject line of a message, so it's a good idea not to type your subject text in ALL CAPITAL LETTERS or use multiple exclamation points!!! Otherwise your recipient's spam filter may inadvertently flag your message as spam and delete it before anyone can even read it.

6. **Click in the message text box and type your message.**

   If you click the Save icon on the Quick Access toolbar (or press Ctrl+S), you can store the message in your Drafts folder so you can edit and send it at a later time.

7. **Click the Send icon to send your message.**

Replying to an e-mail message

Oftentimes, you may receive a message from someone else and want to send a reply to that person. When you send a reply, Outlook automatically copies the original message as part of your e-mail; that way, the recipient can read the original message that you're responding to.

Even better, when you reply to a message, you won't have to retype the recipient's e-mail address and risk misspelling it. To reply to an e-mail message, follow these steps:

1. **Click the Mail icon in the bottom-left corner of the Outlook window.**

2. **Click the Home tab.**

   Outlook displays the Mail pane.

3. **Click a message that you want to reply to.**

   Outlook displays the contents of that message in a pane on the right side of the Outlook window.

4. **Click the Reply icon in the Respond category.**

   Outlook displays a message window with the recipient's e-mail address and subject line already typed in, along with a copy of the original message.

If you click the Forward icon instead of the Reply icon, you can send a message to another person instead of the person who originally sent you the message.

5. Click in the message text box and type your message.

If you click the Save icon on the Quick Access toolbar in the upper-left corner of the screen, you can store the message in your Drafts folder so you can edit and send it at a later time.

6. Click the Send icon.

Using a stored e-mail address to create a new e-mail message

If you send e-mail to certain people regularly, you can type a particular person's e-mail address once, store it, and then have Outlook type that e-mail address whenever you need it again.

To store an e-mail address, follow these steps:

1. Click the Mail icon in the bottom-left corner of the Outlook window.

2. Click the Home tab and click the Address Book icon in the Find category.

The Address Book: Contacts window appears, as shown in Figure 14-3.

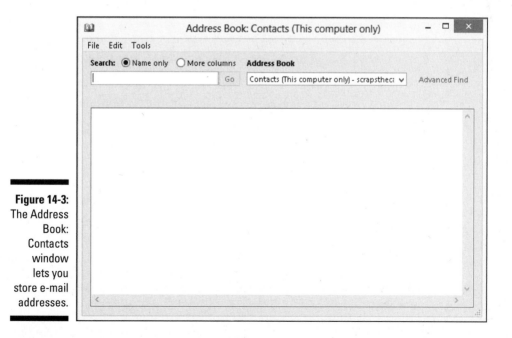

Figure 14-3:
The Address Book: Contacts window lets you store e-mail addresses.

3. **Choose File⇨New Entry.**

   A New Entry dialog box appears.

4. **Choose New Contact and click OK.**

   A Contact window appears, as shown in Figure 14-4.

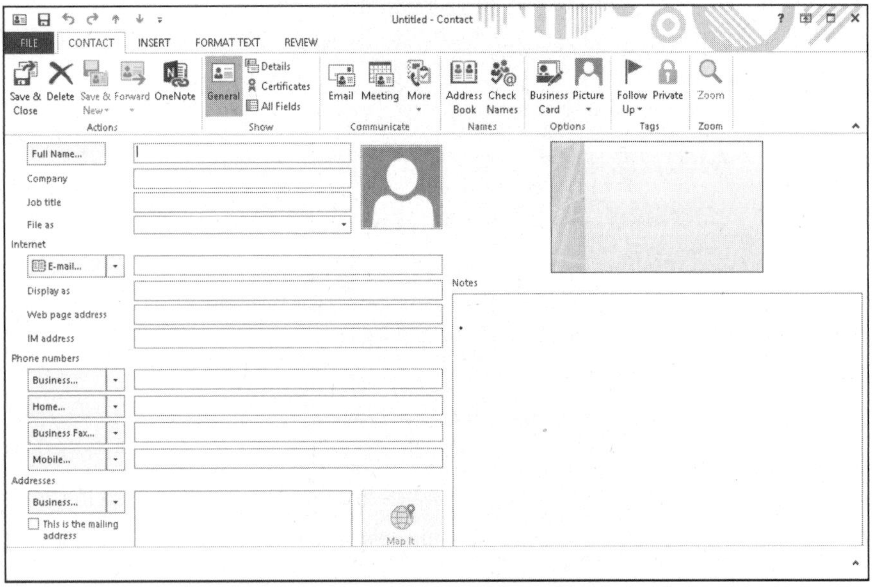

Figure 14-4:
The Contact
window
lets you
add a name
and e-mail
address.

5. **Click in the Full Name text box and type a person's name.**

6. **Click in the E-mail text box and type a person's e-mail address.**

7. **Click the Save & Close icon.**

   Your newly added name appears in the Address Book: Contacts window.

8. **Choose File⇨Close.**

After you have stored at least one name and e-mail address, you can retrieve that e-mail address to send a message by following these steps:

1. **Click the Mail icon in the bottom-left corner of the Outlook window.**

2. **Click the Home tab and click the New Email icon in the New category.**

   The Message window appears.

3. **Click the To button.**

   The Select Names: Contacts dialog box appears, listing all your stored names and e-mail addresses.

4. **Click a name to select it.**

5. **Click the To button at the bottom of the Select Names: Contacts dialog box.**

6. **Click OK.**

   Outlook automatically enters your chosen e-mail address in the To text box.

7. **Click in the Subject text box and type a brief description of your message.**

8. **Click in the message text box and type your message.**

   If you click the Save icon on the Quick Access toolbar, you can store the message in your Drafts folder so you can edit and send it at a later time.

9. **Click the Send icon to send your message.**

Attaching Files to Messages

Rather than just send plain text, you can also *attach* a file to your message. This file can be anything from a picture, a song (stored as an audio file), a program, a video file, or even another e-mail message.

Be careful when attaching files to messages because many Internet service providers (ISPs) put a limit on the maximum size of an e-mail message, such as 10MB. Also try to keep any file attachments small because if the recipient has a slow Internet connection, downloading a large file attachment can take a really long time.

If you want to send someone a picture, video, audio file, compressed file, or even an entire program, you need to attach that file to a message by following these steps:

1. **Follow the steps in the earlier section, "Creating E-Mail," to create a new e-mail message, type a subject, and type an e-mail address.**

2. **Click the Insert tab.**

3. **Click the Attach File icon in the Include group.**

   The Insert File dialog box appears.

4. **Click the file you want to attach to your message and then click Insert.**

   Outlook displays an Attached text box in the message window, as shown in Figure 14-5.

   If you hold down the Ctrl or Shift key while clicking a file, you can select multiple files at once.

Figure 14-5:
Every message with a file attachment displays an Attached text box that displays the filename attached to the message.

5. **(Optional) Right-click any file in the Attached text box; when a pop-up menu appears, choose Remove if you change your mind about attaching a file to a message.**

6. **Click the Send icon.**

Rather than select multiple files to attach to a message, you can compress or *zip* multiple files into a single compressed file by using a separate program such as the free Jzip program (www.jzip.com) or by using the built-in Zip compression feature in Windows.

Reading and Organizing E-Mail

One of the biggest problems with receiving e-mail is trying to sort through all the important messages. To help you organize your e-mail, Outlook offers several ways to group related messages together and search for specific text in messages so you can find exactly what you need.

Grouping messages into categories

Outlook can display messages with the newest message on top and the oldest message at the bottom (or vice versa). In addition, Outlook can also group messages according to Date, Subject, Size, or even by e-mail accounts.

To view and sort your e-mail messages, follow these steps:

1. **Click the Mail icon in the bottom-left corner of the Outlook window.**

2. **Click the View tab.**

   The different ways to arrange e-mail messages appears in the Arrangement category, as shown in Figure 14-6.

Figure 14-6:
The Arrangement category lets you choose how to organize your e-mail messages.

3. **Click a category such as Date, Size, From, or Account.**

   Outlook sorts your messages.

4. **(Optional) Click Reverse Sort.**

   Outlook sorts your messages in reverse order, such as oldest to newest or newest to oldest.

Changing the appearance of the Reading Pane

To make reading e-mail messages easier, Outlook can display your messages in three different ways:

✔ **Right:** Lists of messages appear in the left side of the Outlook window and the currently selected message appears in the right side of the Outlook window.

✔ **Bottom:** Lists of messages appear in the top of the Outlook window and the currently selected message appears in the bottom of the Outlook window.

✔ **Off:** Only lists of messages appear in the Outlook window. To see the contents of a single message, you have to double-click that message.

To change the way Outlook displays your e-mail messages, follow these steps:

1. **Click the Mail icon in the bottom-left corner of the Outlook window.**

2. **Click the View tab.**

3. **Click the Reading Pane icon in the Layout category.**

    A menu appears, as shown in Figure 14-7.

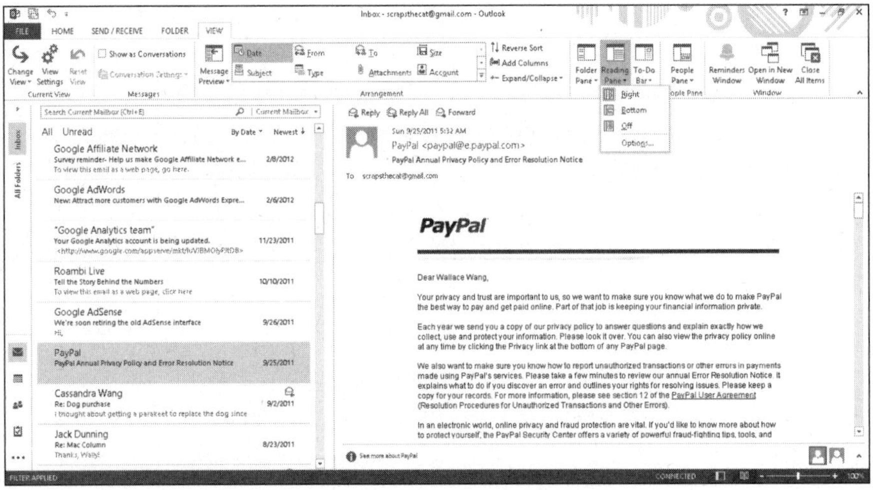

Figure 14-7: The Reading Pane menu.

4. **Choose an option such as Right, Bottom, or Off.**

    Outlook displays your messages in your chosen configuration, as shown in Figure 14-8.

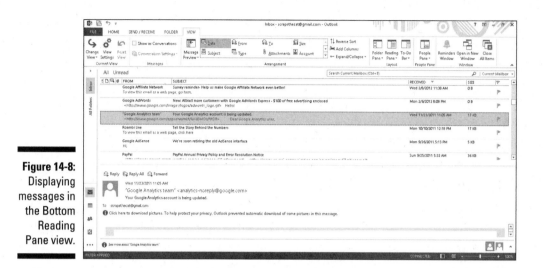

Figure 14-8:
Displaying
messages in
the Bottom
Reading
Pane view.

Retrieving a file attachment from a message

Rather than just send text, people may send you pictures, word-processor documents, or databases as file attachments. When you receive a message with a file attachment, Outlook displays a paper clip icon next to the message.

Never open a file attachment unless you absolutely trust its contents. Many malicious hackers send viruses, worms, spyware, and Trojan horses as file attachments, so if you aren't careful, you can accidentally infect your computer and lose your data.

To open a file attachment, follow these steps:

1. **Click a message that displays a paper-clip icon.**

    Outlook displays the message's contents with the file attachments listed, as shown in Figure 14-9.

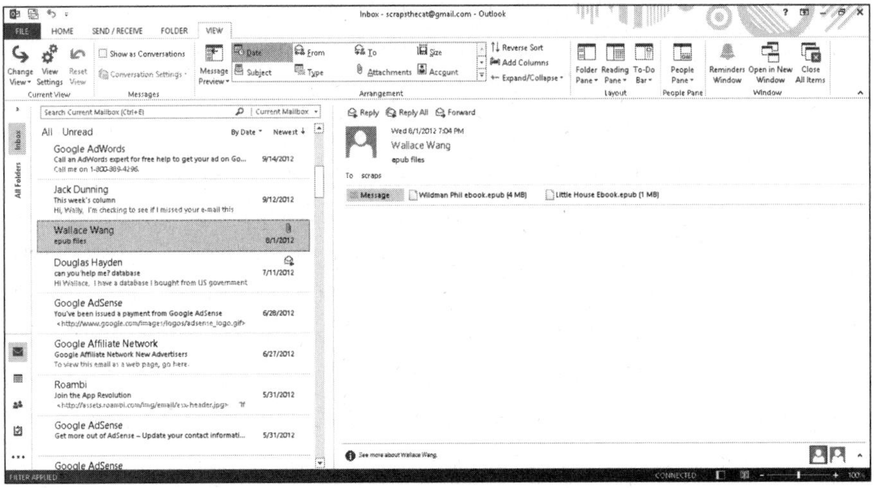

Figure 14-9:
Each file
attachment
appears as
a tiny icon.

2. **Double-click the file (paper clip) icon displayed in the message.**

An Opening Mail Attachment dialog box appears, giving you the option
to open the file directly or save it as shown in Figure 14-10. Unless you
trust the file contents, it's usually best to save the file in a directory and
scan it with your antivirus program.

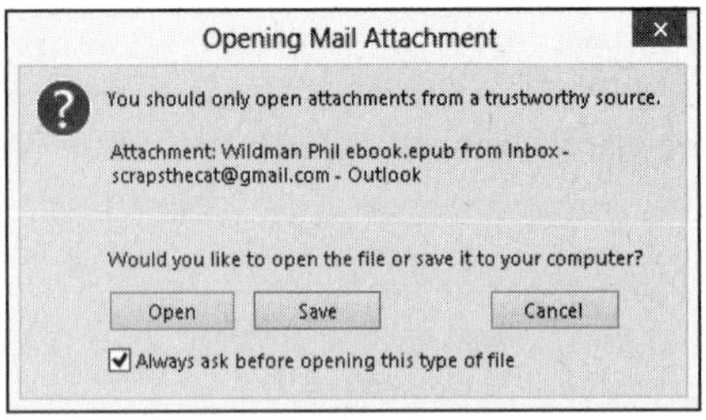

Figure 14-10:
The Opening
Mail
Attachment
dialog box
lets you
choose to
open or
save a file
attachment.

If you right-click a file attachment icon, a pop-up menu appears. Then you can
click Preview and see a preview of the file contents without opening it. This
only works with popular file formats, such as text files or Word documents.

Deleting E-Mail Messages

To keep your Inbox folder from getting too cluttered, you can always delete messages that you're sure you'll never need to read again. To delete a message, follow these steps:

1. **Click the Mail icon in the bottom-left corner of the Outlook window.**

2. **Click the Home tab.**

3. **Click the message you want to delete.**

4. **Press Delete or click the Delete icon in the Delete group.**

If you accidentally delete the wrong e-mail message, you can undelete it by pressing Ctrl+Z or clicking the Undo icon in the Quick Access toolbar.

To help avoid unwanted e-mail messages, give out your e-mail address sparingly. To find how to filter out unwanted messages, see Chapter 19 for tips on configuring Outlook to detect and block spam.

Chapter 15

Calendars, Contacts, and Tasks

- -

- -

*O*utlook 2013 is more than just an e-mail program; it's also a complete personal organizer to help you keep track of appointments, names and addresses, and to-do tasks. With Outlook helping keep your life organized, you no longer have an excuse not to get anything done on time — unless, of course, you really don't want to do it.

Setting Appointments

Everyone can get busy and miss deadlines and appointments. To avoid this problem, let Outlook keep track of your schedule. That way, you'll know what days and times you'll be busy and when you'll be free to do anything else.

Making an appointment

Before you can add an appointment to Outlook, you need to decide which day that appointment will occur and what time it will start. You can also add details such as how long it should last and where it takes place, but the important part is to define the date and time. To do this, you need to look at the Outlook calendar.

Outlook offers several ways to display its calendar:

- ✔ **Day:** Displays a single time divided into 24 hours

- ✔ **Week:** Displays a single week divided into five or seven days

- ✔ **Month:** Displays a single month divided into days

Outlook lets you define starting and ending times of an appointment in half-hour increments such as 1:30 or 11:00 whether you're using the day, week, or month calendar. To set an appointment, follow these steps:

1. **Click the Calendar icon in the bottom-left corner of the Outlook window.**

   Outlook displays the Calendar view.

2. **Click the Home tab and then click the Day, Work Week (5 days), Week (7 days), or Month icon in the Arrange category.**

   Outlook displays the Calendar based on the time frame you chose, such as Work Week or Month, as shown in Figure 15-1.

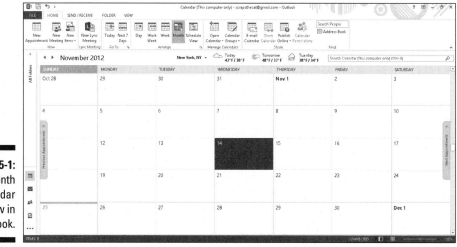

Figure 15-1:
The month
Calendar
view in
Outlook.

You can also click the New Appointment icon on the Home tab to define an appointment.

3. **Double-click the day (or time if you're in the Day calendar) where you want to schedule an appointment.**

   Outlook displays the Appointment window, as shown in Figure 15-2.

4. **Click in the Subject text box and type a brief description of your event, such as** Another meeting with Mike **or** Meet with client.

5. **(Optional) Click in the Location text box and type the location of your appointment, such as** Break Room 10 **or** Back alley near the dumpster.

If you often set appointments for specific locations, Outlook will remember these locations. In the future, just click the downward-pointing arrow in the Location text box and then click a previously used location in the list that appears.

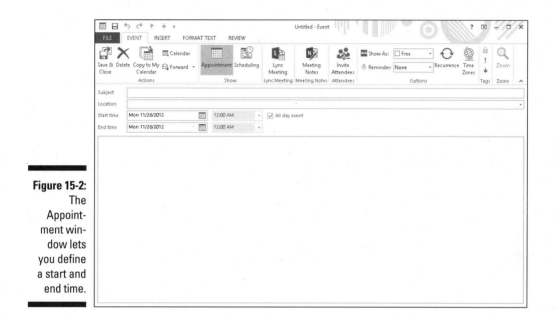

Figure 15-2:
The
Appoint-
ment win-
dow lets
you define
a start and
end time.

6. **Click in the Start Time list box and choose a time.**

You can also type a time directly in the Start Time list box, such as 9:53, or even choose a different date.

If the Start Time and End Time list boxes appear dimmed, make sure you clear the All Day Event check box.

7. **Click in the End Time list box and choose a time.**

You can also type a time directly in the End Time list box, such as 2:23, or even choose a different date.

8. **Click in the big text box and type any additional information you want to store about your event, such as items you need to bring or information you want to recall about the person you're meeting.**

9. **Click the Save & Close icon in the Actions group.**

Outlook displays your appointment in Day, Week, or Month view of the calendar, as shown in Figure 15-3.

If you need to edit an appointment, just double-click it to display the Appointment window again. You can also drag an appointment from one location on the calendar to another to switch it to a different time or date.

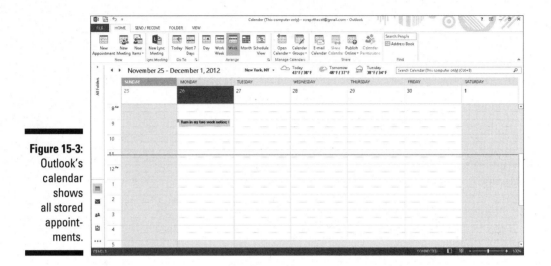

Figure 15-3:
Outlook's
calendar
shows
all stored
appoint-
ments.

Viewing appointments

If you store several appointments on the same day, you may find it hard to keep track of them all. To help you out, Outlook can display your appointments as a picture so you can see the times and dates when you have something planned.

To see your appointments onscreen, click the Home tab and then click the Schedule View icon in the Arrange group. Outlook displays your appointments so you can quickly spot your free and busy times, as shown in Figure 15-4.

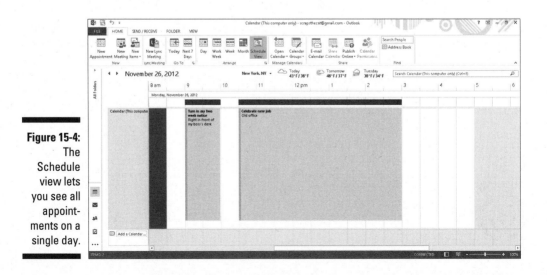

Figure 15-4:
The
Schedule
view lets
you see all
appoint-
ments on a
single day.

You can also view your appointments by moving the mouse pointer over the Calendar icon in the bottom-left corner of the Outlook window, and when a calendar pops up, click a date to view your appointments for that day (as shown in Figure 15-5).

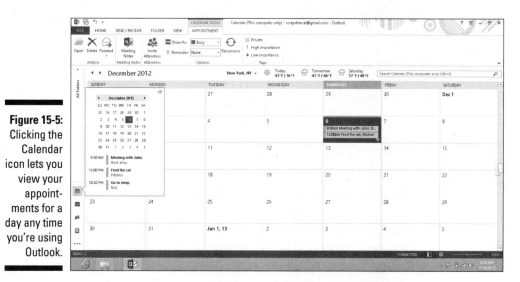

Figure 15-5: Clicking the Calendar icon lets you view your appointments for a day any time you're using Outlook.

Deleting an appointment

After an appointment has passed or been canceled, you can delete it to make room for other appointments. To delete an appointment, follow these steps:

1. **Double-click an appointment to open the Appointment window.**

2. **Click the Delete icon (or press Ctrl+D).**

   Outlook deletes your appointment.

For another way to delete an appointment, follow these steps:

1. **Click an appointment on the calendar.**

   Outlook displays a black border around your chosen appointment and displays the Appointment tab.

2. **Click the Delete icon.**

   Outlook deletes your appointment.

If you delete an appointment by mistake, press Ctrl+Z to recover it.

Storing Names and Addresses

Everyone has important names, addresses, e-mail addresses, and phone numbers that need to be saved. Rather than use Access or another complicated database program to store this type of information, it's much easier to use Outlook.

Adding a name

To store a name in Outlook, follow these steps:

1. **Click the People icon in the bottom-left corner of the Outlook window.**

   Outlook displays the Contacts view.

2. **Click the Home tab and click the New Contact icon in the New group.**

   Outlook displays a Contact window, as shown in Figure 15-6.

3. **Type the information you want to store about each person, such as the name in the Full Name text box.**

   You can store as much or as little data about a person as you want. For example, you may not want to store someone's home phone number or IM (instant messaging) address.

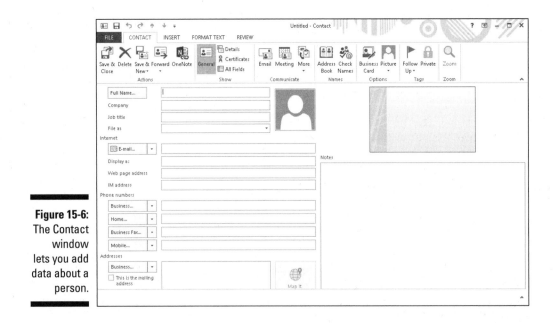

Figure 15-6: The Contact window lets you add data about a person.

4. **Click the Save & Close icon.**

   Outlook saves your information.

If you click the Save & New icon instead of the Save & Close icon in Step 4, another blank Contact window appears so you can keep adding new names to your Outlook contact list.

Viewing names

After you've stored one or more names in Outlook, you'll probably need to find it again. If you just want to browse through your list of names, follow these steps:

1. **Click the People icon in the bottom-left corner of the Outlook window.**

   Outlook displays the Contacts view.

2. **Click the Home tab and click the People, Business Card, Card, Phone, or List icon in the Current View group.**

   The People view displays lists of people alphabetically. The Business Card displays names and additional information as large windows, as shown in Figure 15-7. The Card view displays names as smaller windows, allowing you to see more names on the screen. The Phone view helps you find a specific phone number. The List view organizes people by company.

Figure 15-7:
The
Business
Card view.

If you click a name, you can delete it by clicking the Delete icon on the Home tab.

3. **Double-click a name to open the Contacts window.**

The Contacts window opens, allowing you to edit or add new information to your chosen contact.

Searching names

If you know all or part of a name or other information about a person, you can exhaustively browse through your entire list of stored contacts. However, it's much easier to just search for that information instead.

That way, if you know you want to find a person named Bill, you just have to search for "Bill." Likewise, if you know you need to call someone located in the 408 area code, you can just search for "408," and Outlook will show you all contacts with a phone number in that particular area code.

Searching makes it easier to find a particular name. To search for a name, follow these steps:

1. **Click People icon in the bottom-left corner of the Outlook window.**

Outlook displays the Contacts view.

2. **Click the Home tab and click in the Search Contacts text box in the Find group (or press Ctrl+ E).**

The cursor appears in the Search Contacts text box.

3. **Type as much data as you can about the person you want to find, typing (for example) all or part of a name or phone number.**

4. **Press Enter.**

Outlook displays all contacts that match your search criteria that you typed in Step 3.

5. **Click the Close icon (it looks like an X) that appears at the far right of the Search Contacts text box.**

Outlook displays all your contacts once more.

You can also search for a name by clicking on the People icon in the bottom-left corner of the Outlook window. A window pops up with a search text box on top; there you can type all or part of a name (as shown in Figure 15-8).

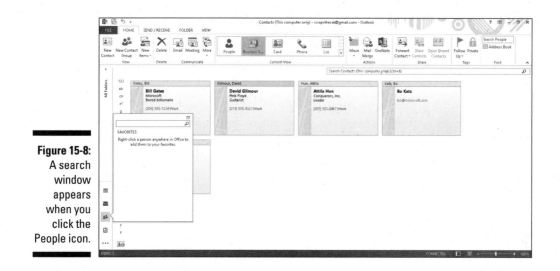

Figure 15-8:
A search
window
appears
when you
click the
People icon.

Managing Tasks

Everyone's busy. However, the big difference between busy, efficient people and overwhelmed people is that busy people simply know how to manage their tasks so they get things done.

To help you manage your tasks, Outlook lets you store your most important tasks and assign due dates and priorities. Now at a glance, you can see what's most important for you to focus on. By spending more of your time on important tasks and less of your time on trivial matters, you'll become more efficient (provided you actually do the work you're supposed to be doing).

Storing a task

A goal is simply a dream with a deadline. When storing tasks in Outlook, you need to define what it is that you want to do and set a date for when you want to complete it.

To store a task in Outlook, follow these steps:

1. **Click Tasks in the bottom-left corner of the Outlook window.**

   Outlook displays the Tasks view (as shown in Figure 15-9).

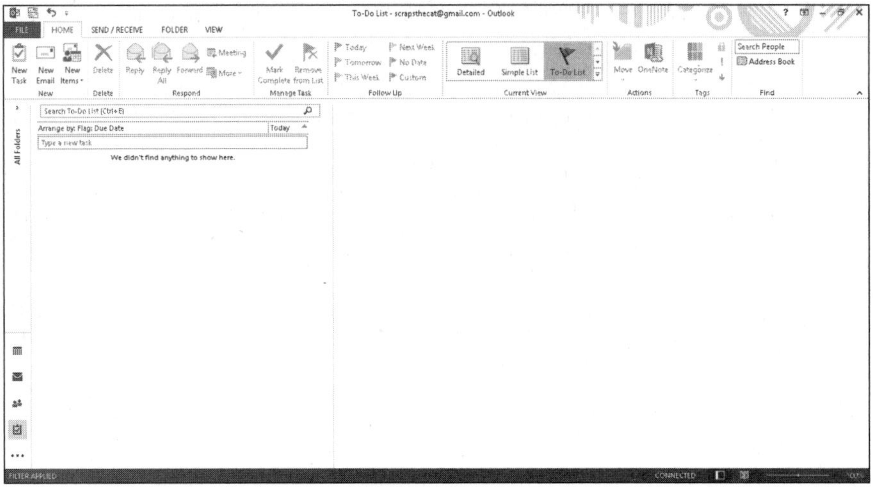

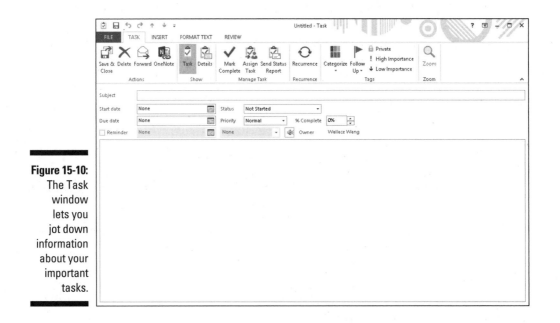

Figure 15-9:
Type a new
task in this
window.

If you just need to store a quick task, click in the Type A New Task text
box in the middle pane, type a brief description of your task, and press
Enter.

2. **Click the Home tab and click the New Tasks icon in the New group.**

Outlook displays a Task window, as shown in Figure 15-10.

Figure 15-10:
The Task
window
lets you
jot down
information
about your
important
tasks.

3. **Click in the Subject text box and type a brief description of your task, such as** Sell produce to my neighbor **or** Meet with informant.

4. **(Optional) Click in the Start Date list box and click a date to start your task. Then click in the Due Date list box and click a date when you want to complete that task.**

You don't have to add a start and end date, but it's a good idea to do so to help you measure your progress (or lack of progress) on your task.

5. **(Optional) Click in the Status list box and choose an option, such as In Progress or Waiting On Someone Else.**

6. **(Optional) Click in the Priority list box and choose an option, such as Low or High.**

7. **(Optional) Click in the % Complete box and click the up/down arrows to define what percentage you've completed of the task.**

8. **Click in the big text box to describe more details about your task.**

9. **Click the Save & Close icon.**

Outlook displays your task, as shown in Figure 15-11.

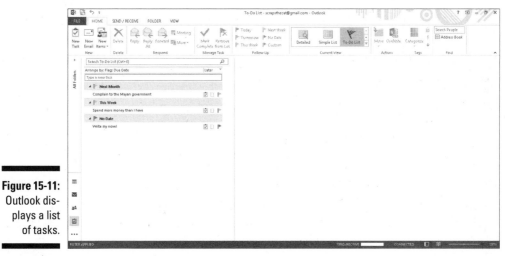

Figure 15-11:
Outlook dis-
plays a list
of tasks.

If you double-click a task, you can open the Tasks window so you can edit or add information to your chosen task.

Microsoft OneNote 2013

If you need to take notes in meetings, you're probably dragging your laptop around and typing notes in a Microsoft Word document. There's nothing wrong with that, except that by the end of the meeting, your notes will appear in one long document and you'll need to edit those notes so you can keep track of everything you wrote.

While you can use Microsoft Word to jot down notes, you may prefer using a more specialized note-taking program called Microsoft OneNote 2013. Like Microsoft Word, Microsoft OneNote lets you type and store notes. However, the program goes much farther than that.

OneNote lets you divide your notes into sections to help you find what you need. Instead of typing everything on a single page (as Microsoft Word forces you to do), OneNote lets you create one section for action items and another section for upcoming meetings to keep the project on track.

Now when you want to read your notes, you don't have to scroll through endless pages (the way you do in Microsoft Word). Instead, you can just flip to the section that contains the information you want to find. Think of the difference between trying to find information printed on a scroll of paper (Microsoft Word) or information organized in separate sections like tabs in a notebook (OneNote).

If you have a microphone and a webcam, you can even capture audio and video to store in your notes. That way you can capture an entire classroom lecture or meeting in audio or video, and then jot down notes at the same time. To review, you can study your written notes as well as replay the audio or video to catch something you may have missed earlier.

Because notes don't always rely on words, OneNote also lets you draw pictures, which can be handy for capturing ideas visually. Now you can use both your left brain (words) and right brain (pictures) to capture notes during any classroom lecture or meeting.

More important, OneNote can link to Outlook to share data. If you're in a meeting, you may need to write down a task for yourself and a future appointment. Now, you can retype all that information into Outlook later, or you can just transfer that data from OneNote to Outlook with a click of the mouse. When you work with Outlook, OneNote lets you capture information and store it in Outlook so you can keep track of your busy schedule.

OneNote can be a great note-taking program by itself, but when combined with Outlook, the two programs make an efficient information-gathering system.

Searching tasks

If you have a lot of tasks, you may want to find a particular one. To find a particular task, you can search for it. That way, if you know you want to find a task involving "Chemicals," you can just search for "chemicals," and Outlook will display that task right away.

To search for a task, follow these steps:

1. **Click Tasks in the bottom-left corner of the Outlook window.**

   Outlook displays the Tasks view. You can browse through this list of tasks to find the one you want. However, if you have many tasks, you may want to let Outlook search for them instead.

2. **Click the Home tab and click in the Search To-Do List text box (or press Ctrl+ E).**

   The cursor appears in the Search To-Do text box.

3. **Type as much data as you can about the task you want to find.**

   Outlook displays all tasks that match the search criteria that you typed in Step 3.

4. **Click the Close icon in the Search text field.**

   Outlook displays all your tasks once more.

Viewing tasks

As you store tasks in Outlook, you'll have tasks in various levels of completion, tasks involving different people, tasks coming due sooner than others, and tasks associated with certain people. To help you see only certain types of tasks, such as tasks due in the next seven days, Outlook can show different views of your task list.

To change views of your list of tasks, follow these steps:

1. **Click Tasks in the bottom-left corner of the Outlook window.**

   Outlook displays the Tasks view.

2. **Click the Home tab.**

3. **Click the More button in the Current View list.**

   Outlook displays a list of different ways to view your tasks (as shown in Figure 15-12).

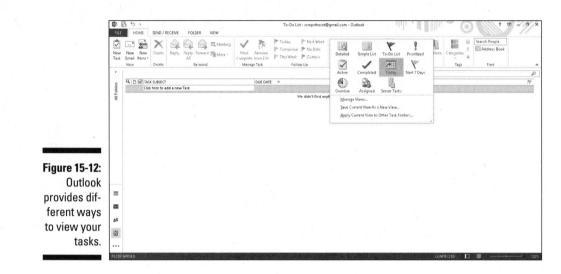

Figure 15-12:
Outlook
provides dif-
ferent ways
to view your
tasks.

4. **Click on a view icon such as Next 7 Days or Overdue.**

   Outlook displays all your tasks that meet your chosen criteria.

Part VI

Storing Stuff in Access

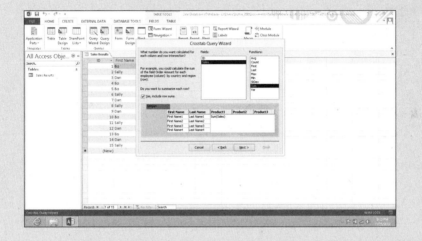

Visit www.dummies.com/extras/office2013 for great Dummies content online.

In this part . . .

- ✔ Designing a database
- ✔ Editing a database
- ✔ Searching and filtering a database
- ✔ Sorting data
- ✔ Creating reports
- ✔ Visit `www.dummies.com/extras/office2013` for great Dummies content online.

Chapter 16

Using a Database

A *database* is a program that stores information, such as names, addresses, and phone numbers, or inventory part numbers, shipping dates, customer codes, and any other type of information that you think is worth saving.

To help you store information in a database, Office 2013 comes with the *Access* database program. Access provides two huge advantages over storing information on paper. First, Access can store literally billions of chunks of information (try doing that with a filing cabinet). Second, Access makes it easy to search and sort through your information in the blink of an eye.

The three main advantages of a computer database over a paper database are

- ✔ **Massive storage:** The largest computer database can fit on a hard drive, but a paper database may take a roomful of file cabinets.

- ✔ **Fast retrieval:** Searching for a single name in a computer database is fast and easy. Doing the same thing in a paper database is difficult, error prone, and nearly impossible with a large database.

- ✔ **Reporting:** A *report* can help you make sense out of your data, such as showing a list of customers who earn a certain amount of money and live in a specific area. Trying to find this information in a paper database is time-consuming and error-prone.

Understanding the Basics of a Database

A database is nothing more than a file that contains useful information that you need to save and retrieve in the future. A database can consist of a single name and address, or several million names and addresses.

A typical Access database file consists of several parts:

- ✔ **Fields:** A *field* contains a single chunk of information, such as name, street address, or phone number.

- ✔ **Records:** A *record* consists of one or more fields. A business card is a paper version of a database record that stores fields (name, address, phone number, and so on) about a single person (record).

- ✔ **Tables:** A *table* displays records in rows and columns, much like a spreadsheet. Tables group related records, such as records of all your customers or records of all your invoices.

- ✔ **Forms:** A *form* displays all the fields of a single record onscreen, mimicking a paper form, so that you can add, edit, or view a single record at a time.

- ✔ **Queries:** A *query* lets you retrieve certain information based on your criteria, such as only retrieving names and addresses of people who earn more than $50,000 a year and have children.

- ✔ **Reports:** A *report* arranges your data in a certain way, such as showing all customers who placed more than 1,000 orders last year or all customers who live within a certain zip code.

Access is known as a *relational* database. Basically, this means that you can store data in separate tables and link or "relate" them together to avoid duplicating data in multiple tables. One table may contain customer names and addresses while a separate, related table may contain those same customers' purchase orders.

Here are the two basic steps to using a database. First, you need to design your database, which means deciding what type of information your database will hold, such as names, addresses, e-mail addresses, telephone numbers, and so on.

After you design a database, the second step is filling it with actual data, such as typing the name **Bob Jones** in the Name field or the e-mail address **BJones@somecompany.com** in the E-mail field.

When you first create a database, you'll probably start out with a single table that contains customer information. Inside the Customer Information table will be multiple records where each record represents a single customer. Each record will consist of multiple fields, such as Last Name, Company Name, Phone Number, and E-mail Address.

To help you edit and view your database table information, you may eventually want to create a form that displays your fields onscreen, mimicking a paper form that's easy to read.

If you find yourself searching for the same type of information on a regular basis, such as looking for the names of your best customers (say, those who order more than $1,000 worth of products from you a week), you can store this search criteria as a query. Then you can just click the query name and make Access show you exactly what you want to find.

Finally, you may want to print your data in a way that makes sense to you, such as printing a quarterly sales report. By saving your printing criteria in a report, you can make Access print selected data on a page that's easy for you to read and understand.

Features such as forms, queries, and reports are optional but handy. Features like tables, records, and fields are necessary to store your information in your database.

Designing a Database

To design a database, you need to first create a database table and then define the names of all the fields you want to store in that particular table. Database tables let you divide a file into separate parts. For example, one database table may hold the names and addresses of all your customers, a second database table may hold the names and addresses of all your employees, and a third database table may hold the names and addresses of your suppliers. Access stores all this related information in a single Access file that's saved on your hard drive, as illustrated in Figure 16-1.

Figure 16-1:
You can divide an Access file into separate tables that contain different fields.

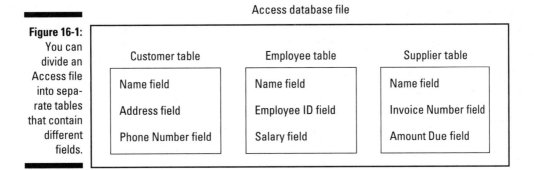

Access database file

To design your database, you can create a database from scratch or use an existing template, which you can modify. *Designing* a database means defining both the number of fields to use for storing information and the maximum amount of data each field can hold.

If you have a field that stores numbers, what are the maximum and minimum limits on the numbers you want to save in that field? If you're storing someone's age, you probably don't want the field to contain negative numbers or numbers beyond 200. If your field needs to hold salaries, the field may need to hold large numbers but no negative numbers.

In general, store information in separate fields. So rather than create a single field to hold someone's full name, create two separate fields: One field holds a first name, and the second field holds the last name. By storing last names in a separate field, you can easily yank last names out of your database to create form letters that state, "The <u>Smith</u> family has just won $200,000 dollars in the Publisher's Umpteenth Sales Pitch Sweepstakes!"

Access can create a blank database or a special database by using one of many templates available from the Microsoft website. No matter how you create a database, you will likely need to modify it to customize it for the type of data you want to store.

When you start Access, it gives you a choice of opening an existing database or creating a new one.

To create a database with Access already running, follow these steps:

1. **Click the File tab.**

2. **Choose New.**

   Access displays a variety of options, as shown in Figure 16-2.

3. **Click an icon such as Blank desktop database or any database template.**

   If you click a template, the right pane shows a preview of your template.

4. **Click in the File Name text box and type a descriptive name for your database.**

   If you click the folder icon that appears to the right of the File Name text box, you can open a dialog box that will let you define a specific drive and folder in which to store your database file.

5. **Click the Create button to create your database file.**

   Access displays a blank database with a generic field name of `Field1`, as shown in Figure 16-3.

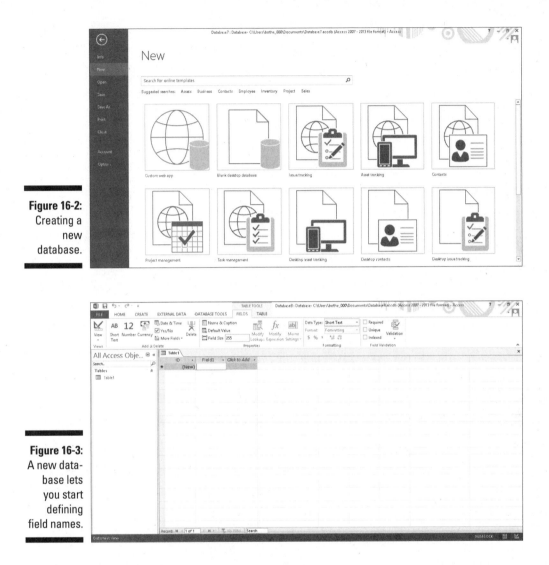

Figure 16-2:
Creating a
new
database.

Figure 16-3:
A new data-
base lets
you start
defining
field names.

6. **Double-click the Field1 column heading and type a name for your field (such as** First Name **or** Salary**).**

7. **Click the Click To Add column heading to define another field for your database.**

   A menu appears, letting you choose the type of data to store in that field as shown in Figure 16-4.

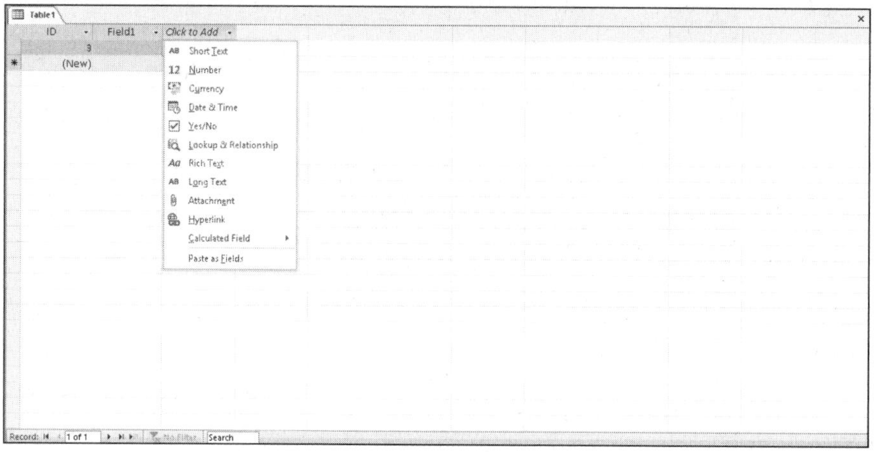

Figure 16-4:
The Click to
Add column
heading
displays a
menu of dif-
ferent data
types.

8. **Click a data type to store in your field such as Number, Currency, or Long Text.**

9. **Double-click the Field column heading and type a name for your field such as** Last Name.

10. **Repeat Steps 7 through 9 for each additional field you want to create.**

Editing and Modifying a Database

After you create a database from scratch or from a template, you may need to modify it by giving each field a descriptive name, defining the size of each field, or adding and deleting a field.

Naming a field

If you create a database from scratch, Access displays generic field names such as *Field1*. If you create a database from a template, you'll see the descriptive field names, but you may still want to rename the fields to something else.

To rename a field, follow these steps:

1. **In the All Access Objects pane on the left of the screen, double-click the table that contains the fields you want to rename.**

   Access displays the Datasheet view of your database.

2. **Double-click the field (column head) that you want to rename.**

   Access highlights the column heading.

3. **Type a new name for your field and then press Enter when you're done.**

Adding and deleting a field

Sometimes you may need to add a field to make room to store new information. At other times, you may want to delete a field that you don't really want after all. To add a field to a database table, follow these steps:

1. **Click the downward-pointing arrow that appears to the right of the Click to Add heading.**

   A menu appears (see Figure 16-4).

2. **Choose the type of field you want to add, such as Currency or Text.**

   Access inserts your field and gives it a generic name like `Field3`.

To delete a field from a database table, follow these steps:

1. **Click the field (column head) you want to delete.**

   Access highlights the entire column in your database table.

2. **Click the Delete button in the Add & Delete group.**

   If you have stored data in that field, a dialog box appears, asking whether you want to permanently delete all the data in the field.

   If you delete a field, you also delete any data that may be stored in that field. Depending on how much data you have stored, you can wipe out a lot of information by deleting a single field, so be careful.

3. **Click Yes (or No).**

   If you click Yes, Access deletes your chosen field.

Defining the type and size of a field

The *data type* of a field defines what kind of data the field can hold (numbers, text, dates, and so on), and the *size* of a field defines the amount of data the field can hold (no numbers larger than 250 digits, any text string with fewer than 120 characters, and so on).

The purpose of defining the type and size of a field is to make sure that you store only valid data in a particular field. If a field is meant to store names, you don't want someone typing in a number. If a field is meant to store a person's age, you don't want the field to accept negative numbers.

To define the type and amount of data a field can store, follow these steps:

1. **Click the Home tab.**

2. **In the All Access Objects pane on the left of the screen, double-click the table that contains the fields you want to define.**

   Access displays the Datasheet view of your table.

3. **Click the column heading of the field you want to define.**

   Access highlights the entire column.

4. **Click the Fields tab that appears under the Table Tools heading on the Ribbon interface.**

   The Fields tab displays options for modifying your field (as shown in Figure 16-5).

5. **Click the arrow that appears to the right of the Data Type combo box.**

   A pull-down menu appears, listing all the different types of data you can define to store in a field, as shown in Figure 16-6.

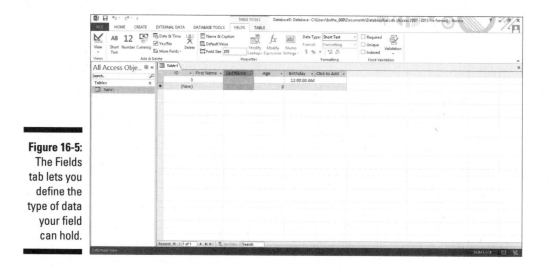

Figure 16-5:
The Fields tab lets you define the type of data your field can hold.

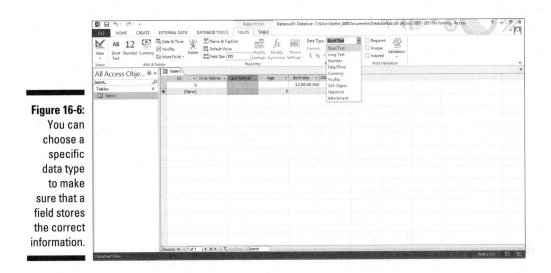

Figure 16-6:
You can
choose a
specific
data type
to make
sure that a
field stores
the correct
information.

6. **Choose a data type, such as Number, Text, or Date/Time.**

   Depending on the data type you choose, you can choose additional
   options by clicking in the Format combo box.

Typing Data into a Database

After you create a database table and define fields within that table to hold
chunks of information, you're ready to type in actual names, phone numbers,
and e-mail addresses into each field. Access gives you two ways to enter data:

- ✔ Through Datasheet view
- ✔ Through Form view

Datasheet view displays information in rows and columns, where each row
represents a single record and each column defines a specific field name.
Datasheet view can be especially handy for examining multiple records at
once.

Form view displays all the fields of a single record onscreen. Form view is
most useful when you just need to view or edit a single record, as when
you're typing in the phone number of your cousin or boss.

Using Datasheet view

Datasheet view displays all your database information in rows and columns, much like a spreadsheet. To view and enter data in Datasheet view, follow these steps:

1. **In the All Access Objects pane on the left of the screen, double-click a table name.**

   Access displays the Datasheet view of your table.

2. **Click the bottom half of the View icon (that displays a downward-pointing arrow), which appears in the Views group.**

   A pull-down menu appears.

3. **Click Datasheet View.**

   Access displays the Datasheet view of your database table.

4. **Click in a field defined by the column and row.**

   Each column defines a field, such as a name or address. Each row represents a single record.

   If you click in a field that already contains data, you can edit or delete that data.

5. **Press Tab to select the next field (or Shift+Tab to select the preceding field).**

6. **Type or edit the data in the field.**

Using Form view

The biggest problem with Datasheet view is that it can be confusing to find a field for a specific record. Because most people are familiar with paper forms or index cards that arrange related data (fields) on a page, Access offers you Form view.

Form view simply displays the fields of a single record onscreen, arranged like the information typically stored on a business card. To use Form view, you must first create a form and arrange your fields on that form. After you create a form, you can add, edit, and view data through that form.

Creating a form

The simplest way to create a form is to let Access design one for you, which you can modify. To create a form quickly, follow these steps:

1. **In the All Access Objects pane on the left of the screen, double-click a table.**

   Access displays the Datasheet view of your database.

2. **Click the Create tab.**

3. **Click the Form icon in the Forms group.**

   Access creates a form, as shown in Figure 16-7. Notice that the form name automatically uses the name of the database table you chose in Step 3.

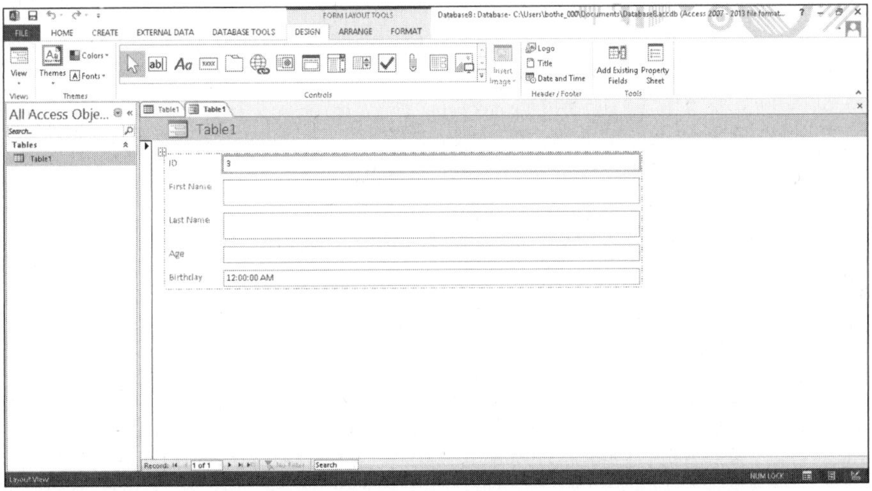

Figure 16-7:
Form view displays multiple fields of a single record.

4. **Click the Save icon on the Quick Access toolbar (or press Ctrl+S).**

   The Save As dialog box appears, asking you to type a name for your form.

5. **Type a descriptive name for your form in the Form Name text box and then click OK.**

   Access displays your form's name underneath the All Tables pane. The next time you open this database and want to view the form, you can double-click the form's name in the left pane.

Viewing and editing data in a form

After you create a form, you can use it to edit and add data at any time. To view a form, follow these steps:

1. **In the All Access Objects pane on the left of the screen, double-click the name of the form you want to use.**

    Access displays the Form view of your database.

2. **Click one of the following icons (they appear near the bottom of the screen) to display a record:**

    • *First Record:* Displays the first record stored in your file

    • *Previous Record:* Displays the preceding record in the file

    • *Next Record:* Displays the next record in the file

    • *Last Record:* Displays the last record that contains data

    • *New (Blank) Record:* Displays a blank form so you can type in data that will create a new record in your file

3. **Click in a field and type the information you want to store, such as a name or phone number.**

You don't need to use the Save command to save your changes because Access automatically saves any data you add or edit in your file as soon as you type or edit the data and move the cursor to a new field or record.

Editing a form

A form can be a convenient way to view all the fields of a single record. However, you can always rearrange the position of certain fields onscreen (to make them easier to find), or you can delete one or more fields altogether. This can be handy to create a form that shows only a filtered view of your data, such as a form that shows you only employee names, phone numbers, and e-mail addresses instead of also showing you their salaries and employee ID numbers at the same time.

Deleting a field

If you delete a field from a form, you simply prevent the form from displaying any data stored in that field. For example, if you don't want to see each person's hire date, you can delete the Hire Date field from your form.

Deleting a field on a form doesn't erase any data; it just keeps you from seeing that data on a particular form.

To delete a field from a form, follow these steps:

1. **In the All Access Objects pane on the left of the screen, double-click the name of the form you want to use.**

    Access displays the Form view of your database.

2. **Click the Home tab.**

3. **Click the downward-pointing arrow underneath the View icon in the Views group.**

    A pull-down menu appears.

4. **Choose Design View.**

    Access shows your chosen form in Design view, which displays a background grid to help you align fields on your form (as shown in Figure 16-8).

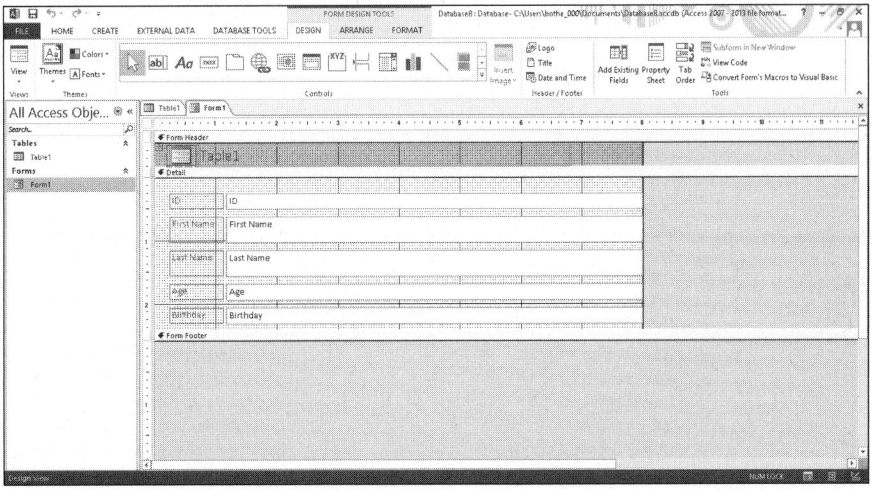

Figure 16-8:
Form view displays multiple fields of a single record.

5. **Hold down the Ctrl key and click the field label and field that you want to delete.**

    Access highlights your chosen field.

    Each field consists of a field label *and* the actual field itself. The *field label* contains descriptive text that defines the data, such as Name, Age, or Sales. The field is the text box that holds the actual data, such as "Fred," 47, or $34.08.

6. **Click the Home tab, and then click the Delete icon in the Records group.**

    Access deletes your chosen field.

    If you press Ctrl+Z right away, you can undelete any field that you just deleted.

7. **Click the downward-pointing arrow underneath the View icon in the Views group.**

   A pull-down menu appears.

8. **Choose Form View.**

   Access shows your form with the deleted field missing.

Adding a field

Before you can add a field to a form, you must make sure that the field already exists in your database table. For example, if you want to add a field on a form that displays phone numbers, you must first create that field in your database table and then stuff it with actual data.

To add a field to a form, follow these steps:

1. **In the All Access Objects pane on the left of the screen, double-click the name of the form you want to use.**

   Access displays the Form view of your database.

2. **Click the Home tab.**

3. **Click the downward-pointing arrow underneath the View icon in the Views group.**

   A pull-down menu appears.

4. **Choose Design View.**

   Access displays your form in Design view.

5. **Click the Design tab.**

6. **Click the Add Existing Fields icon in the Tools group.**

   The Field List pane appears on the right side of the screen, as shown in Figure 16-9.

7. **Double-click a field.**

   Access displays the field label and a field on your form.

8. **Move the mouse pointer over the edge of the field and drag the mouse (hold down the left mouse button and move the mouse) to move the field and field label on your form.**

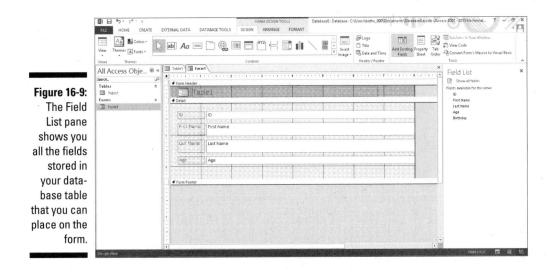

Figure 16-9:
The Field
List pane
shows you
all the fields
stored in
your data-
base table
that you can
place on the
form.

9. **Click the downward-pointing arrow underneath the View icon in the Views group and choose Form View.**

    Access displays the Form view. Notice that the form displays both your newly added field and any data stored in that field.

Closing and Saving a Database

When you're done using a database file, you can either close it or exit Access altogether. Access gives you two options for closing a database:

- ✔ Close a database.
- ✔ Close and exit from Access.

Closing a database

Closing a single database table simply removes the data from view. After you close a database table, you can open another one. (You don't have to close a database table to open another one, but if you know you won't need to view a particular database table, you may as well close it to get it out of the way.)

To close a database table, follow these steps:

1. **Click the File tab.**

2. **Choose Close.**

   If you haven't saved any changes you made to your form or datasheet, Access displays a dialog box, asking whether you want to save your changes.

3. **Click Yes or No.**

   Access closes your chosen database table.

When you save an Access database, you're saving only the changes you made to the database table or form. Access automatically saves any data you type or edit in your database file. (When you type or edit data, Access saves it as soon as you move the cursor to a new field or record.)

Exiting Access

When you're done using Access, you can close the program altogether and shut down any databases you may have open. To exit Access and close any open databases, follow these steps:

1. **Choose one of the following.**

   • Press Alt+F4.

   • Click the Close icon that appears in the upper-right corner of the Access window.

   If you made any changes to your database structure such as moving the location of a field on a form or adding (or deleting) a field, a dialog box appears, asking whether you want to save your changes.

2. **Click Yes or No.**

Chapter 17

Searching, Sorting, and Querying a Database

*I*f you need to find a specific name in your database, searching through the database alphabetically may be tedious but possible. However, if you need to find the names of everyone in California who ordered more than $50,000 worth of supplies in the past three months, trying to find this information yourself would prove tedious and time consuming. Yet, Access can search for this information at the blink of an eye.

If you search for specific types of data on a regular basis, you probably don't want to keep telling Access what to search for over and over again. To simplify this, you can create a *query*. A query lets you define specific ways to search your data and save those parameters so you can retrieve data instantly the next time you need it.

Besides searching through data, Access can also sort data. *Sorting* can be as simple as organizing names alphabetically, or it can be more complicated, such as sorting names according to zip code, annual salary, and alphabetically by last name. Sorting simply rearranges your data so you can study it from a new point of view.

By searching, sorting, and querying your data, you can extract useful information about your data.

Searching a Database

A paper database is useful for storing information, but not so useful for finding it again. If you have a thousand business cards stored in a Rolodex file, how much time do you want to waste trying to find the phone number of a single person?

Searching a database is crucial to make your data useful, so Access provides two ways to search a database:

- ✔ Search for a specific record.
- ✔ Use a filter to show one or more records that meet a specific criterion.

Searching for a specific record

The simplest type of search looks for a specific record. To search for a record, you need to know the data stored in at least one of its fields, such as a phone number or e-mail address.

The more information you already know, the more likely Access will find the one record you want. If you search for all records that contain the first name *Bill,* Access could find dozens of records. If you just search for all records that contain the first name *Bill,* the last name *Johnson,* and a state address of *Alaska,* Access will likely find just the record you want.

To search for a specific record in a database table, follow these steps:

1. **In the All Access Objects pane on the left of the screen, double-click the name of the database table you want to search.**

   Access displays the Datasheet view of your database.

2. **Click the Home tab.**

3. **Click the Find icon in the Find group.**

   The Find and Replace dialog box appears, as shown in Figure 17-1.

4. **Click in the Find What text box and type in the data you know is stored in the record you want to find.**

   For example, if you want to find the phone number of a person but you know only that person's last name, you type that person's last name in the Find What text box.

5. **Click the Look In list box and choose Current field or Current document (searches in all fields).**

6. **(Optional) Click in the Match list box and choose one of the following:**

   - *Any Part of Field:* The Find What text can appear in any part of a field.

   - *Whole Field:* The Find What text is the only text stored in a field.

   - *Start of Field:* The Find What text can be only at the beginning of a field.

7. **(Optional) Click in the Search list box and choose one of the following:**

   - *Up:* Searches from the record where the cursor appears, up to the beginning of the database table

   - *Down:* Searches from the record where the cursor appears, down to the end of the database table

   - *All:* Searches the entire database table

8. **Click Find Next.**

   Access highlights the field where it finds the text you typed in Step 4.

9. **Repeat Step 8 to search for more records that may contain the text you typed in Step 4.**

10. **Click Cancel or the Close button.**

Filtering a database

Searching a database is easy but somewhat limited because you can retrieve only a record that matches any text that you want to find. If you want to find multiple records, you can use a filter.

A *filter* lets you tell Access to display only those records that meet certain criteria, such all records that contain people who earn more than $200,000 a year, are currently married, live in Las Vegas, Nevada, and own two or more cats.

To filter a database table, you must tell Access which field to use as a filter, and then you must define the criteria for that filter. For example, if you want to filter your database table to see only those records listing the names of people who are at least 65, you filter the Age field and set the criterion to *Greater than or equal to 65.*

Filtering simply hides all records in a database table that don't match your criteria. Filtering doesn't delete or erase any records.

Using an exact match for a filter

The simplest filtering criterion searches for an exact match. When you filter a field by an exact match, you're telling Access, "I want to see only those records that contain this specific chunk of data in this particular field." By using an exact match filter, you can display only those records that contain CA in the State field.

To filter a database table, follow these steps:

1. **In the All Access Objects pane on the left of the screen, double-click the name of the database table you want to filter.**

   Access displays the Datasheet view of your database.

2. **Click the Home tab.**

3. **Click in the field (column) that you want to use as a filter.**

4. **Click the Filter icon in the Sort & Filter group.**

   A pop-up menu appears, as shown in Figure 17-2.

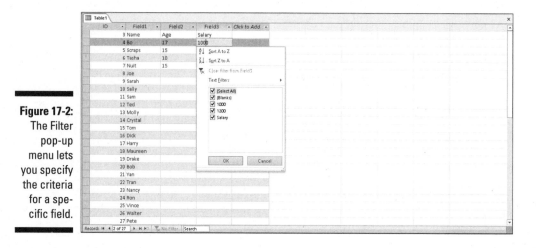

Figure 17-2:
The Filter pop-up menu lets you specify the criteria for a specific field.

5. **(Optional) Clear one or more of the check boxes that appear to the left of the list of data that appears in the field you chose in Step 3.**

6. **Click OK.**

   Access displays the filtered view of your database table of only those items that appeared selected in Step 5.

7. **Repeat Steps 3 through 6 for each additional field you want to filter.**

You can click the Toggle Filter on the Home tab in the Sort & Filter group to view all the data in your database table.

Filtering by form

One problem with defining filters in Datasheet view is that you have all your database table records cluttering the screen. To avoid this problem, Access lets you define filters by using a *form,* which basically displays an empty record so you can click the fields that you want to use to filter your database table.

To define a filter by form, follow these steps:

1. **In the All Access Objects pane on the left of the screen, double-click the name of the database table that you want to filter.**

   Access displays the Datasheet view of your database.

2. **Click the Home tab.**

3. **Click the Advanced icon in the Sort & Filter group.**

   A pull-down menu appears.

4. **Choose Filter By Form, as shown in Figure 17-3.**

   Access displays a blank record.

Figure 17-3: The Advanced pop-up menu lets you specify the criteria for a specific field.

5. **Click in any field.**

   A downward-pointing arrow appears.

6. **Click the downward-pointing arrow.**

   A pull-down menu appears, listing all the data currently stored in that field, as shown in Figure 17-4.

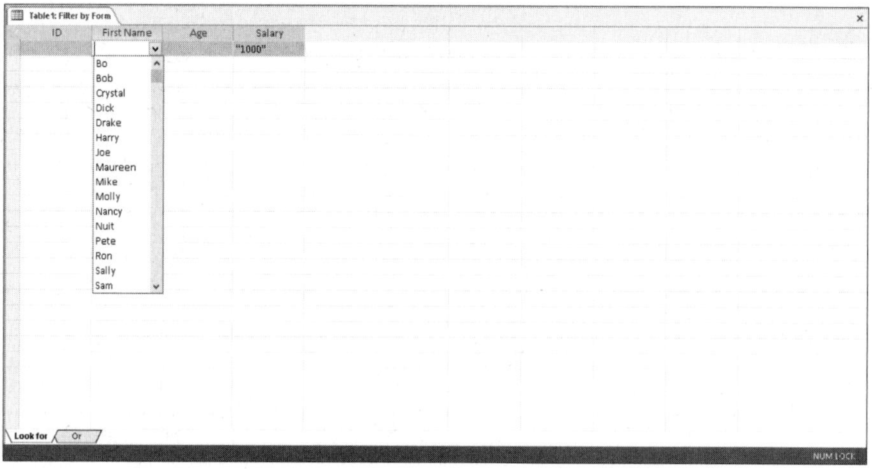

Figure 17-4:
Filtering by form lets you choose the type of data you want to view from a pull-down menu.

7. **Click the data you want.**

   You can only click one entry in the list.

8. **Click the Toggle Filter icon in the Sort & Filter group.**

   Access displays a filtered view of your database table.

You can click the Toggle Filter icon again to view all the data in your database table.

Using a filter criteria

Searching for an exact match in a field can be handy, but sometimes you may want to see records that meet certain criteria, such as finding the names of everyone whose salary is greater than $50,000 a year. Instead of filtering by an exact match, you have to define the filter criteria.

The type of data stored in each field determines the type of criteria you can create. Three common types of data stored in fields include Text, Numbers, and Dates, which you can filter in different ways, as shown in Tables 17-1, 17-2, and 17-3.

Table 17-1   Common Criteria for Filtering Text Data

Filtering Criteria	Description
Equals	Field must match filter text exactly.
Does Not Equal	Field must not match filter text.
Begins With	Field must start with the filter text.
Does Not Begin With	Field must not begin with the filter text.
Contains	Field must contain the filter text.
Does Not Contain	Field must not contain any part of the filter text.
Ends With	Field ends with the filter text.
Does Not End With	Field does not end with the filter text.

Table 17-2   Common Criteria for Filtering Numeric Data

Filtering Criteria	Description
Equals	Field must equal filter number.
Does Not Equal	Field must not equal filter number.
Less Than or Equal To	Field must contain a number less than or equal to the filter number.
Greater Than or Equal To	Field must contain a number greater than or equal to the filter number.
Between	Field must contain a number that falls between two filter numbers.

Table 17-3   Common Criteria for Filtering Field Data

Filtering Criteria	Description
Equals	Field must equal the filter date.
Does Not Equal	Field must not equal the filter date.
On or Before	Field date must be equal or earlier than the filter date.
On or After	Field date must be equal or later than the filter date.

To create the filter criteria, follow these steps:

1. **In the All Access Objects pane on the left of the screen, double-click the name of the database table you want to filter.**

   Access displays the Datasheet view of your database.

2. **Click the Home tab.**

3. **Click in the field (column) that you want to use as a filter.**

4. **Click the Filter icon in the Sort & Filter group.**

   A pop-up menu appears (refer to Figure 17-2).

5. **Select the Filters option, such as Text Filters or Number Filters.**

   A submenu of filter options appears, as shown in Figure 17-5.

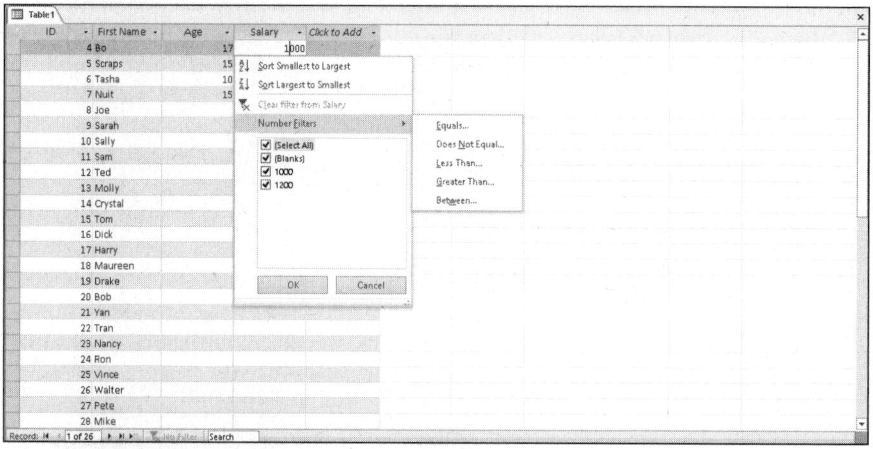

Figure 17-5:
The Filter pop-up menu lets you specify the criteria for a specific field.

6. **Click a filter option, such as Between or Less Than.**

   The Custom Filter dialog box appears, as shown in Figure 17-6. The Custom Filter dialog box contains the name of your filter option, such as Between Numbers or Less Than.

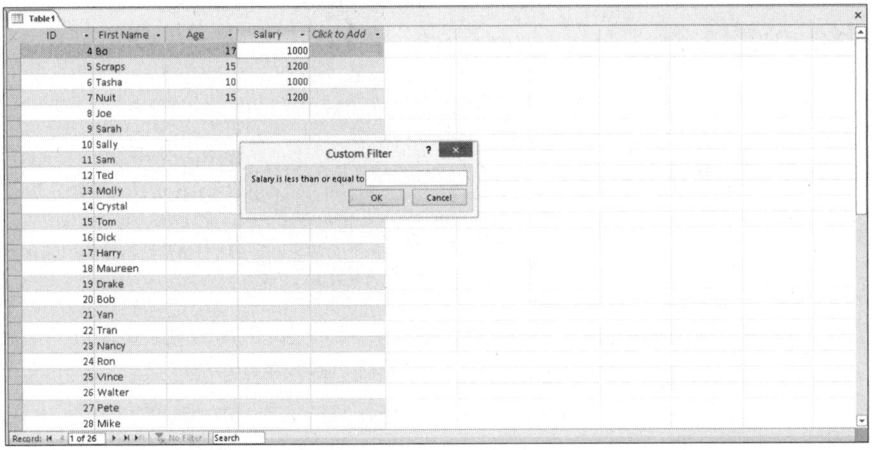

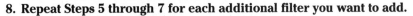

Figure 17-6:
Type in a
value for
your filter
criteria.

7. **Type in one or more values in each text box displayed in the Custom Filter dialog box and then click OK.**

   Access filters your database table according to your criteria.

8. **Repeat Steps 5 through 7 for each additional filter you want to add.**

You can click the Toggle Filter icon again to view all the data in your database table.

Clearing a filter

When you apply a filter to a database table, you see only those records that match that filter. Access displays a Filtered message at the bottom of the screen to let you know when you're looking at a filtered database table.

To remove a filter so you can see all the records, choose one of the following:

- ✔ Click the Toggle Filter icon in the Sort & Filter group.
- ✔ Click the Filtered or Unfiltered button on the status bar near the bottom of the screen.

Access temporarily turns off any filters so you can see all the information stored in your database table.

When you choose the Save command (Ctrl+S) to save a database table, Access also saves your last filter. The next time you open that database table, you'll be able to use the last filter you created. If you want to save multiple filters, you'll have to save them as a query (see the section "Querying a Database" later in this chapter).

Sorting a Database

Sorting simply rearranges how Access displays your information. Sorting can be especially handy for rearranging your records alphabetically by last name, by state, or by country. You can also sort data numerically so that customers who buy the most from you appear at the top of your database table, while customers who don't buy as much appear near the bottom.

To sort a database table, follow these steps:

1. **In the All Access Objects pane on the left of the screen, double-click the name of the database table you want to sort.**

   Access displays the Datasheet view of your database.

2. **Click the Home tab.**

3. **Click in a field (column) that you want to use for sorting.**

4. **Click the Ascending or Descending icon in the Sort & Filter group.**

   Access sorts your records and displays an Ascending or Descending icon in the field name so you know you're looking at a sorted list, as shown in Figure 17-7.

5. **Click the Remove Sorts icon in the Sort & Filter group when you don't want to view your sorted database table any more.**

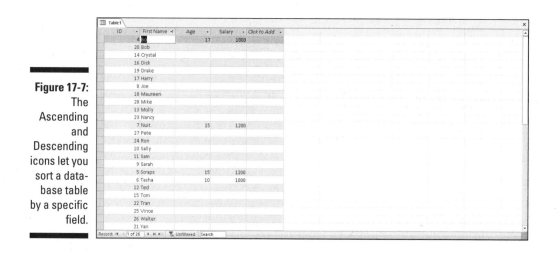

Figure 17-7:
The Ascending and Descending icons let you sort a database table by a specific field.

Querying a Database

One problem with sorting or filtering a database table is that you must constantly define what you want to sort or filter. In case you sort or filter your data a certain way on a regular basis, you can use a query instead.

A *query* is nothing more than a saved version of your sort or filter criteria. By saving the particular sort or filter criteria as a query, you can select that query by name later.

Creating a simple query

If your database table contains dozens of different fields, you may find it confusing to make sense of all your information. As an aid, a *simple query* strips away fields so you see only the fields containing data you want to see, such as a person's name and phone number but not her hire date or employee number.

To create a query, follow these steps:

1. **Click the Create tab.**

2. **Click the Query Wizard icon in the Queries group.**

   The New Query dialog box appears, as shown in Figure 17-8.

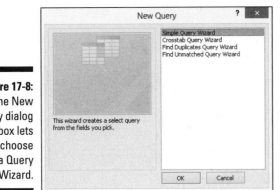

Figure 17-8:
The New Query dialog box lets you choose a Query Wizard.

3. **Click Simple Query Wizard and then click OK.**

   The Simple Query Wizard dialog box appears, as shown in Figure 17-9.

4. **Click a field name listed in the Available Fields box and then click the > button.**

   Access displays your chosen field in the Selected Fields box.

5. **Repeat Step 4 for each field you want to use in your query.**

6. **Click Next.**

   Another dialog box appears, as shown in Figure 17-10. This dialog box asks whether you want to display a Detail (shows every record) or Summary (shows numerical information such as the total number of records found, the average value, and the minimum/maximum value) view of your data.

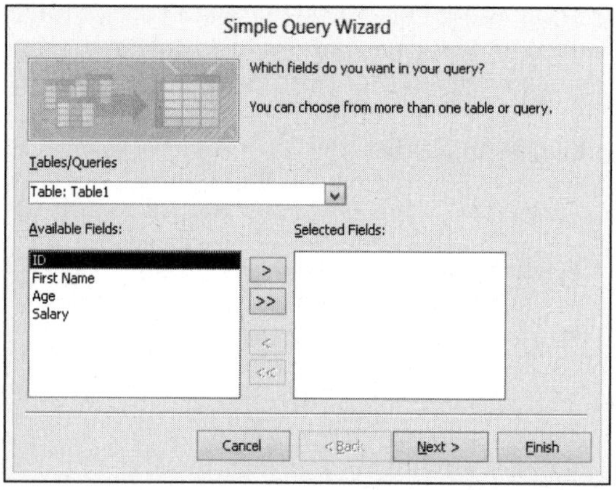

Figure 17-9:
The Simple Query Wizard dialog box lets you pick the fields to use for your query.

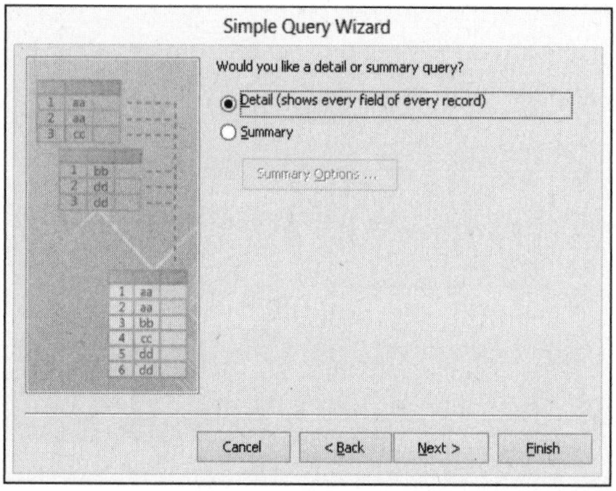

Figure 17-10:
Choose between viewing Detail or Summary view.

7. **Select the Detail or Summary radio button and then click Next.**

    Another dialog box appears, asking you to type a descriptive name for your query.

8. **Click in the text box, type a descriptive name for your query, and then click Finish.**

    Access displays the results of your query as a separate tab. If you add or delete information from your database, you can click this query tab to get a quick look at the results of your query without having to define everything all over again.

9. **Click the File tab and then choose Save to save your query.**

Creating a crosstab query

A *crosstab query* lets you combine two or more fields to calculate and display a calculation based on a third field. For example, if your database contains the names of salespeople and the products they sold, you can use those two fields to create a crosstab that tells you how much each salesperson sold of each product, as shown in Figure 17-11.

Figure 17-11:
A cross-tab query extracts information by cross-referencing two or more fields.

To create a crosstab query, you need to identify three types of fields:

- ✔ One to three fields to identify each record (such as the First Name and Last Name fields)

- ✔ A single field to display specific data from each record (such as the Product field, which displays the actual product names like Purses, Unicorn Meat, or Missiles)

- ✔ A crosstab field that displays a calculated result (such as Sales)

To create a crosstab query, follow these steps:

1. **Click the Create tab.**

2. **Click the Query Wizard icon in the Queries group.**

   The New Query dialog box appears (refer to Figure 17-8).

3. **Click Crosstab Query Wizard and then click OK.**

   The Crosstab Query Wizard dialog box appears, as shown in Figure 17-12.

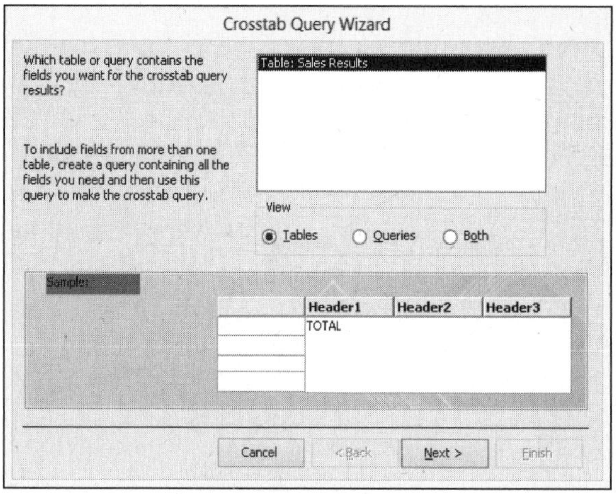

Figure 17-12: The Crosstab Query Wizard dialog box asks you to choose which database table to use.

4. **Click a database table and then click Next.**

   Another Crosstab Query Wizard dialog box appears that asks for between one and three fields to identify each row (record), as shown in Figure 17-13.

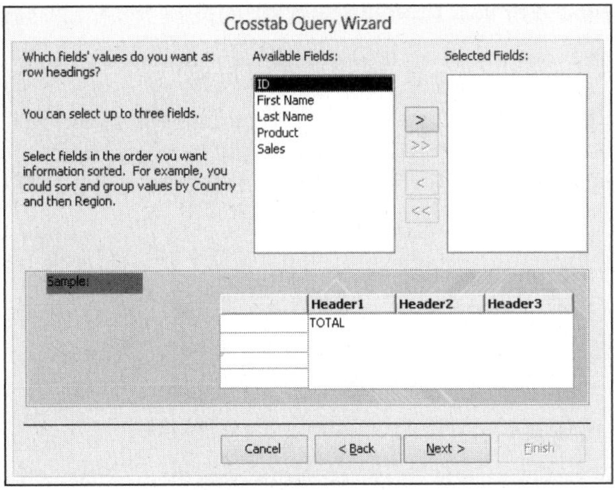

Figure 17-13:
The first
step to
creating a
crosstab
query is
to choose
up to three
fields to
identify
each
record.

5. **Click a field in the Available Fields box and then click the > button to move your chosen field to the Selected Fields box.**

6. **Repeat Step 5 for each additional field you want to include.**

7. **Click Next.**

   Another dialog box appears, asking for a single field to use to cross-tabulate data with the fields you chose in Steps 5 and 6, as shown in Figure 17-14.

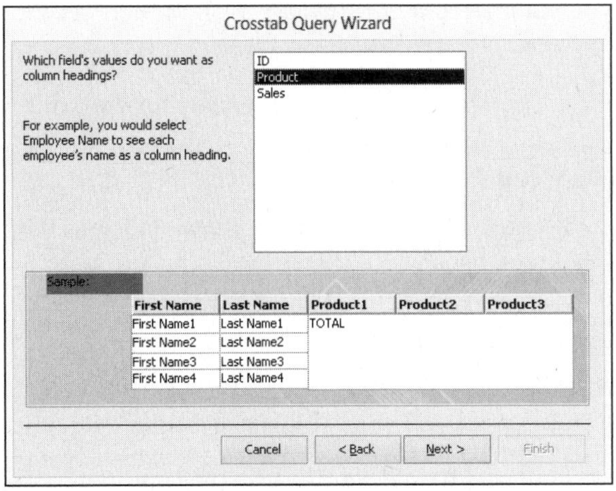

Figure 17-14:
To cross-
tabulate
your data,
you need
to choose
another
field.

8. **Click a field name and then click Next.**

   Ideally, this field should consist of text information that lists different data, such as sales regions (East, West, North, or South) or products (Missiles, Unicorn Meat, and so on). If you choose a field that contains numerical data, your crosstab query displays only those numbers in the column headings, which will seem meaningless. Another dialog box appears, as shown in Figure 17-15.

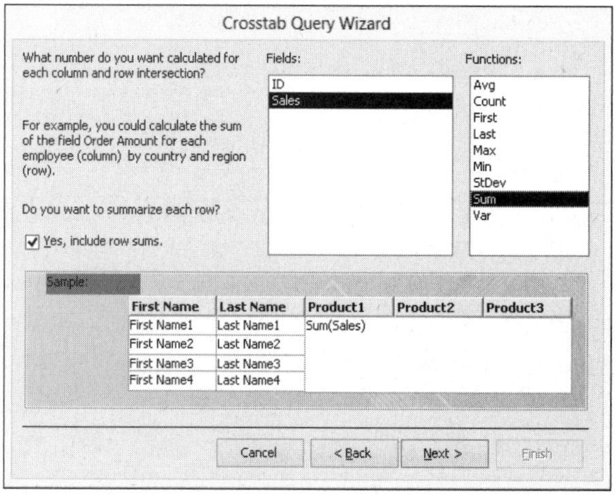

Figure 17-15:
The
Crosstab
Query
Wizard
dialog box
displays a
list of math-
ematical
functions
you can
choose.

9. **Click a field from the Fields box and then click a mathematical function that you want Access to calculate, such as Sum, Avg, or Count.**

10. **Click Next.**

    Another dialog box appears, asking for a name for your query.

11. **Type a descriptive name for your query in the text box at the top of the dialog box and then click Finish.**

    Access displays your crosstab query, as shown in Figure 17-16.

12. **Click the File tab and choose Save to save your query.**

Figure 17-16:
The
Crosstab
Query can
display
calculations
on your
database
information.

Creating a query that finds duplicate field data

Suppose you sell a hundred different products. How can you tell which products customers are buying the most? To find the answer to this type of question, you can search your database manually to find a Products Sold field and then count how many times each product appears.

As a simpler solution, you can create a query that finds and counts how many times duplicate data appears. To create a query to find duplicate field data, follow these steps:

1. **Click the Create tab.**

2. **Click the Query Wizard icon in the Queries group.**

   The New Query dialog box appears (refer to Figure 17-8).

3. **Click Find Duplicates Query Wizard and then click OK.**

   The Find Duplicates Query Wizard dialog box appears, asking you to choose the database table to search.

4. **Click a database table and then click Next.**

   Another dialog box appears, asking you to choose the fields to examine for duplicate data.

5. **Click a field name and then click the > button. Repeat this step for each additional field you want to search.**

6. **Click Next.**

   Another dialog box appears, asking whether you want to display any additional fields. If you choose to look for duplicate data in a Product field (Step 5) to see which products are most popular, you can display additional fields such as each salesperson's name so you can also see who is responsible for selling the most products.

7. **Click a field and click the > button. Repeat this step for each additional field you want to display.**

8. **Click Next.**

   A dialog box appears, asking whether you want to give your query a descriptive name.

9. **Type a descriptive name in the top text box and then click Finish.**

   Access displays your query as a separate tab.

10. **Click the File tab and then choose Save to save your query.**

Creating an unmatched query

Access can store huge amounts of data, but the more data you store, the harder it can be to view your data. To help you organize your data, you can divide data into separate tables. One table may contain a list of customers, and a second table may contain a list of salespeople.

When you store data in separate tables, each table may share one or more common fields. For example, a table containing customers may contain a SalesPerson field that shows which salesperson deals exclusively with which customer. A second table listing salespeople can contain the Customer field (along with additional information such as each salesperson's phone number, address, sales region, and so on).

An unmatched query examines two (or more) database tables to look for missing information. For example, you can also use an unmatched query to find customers who haven't ordered anything in the past six months, sales regions that haven't ordered certain products, or salespeople who have not been assigned to a sales region. Basically, an unmatched query can help you find missing pieces or holes in your entire database file.

To create an unmatched query, follow these steps:

1. **Click the Create tab.**

2. **Click the Query Wizard icon in the Queries group.**

   The New Query dialog box appears (refer to Figure 17-8).

3. **Click Find Unmatched Query Wizard and then click OK.**

   The Find Unmatched Query Wizard dialog box appears, asking you to choose a database table that contains the unmatched records you want to find.

4. **Click a database table and then click Next.**

   Another dialog box appears, asking you to choose a database table that contains at least one field that also appears in the table you chose in Step 3.

5. **Click a second database table and then click Next.**

   Another dialog box appears, asking you to identify the field that both database tables have in common.

6. **Click the common field that both database tables share.**

7. **Click the gray <=> button that appears between the two fields and then click Next.**

   A dialog box appears, asking you to identify the fields you want to display from the database table you chose in Step 4.

8. **Click a field and then click the > button. Repeat this step for each additional field you want to display.**

9. **Click Next.**

   A dialog box appears, asking you to give your query a descriptive name.

10. **Type a descriptive name in the text box and then click Finish.**

    Access displays your query results, which show you only the data in fields you selected in Step 8.

11. **Click the File tab and choose Save to save your query.**

Viewing, renaming, closing, and deleting queries

Each time you create and save a query, Access stores it for future use. After you create and save a query, you can add or delete data from your tables and then apply your queries on the newly modified data.

To view a query, just double-click the query name in the left pane. In case you need to rename your query to give it a better descriptive name, follow these steps:

1. **Right-click the query name in the left pane.**

   A pull-down menu appears.

2. Choose Rename.

Access highlights the query name.

3. Type a new name and then press Enter.

Each time you view a query, it displays a tab. Eventually, you'll probably want to get rid of a query, so to close a query, follow these steps:

1. Right-click the query name that appears in the tab.

A pull-down menu appears.

2. Choose Close.

Access closes your chosen query and removes its tab from view.

Queries can be handy, but eventually, you may no longer need a query. To delete it, follow these steps:

1. Right-click a query name; when a pop-up menu appears, choose Delete.

You won't be able to delete a query unless you close it first.

A dialog box appears, asking whether you really want to delete your query.

2. Click Yes (or No).

Chapter 18

Creating a Database Report

- -

In This Chapter

▶ Creating a report with the Report Wizard

▶ Displaying and printing reports

▶ Modifying the appearance of a report

▶ Erasing a report

- -

Data is useless if you can't understand what it means, so that's why Access lets you create reports. A *report* simply provides a printed version of your data arranged in some useful way.

A report can dig through your data and print a list of your top ten salespeople. Another report may print out the top ten products you sold last year. Reports simply provide a way to make sense of your data and print it so you can examine your data on paper.

Using the Report Wizard

The easiest way to create a report is to use the Report Wizard, which guides you step by step through arranging and selecting which data to print on a report, along with sorting your data at the same time. To use the Report Wizard, follow these steps:

1. **Click the Create tab.**

2. **Click the Report Wizard icon in the Reports group.**

   The Report Wizard dialog box appears, as shown in Figure 18-1.

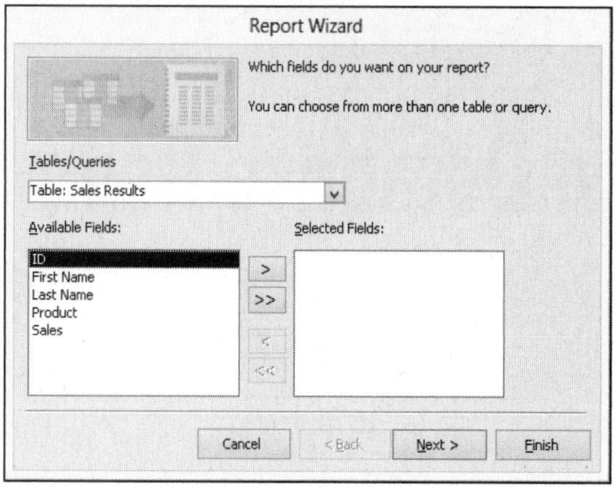

Figure 18-1:
The Report Wizard lets you choose where to retrieve your data for your report.

3. **Click in the Tables/Queries list box and choose the table or query that contains the data you want to print in a report.**

4. **Click in a field in the Available Fields box and then click the > button. Repeat this step for each additional field you want to display in your report.**

5. **Click Next.**

   Another dialog box appears, asking whether you want to group your data by a specific field, such as by Last Name or Employee Number, as shown in Figure 18-2.

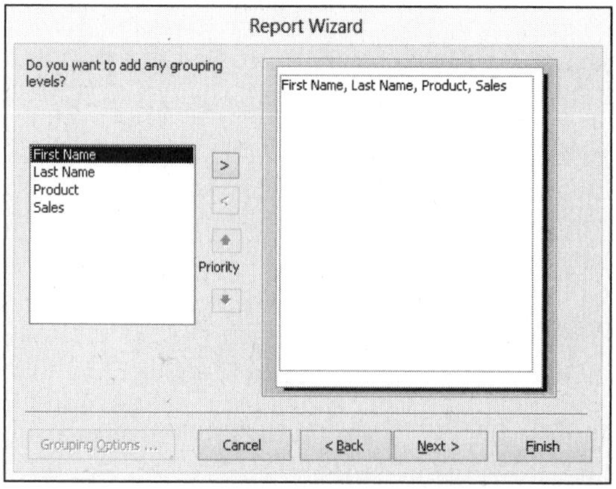

Figure 18-2:
A report can group data under categories so you can see all your data arranged by a specific field.

6. **Click a field name displayed in the box and then click the > button. Repeat this step for each additional field you want to use to group your data on the report.**

7. Click Next.

Another dialog box appears, asking you to choose up to four fields to use for sorting your data in your report, as shown in Figure 18-3.

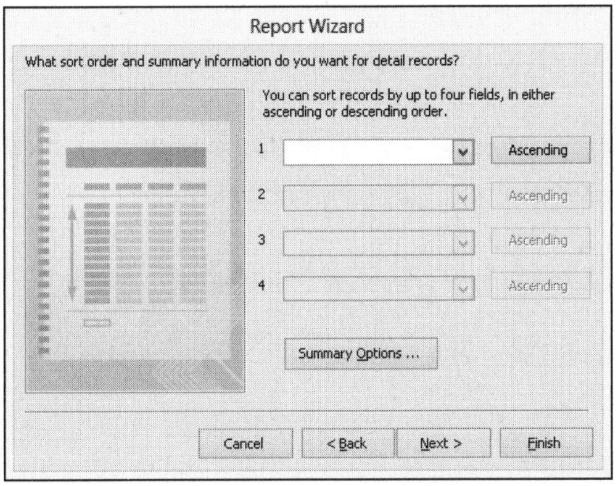

Figure 18-3:
You can sort the data in your report, using up to four fields.

8. Click in a list box and choose a field to sort your data.

Data will be sorted by the order chosen here for each additional field you sort on.

9. (Optional) Click the Ascending button to change the sorting criteria from Ascending to Descending and vice versa.

10. Click Next.

Another dialog box appears, asking you how to lay out your report, as shown in Figure 18-4.

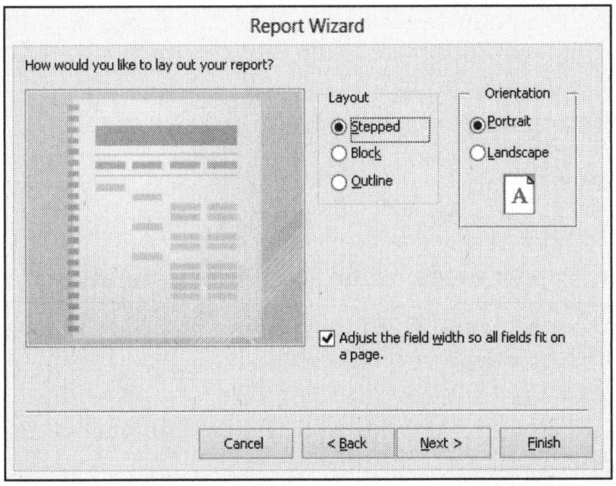

Figure 18-4:
The Report Wizard offers different options for making your report look readable.

11. **Select a radio button under the Layout group, such as Stepped or Block.**

12. **(Optional) Select a radio button in the Orientation group, such as Portrait or Landscape.**

13. **Click Next.**

    Another dialog box appears, asking for a descriptive name for your report.

14. **Type a descriptive name for your report and then click Finish.**

    Access displays your report, as shown in Figure 18-5.

Sales Results			
Product	Last Name	First Name	Sales
Magic wands			
	Smith	Sally	$774.31
	Smith	Sally	$490.78
	Katz	Bo	$783.74
	Katz	Bo	$349.50
			$2,398.33
Sugar			
	Smith	Sally	$230.91
	Katz	Bo	$90.42
	Katz	Bo	$490.68
	Brickman	Dan	$773.80
	Brickman	Dan	$793.21
	Brickman	Dan	$893.45
			$3,272.47
White flags			
	Smith	Sally	$89.93
	Smith	Sally	$892.31
	Katz	Bo	$893.93
	Brickman	Dan	$883.90
	Brickman	Dan	$445.??

Figure 18-5: Access displays your report onscreen.

To view your report again, double-click the report name in the left pane of the Access window.

If you change any data, you can see those updated changes in your report by following these steps:

1. **Right-click the tab that represents your currently displayed report.**

    A pop-up menu appears.

2. **Choose Close.**

3. **Double-click the report name in the left pane of the Access window.**

    Your chosen report appears again, displaying any data you updated or modified since the last time you viewed the report.

Access won't automatically update your reports just because you modified any data that the report displays.

Manipulating the Data in a Report

After you create a report, you can manipulate the data displayed in that report, such as sorting data in ascending or descending order, or applying a filter that only displays data that meets a certain criteria.

By using a report, you get a different view of your data. By manipulating the data in a report, you create alternate views of the same report. Some common ways to extract information from a report include *counting, sorting,* and *filtering*.

Switching a report to Layout view

To manipulate data in a report, you must first display your report in Layout view, which you can do by following these steps:

1. **Double-click the report name in the All Access Objects pane.**

   Access displays your chosen report.

2. **Click the Home tab and click the downward-pointing arrow underneath the View icon in the Views group.**

   A pull-down menu appears.

3. **Choose Layout View.**

   Access displays your report in Layout view, which highlights an entire column (field) at a time, as shown in Figure 18-6.

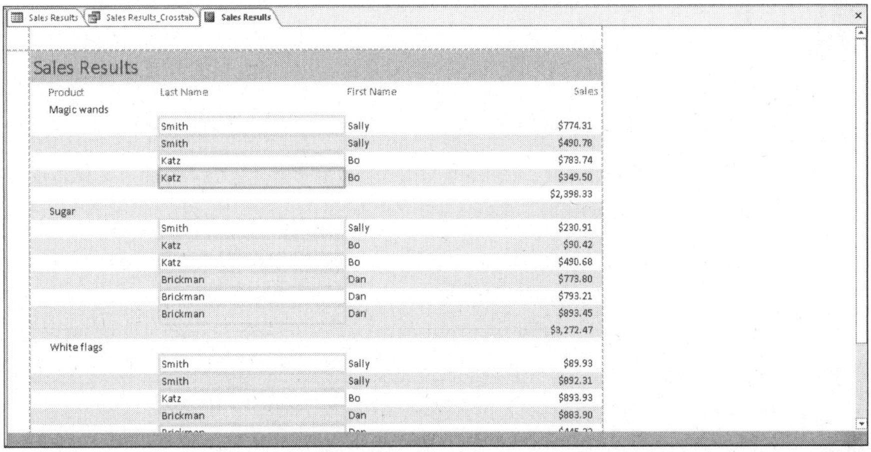

Figure 18-6: Layout view highlights a single column of your report so you can manipulate the data within the highlighted field.

Counting records or values

To make reports more useful, you can have Access count and display information, such as which products are selling the best or the total dollar amount of each sale so you can tell exactly how much money your company made during March. By counting records or adding up values stored in fields, Access can help you better interpret the data displayed in a report.

To count the number of records or values in a report, follow these steps:

1. **Switch to the Layout view of your report by following the steps in the preceding section, "Switching a report to Layout view."**

2. **Right-click in the column (not the column heading) that you want to count.**

   Access highlights your chosen column and displays a pop-up menu, as shown in Figure 18-7.

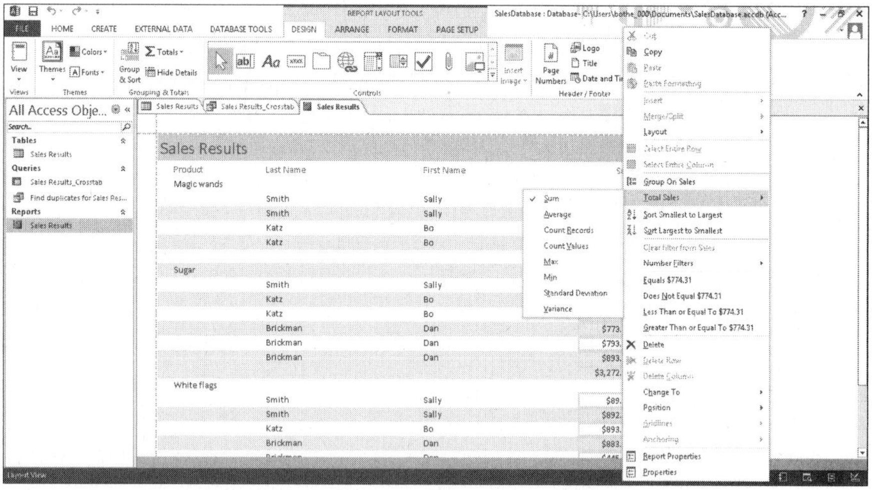

Figure 18-7: Right-clicking a column displays a pop-up menu for manipulating your data.

3. **Click Total.**

   The menu command displays the Total command along with the field name you right-clicked, such as Total Last Name or Total Sales.

   Access displays a submenu that displays Count Records or Count Values.

4. **Choose either Count Records or Count Values.**

   Access displays the total count in your report.

If you choose the Count Records or Count Values command again, you can hide the total count in your report.

Sorting a field

Access can sort each field in ascending or descending order. *Sorting a field* simply rearranges the data in your report for your convenience. To sort a column (field) in a report, follow these steps:

1. **Switch to the Layout view of your report by following the steps in the preceding section, "Switching a report to Layout view."**

2. **Right-click in the column (not the column heading) that you want to sort.**

   Access highlights your chosen column and displays a pop-up menu (refer to Figure 18-7).

3. **Choose one of the following:**

   • Sort A to Z (or Sort Smallest to Largest): Sorts in ascending order.

   • Sort Z to A (or Sort Largest to Smallest): Sorts in descending order.

   Access sorts your chosen data in your report.

Filtering a field

Filtering can tell Access to only display data that meets certain criterion, such as a fixed amount. For example, if you have a report that lists all the sales of products, you can filter your report to show only those products that sold over a fixed amount, such as $1,000.

To filter data in a field, follow these steps:

1. **Switch to the Layout view of your report by following Steps 1 through in the previous section, "Manipulating the Data in a Report."**

2. **Right-click in the column (not the column heading) that you want to filter.**

   Access highlights your chosen column and displays a pop-up menu (refer to Figure 18-7).

3. **Choose Filters.**

   Depending on the type of data your column contains, the Filter command may appear as Text Filters or Number Filters.

   A submenu appears, as shown in Figure 18-8.

Figure 18-8:
The Filters
command
displays a
submenu
of different
criteria you
can choose.

4. **Choose a filter criteria, such as Equals or Less Than.**

   Depending on the criteria you choose, a Custom Filter dialog box appears.

5. **Type your criteria in the Custom Filter dialog box and then click OK.**

   Access applies your filter to your report.

You can always turn off your filter by clicking the Home tab and then clicking the Toggle Filter icon in the Sort & Filter group.

Editing a Report

After you create a report, you may want to modify it later to expand the space used to display data or eliminate fields altogether.

To edit a report, you must switch to the Design view of your report, as shown in the sidebar "Switching to Design view." You can modify your report while you view it in Design view.

Resizing fields

When the Report Wizard creates a report, it doesn't always leave enough room to display your actual data. If a field is too small, Access may display data as a series of x's, such as xxxxx. If this occurs, resize a field to make it wider. (If your data turns out to be smaller than the field, you may need to shrink the field.) To resize a field, follow these steps:

1. **Display your report in Design view.**

   Follow the steps in the sidebar "Switching to Design view."

2. **Choose the field you want to resize.**

   Access highlights your chosen field.

Switching to Design view

To see the Design view of a report, follow these steps:

1. **Double-click the name of the report in the All Access Objects pane.**

2. **Click the Home tab.**

3. **Click the downward-pointing arrow underneath the View icon that appears in the Views group.**

   A pull-down menu appears.

4. **Choose Design View.**

   Access displays your report in Design view, as shown here.

At this point, you can move, resize, add, or delete fields on your report:

- Text is bold for labels that print *identifying* text, such as First Name or Sales Region.

- Text in normal typeface (not in bold) represents fields that display *data* in your report.

---

3. **Move the mouse pointer over the left or right edge of the field until the mouse pointer turns into a two-way pointing arrow.**

4. **Drag the mouse to resize and expand or shrink the field.**

   Access displays your report with your modified field size.

Deleting fields

If a report displays data that you no longer want to see, you can delete that field from your report by following these steps:

1. **Display your report in Design view.**

   Follow the steps in the sidebar "Switching to Design view."

2. **Right-click the field you want to delete.**

   Access highlights your chosen field and displays a pop-up menu.

3. **Click Delete.**

   Access deletes your chosen field.

   You can press Ctrl+Z right away to retrieve any fields you may have deleted accidentally.

Making Reports Look Pretty

Reports can be useful for displaying data, but go one step farther and make your reports look visually pleasing as well. One way to change the appearance of a report is to use a predefined theme, which can instantly add color to make even the dullest report look interesting.

Applying themes

A theme simply rearranges the appearance of your entire report so it doesn't look like a boring list of text and numbers. To apply a theme to a report, follow these steps:

1. **Display your report in Design view.**

   Follow the steps in the sidebar "Switching to Design view."

2. **Click the Design tab.**

3. **Click the Themes icon in the Themes group.**

   A menu appears, listing all the available themes (as shown in Figure 18-9).

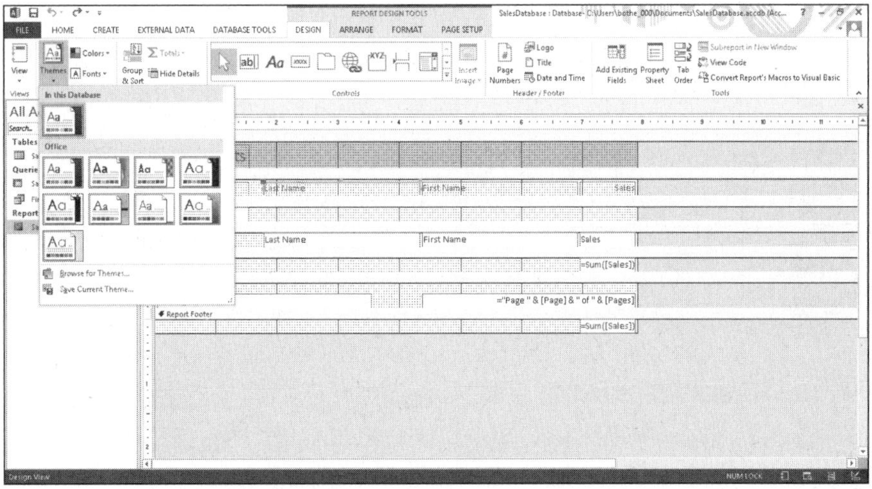

Figure 18-9:
Themes give you a quick way to modify the appearance of a report.

4. **Move the mouse pointer over a theme.**

   Access shows how your report will look with the selected theme.

5. **Select a theme to choose it for your report.**

   Access displays your report with your selected theme.

Creating conditional formatting

A report can display data, but sometimes you may want help in identifying certain types of data. For example, you may want Access to highlight sales figures that are greater than $250,000 so you can spot this information easier. While you can manually examine a report and highlight such information yourself, it's faster and more accurate to let Access do it instead.

Formatting data based on certain criteria is known as *conditional formatting*. The idea is that Access formats data only when certain conditions are met, such as a value greater than $250,000 or less than $10,000.

To use conditional formatting, you need to define the field to format, define a rule to trigger the formatting, and then the type of formatting you want to apply, such as highlighting the field in red or yellow.

To apply conditional formatting to data in a report, follow these steps:

1. **Display your report in Design view.**

   Follow the steps in the sidebar "Switching to Design view."

2. **Select the field to which you want apply conditional formatting.**

   You can apply conditional formatting to a numeric or text field.

3. **Click the Format tab.**

4. **Click the Conditional Formatting icon in the Control Formatting group.**

   A Conditional Formatting Rules Manager dialog box appears, as shown in Figure 18-10.

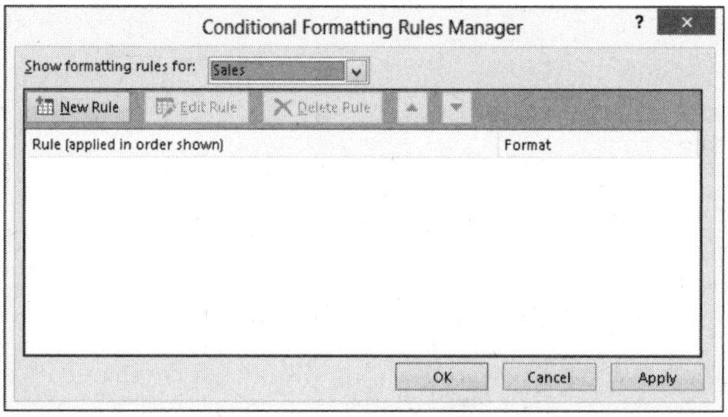

Figure 18-10: The Conditional Formatting Rules Manager dialog box.

Conditional Formatting Rules Manager

Show formatting rules for: Sales

New Rule   Edit Rule   Delete Rule

Rule (applied in order shown)   Format

OK   Cancel   Apply

5. **Click the New Rule button.**

   A New Formatting Rule dialog box appears, as shown in Figure 18-11.

   You can click the Edit Rule or Delete Rule button here to edit or delete a rule that you've created.

6. **Select a rule type:**

   • Check values in the current record or use an expression (you can create a rule that only considers the value of a single field).

   • Compare to other records (you can create a rule that examines the value of the same field stored in other records).

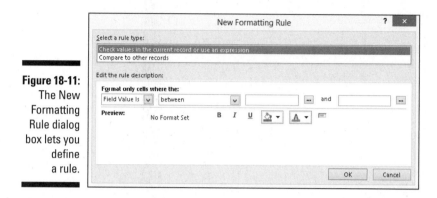

Figure 18-11:
The New
Formatting
Rule dialog
box lets you
define
a rule.

7. Define your rule under the Edit the Rule Description category.

Depending on the option you chose in Step 6, the Edit the Rule Description category may display different options.

8. Choose the type of formatting to display if the data in a field matches your rule that you defined in Step 7.

9. Click OK.

The Conditional Formatting Rules Manager dialog box appears again, displaying your newly created rule.

10. Click OK.

Access now displays your formatting changes in the field if it matches your defined rule.

Deleting a Report

Eventually, you may find that you no longer need a report, so you may as well delete it. To delete a report, follow these steps:

1. Right-click the Report tab.

A pull-down menu appears.

2. Choose Close.

3. In the left pane, right-click the report that you want to delete.

A pull-down menu appears.

4. **Click Delete.**

   A dialog box asks whether you really want to delete your report.

   Make sure that you really want to delete a report. You won't be able to retrieve it afterward.

5. **Click Yes (or No).**

the
part of
tens

Enjoy an additional Office 2013 Part of Tens chapter online at
www.dummies.com.

In this part . . .

- ✔ Discover ten great ways to use Office 2013 successfully.
- ✔ Explore the do's and don'ts that can make any Office 2013 experience heavenly.
- ✔ Enjoy an additional Office 2013 Part of Tens chapter online at www.dummies.com.

Chapter 19

Ten Tips for Using Office 2013

Microsoft Office is famous for burying tons of useful features that most people never know about, so this chapter is about exposing some of Office 2013's features so you can take advantage of them and make Office 2013 more convenient (and safer) for you to use.

Saving Office 2013 Files

Most people dump their documents inside a folder in the Documents folder. Store too many documents in this folder, however, and you'll find it's nearly impossible to find anything. To make retrieving files easier, it's a good idea to store different data in its own folders, such as storing tax-related information in a special Tax Returns folder or invoices in a special 2014 Invoices folder.

Left to its own devices, of course, Office 2013 will cheerfully save all your files in the Documents folder, so you'll need to tell Office 2013 where you want it to save files.

In addition to defining a default folder to store files, you can also define a default file format for your Office 2013 programs. This can be especially useful if you need to share files with others, such as people still stuck using an older version of Microsoft Office (97/2000/XP/2003).

Finally, to protect your data (as much as possible) from inevitable computer crashes and hard drive failures, Office 2013 programs include a special AutoRecover feature, which saves a temporary copy of your file at fixed intervals, such as every ten minutes. That way, if the power goes out, you lose only those changes you made in the last ten minutes and not all your changes.

Access doesn't offer an AutoRecover feature because it automatically saves any changes to your data anyway.

To customize the location, format, and AutoRecover feature of an Office 2013 program, follow these steps:

1. **Load the Office 2013 program you want to customize (such as Word or PowerPoint).**

2. **Click the File tab.**

3. **Click Options.**

    An Options dialog box appears.

4. **Click Save in the left pane.**

    The Options dialog box displays various Save options, as shown in Figure 19-1.

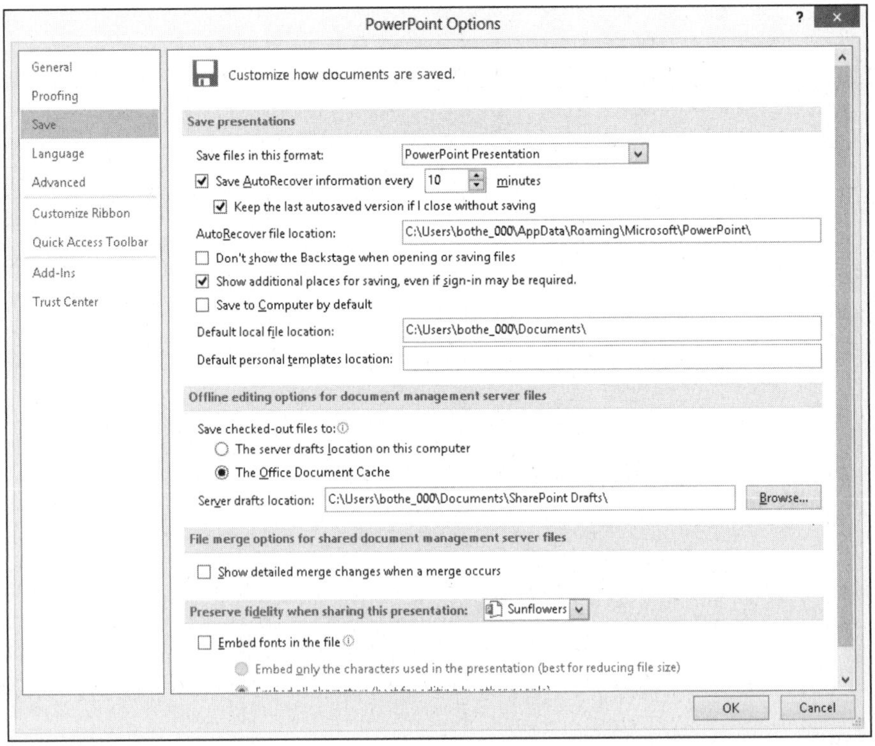

Figure 19-1: The Options dialog box lets you define default settings to save a file.

5. **(Optional) Click in the Save Files in This Format list box and choose a file format, such as the 97–2003 format to save files that are compatible with previous versions of Office.**

6. **(Optional) Click in the Default File Location text box and type the drive and folder that you want to define as your default folder.**

7. **(Optional) Select the Save AutoRecover Information Every check box, click in the Minutes text box, and type a value or click the up/down arrows to define a value, such as 7 minutes.**

8. **Click OK.**

Password-Protecting Your Files

To prevent prying eyes from peeking at your Word, Excel, or PowerPoint files, you can password-protect them. That way, if someone wants to open, view, or edit your files, she must use your password. If someone doesn't know your password, she won't be able to view — let alone edit — your files.

You (or anyone) can buy programs off the Internet that can crack an Office 2013 password-protected file. For real security, don't rely on Office 2013's password-protection feature.

To password-protect a file, follow these steps:

1. **Load Word, Excel, or PowerPoint.**

2. **Click the File tab.**

3. **Choose Save As.**

   The Save As window appears.

4. **Click the Browse button.**

   The Save As dialog box appears.

5. **Click the Tools button.**

   A pull-down menu appears, as shown in Figure 19-2.

6. **Choose General Options.**

   The General Options dialog box appears.

7. **(Optional) Click in the Password to Open text box and type a password.**

   Another dialog box appears and asks you to confirm the password by typing it again.

8. **Type the password again and then click OK.**

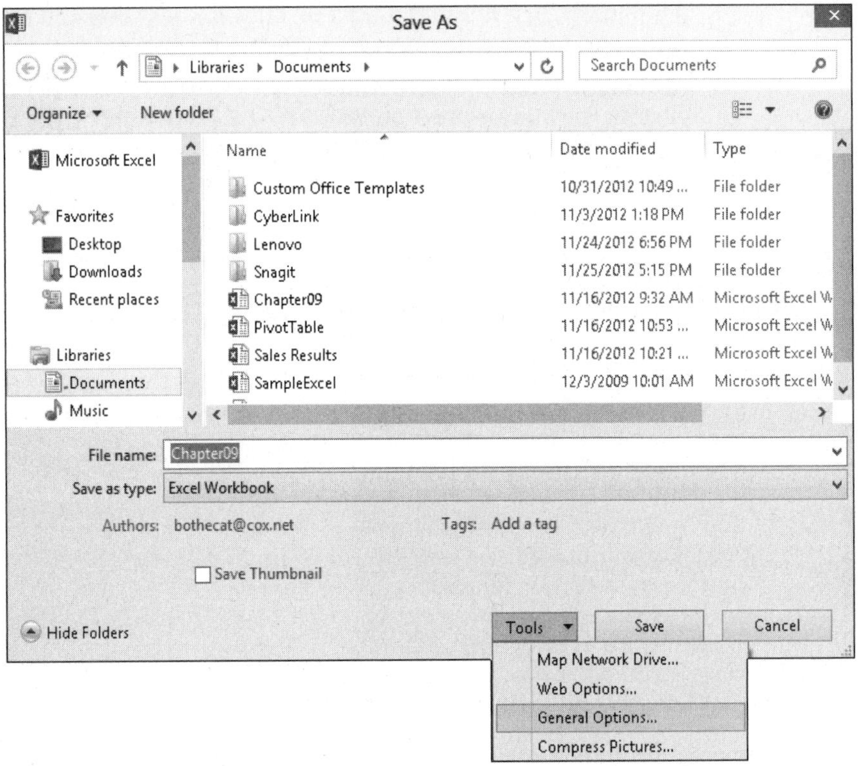

Figure 19-2:
The Tools
button
appears in
the bottom-
right corner
of the Save
As dialog
box.

9. **(Optional) Click in the Password to Modify text box and type a password.**

   This password can be different from the password you typed in Step 6. Another dialog box appears and asks you to confirm the password by typing it again.

10. **Type the password again and then click OK.**

11. **Click Save.**

You can create a password or remove passwords altogether by repeating the preceding steps and retyping a new password or deleting the password completely.

Guarding against Macro Viruses

Macro viruses are malicious programs designed to attach themselves to Word, Excel, and PowerPoint files. When an unsuspecting victim opens an infected file, the virus can spread and do something nasty, such as deleting your files or the entire contents of your hard drive.

To stop these pests from wrecking your files, get an antivirus program, avoid downloading or accepting any files from unknown people, and turn on Office 2013's built-in macro-protection feature, which can disable macros or restrict what macro viruses and worms can do even if they infect your computer.

To turn on macro protection, follow these steps:

1. **Load Word or PowerPoint.**
2. **Click the File tab.**
3. **Click Options.**

   The Options dialog box appears.

4. **Click Trust Center.**

   The Trust Center options appear in the right pane.

5. **Click the Trust Center Settings button.**

   The Trust Center dialog box appears with the Macro Settings options displayed, as shown in Figure 19-3.

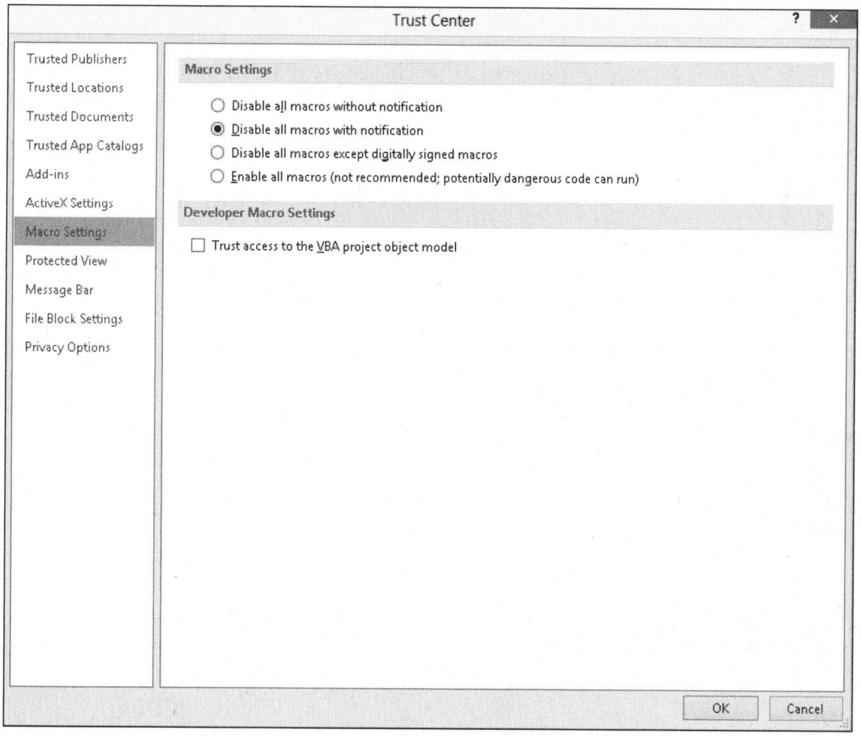

Trust Center

Trusted Publishers
Trusted Locations
Trusted Documents
Trusted App Catalogs
Add-ins
ActiveX Settings
Macro Settings
Protected View
Message Bar
File Block Settings
Privacy Options

Macro Settings

○ Disable all macros without notification
● Disable all macros with notification
○ Disable all macros except digitally signed macros
○ Enable all macros (not recommended; potentially dangerous code can run)

Developer Macro Settings

☐ Trust access to the VBA project object model

OK   Cancel

Figure 19-3:
The Trust
Center
dialog box.

6. **Select one of the following radio buttons:**

   • *Disable All Macros without Notification:* The safest but most restrictive setting, this prevents any macros (valid or viruses) from running when you open the file.

   • *Disable All Macros with Notification:* This is the default setting; it displays a dialog box that lets you turn on macros if you trust that the file isn't infected.

   • *Disable All Macros except Digitally Signed Macros:* Blocks all macros except for the ones "authenticated" (previously defined as "trusted") by the user.

   • *Enable All Macros:* This setting runs all macros, which is the most dangerous setting.

7. **Click OK until you return to the Save As dialog box.**

8. **Click Save.**

Customize the Ribbon

Some people love the Ribbon interface of Office 2013, while others only tolerate it. No matter what your feelings toward the Ribbon interface may be, you can customize which icons appear on it so it only displays those features you need (and use) most often.

To customize the Ribbon interface, follow these steps:

1. **Load an Office 2013 program, such as Word or Excel.**

2. **Click the File tab.**

3. **Click Options.**

   The Options dialog box appears.

4. **Click Customize Ribbon in the left pane.**

   The Options dialog box displays two columns. The left column displays all additional commands you can place on the Ribbon, while the right column lists all currently displayed tabs and commands, as shown in Figure 19-4.

5. **(Optional) Clear a check box in the right column to hide an entire tab from view.**

   Hiding tabs can be handy when you never use a particular group of commands and you want to simplify the Ribbon interface.

Figure 19-4:
You can custom-ize which tabs and commands appear on the Ribbon.

6. **(Optional) Click the New Tab button to create a new tab. Then you can click a command in the left column and click the Add button to place commands on a new tab of your own design.**

7. **(Optional) Click the Reset button.**

   The Reset button lets you restore the default settings of a single tab or the entire Ribbon. Use this feature to make your copy of Office 2013 look like everyone else's.

8. **Click OK.**

Customizing the Ribbon can make your copy of Office 2013 work exactly the way you want. However, if other people need to use your copy of Office 2013 (or if you need to use someone else's copy of Office 2013), you may find that using different Ribbon interfaces can get confusing.

Save to SkyDrive

If you need to access, edit, or create files on a computer, smartphone, or tablet, you may find it easier to save your important files to SkyDrive, which is Microsoft's cloud storage service. By signing up for a SkyDrive account, you can get 7GB of free storage and pay if you need more.

The basic idea behind SkyDrive (and cloud storage in general) is that you store a single file on your SkyDrive. Now — no matter where you are in the world or which device you have with you — you can access that file as long as you have an Internet connection. By editing a file stored in a single location, you can avoid the hassles of copying a file to store on multiple devices and then worrying about which file has your latest changes.

You can download the SkyDrive app from www.windows.microsoft.com/en-US/skydrive/download.

To open a file stored on SkyDrive, follow these steps:

1. **Load an Office 2013 program, such as Word or Excel.**

2. **Click the File tab.**

3. **Click Open.**

   The Open window appears.

4. **Click Add a Place.**

5. **Click SkyDrive.**

   At this point, you'll have to type in your SkyDrive username and password to access your file.

To save a file to SkyDrive, follow these steps:

1. **Load an Office 2013 program, such as Word or Excel.**

2. **Click the File tab.**

3. **Click Save As.**

   The Save As window appears.

4. **Click Add a Place.**

5. **Click SkyDrive.**

   At this point, you'll have to type in your SkyDrive username and password to save your file to your SkyDrive account.

When in Doubt, Right-Click the Mouse

As a shortcut to giving commands to Office 2013, remember this simple guideline: First select, and then right-click.

So if you want to change text or a picture, first select it to tell Office 2013 what you want to modify. Then right-click the mouse to display a pop-up menu of the commands. These pop-up menus display a list of only relevant commands for the item you just selected.

Freezing Row and Column Headings in Excel

One problem with creating large spreadsheets in Excel is that your identifying row and column headings may scroll out of sight if you scroll down or to the right of your worksheet.

To prevent this from happening, you can "freeze" a row or column that contains identifying labels. That way, when you scroll through your worksheet, your frozen row or column always remains visible.

To freeze a row or column in an Excel worksheet, follow these steps:

1. **Click the View tab.**
2. **Click the Freeze Panes icon in the Window group.**
3. **Click one of the following:**
    - *Freeze Panes:* Divides a worksheet into multiple panes
    - *Freeze Top Row:* Always displays the top row, no matter how far down you scroll
    - *Freeze First Column:* Always displays the first column, no matter how far to the right you scroll

To unfreeze a row or column, repeat Steps 1 through 3 but click Unfreeze Panes in Step 2.

Displaying Slides Out of Order in PowerPoint

When you display a PowerPoint presentation, your slides typically appear in the order that you arranged them, starting with the first slide. If you want to display your slides in a different order in the middle of a presentation, follow these steps:

1. **Load your presentation in PowerPoint and press F5.**

   The first slide of your presentation appears.

2. **Type the number of the slide you want to view and press Enter.**

   If you want to jump to the fifth slide in your presentation, type **5** and press Enter. If you jump to the fifth slide, clicking the mouse or pressing the spacebar next displays the sixth slide, and then the seventh, and so on.

Print a list of your slide titles and slide numbers on a sheet of paper so that you know which slide number to type to view a particular slide.

Reduce Spam in Outlook

If you have an e-mail account, you will get *spam,* that unwanted e-mail that clogs millions of Inboxes every day with obnoxious offers for mortgage refinancing, low-cost prescription drugs, or celebrity pornography. Unless you actually enjoy deleting these messages manually, you can use Outlook to filter your e-mail for you.

Setting up Outlook's junk e-mail filter

Outlook can move suspected spam to a special junk e-mail folder automatically. Because Outlook looks for keywords in spam, be aware that it will never be 100-percent effective in identifying spam, but it can identify the more blatant spam and save you the time and effort of deleting the messages yourself.

To define Outlook's spam filter, follow these steps:

1. **Click the Home tab.**

2. **Click the Junk icon.**

   A menu appears, as shown in Figure 19-5.

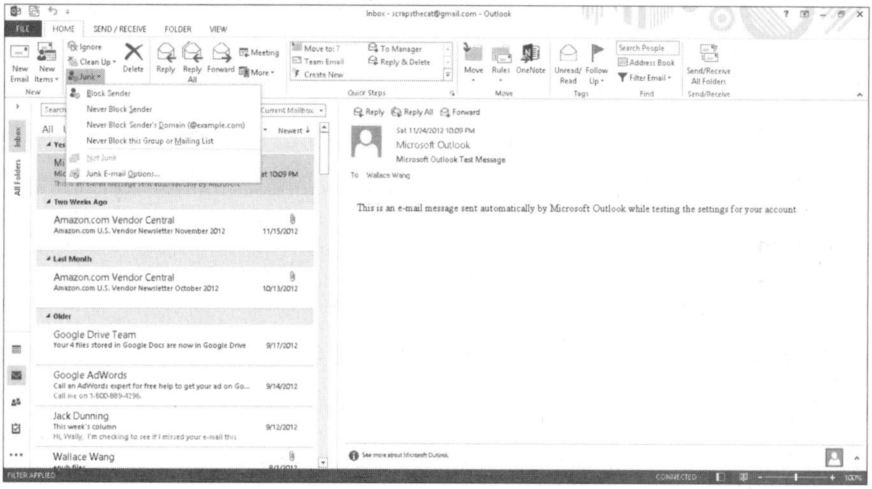

Figure 19-5:
The Junk
menu.

3. **Click Junk E-mail Options.**

   The Junk E-mail Options dialog box appears, as shown in Figure 19-6.

4. **Select one of the following radio buttons:**

   • *No Automatic Filtering:* Turns off the Outlook spam filter.

   • *Low:* Identifies and moves most obvious spam to the Junk E-mail folder.

   • *High:* Identifies and moves nearly all spam into the Junk E-mail folder along with some regular e-mail messages, too, so check the Junk E-mail folder periodically to look for valid messages.

   • *Safe Lists Only:* Identifies and moves e-mail messages into the Junk E-mail folder, except for those messages sent from addresses listed in your Safe Senders List or Safe Recipients List.

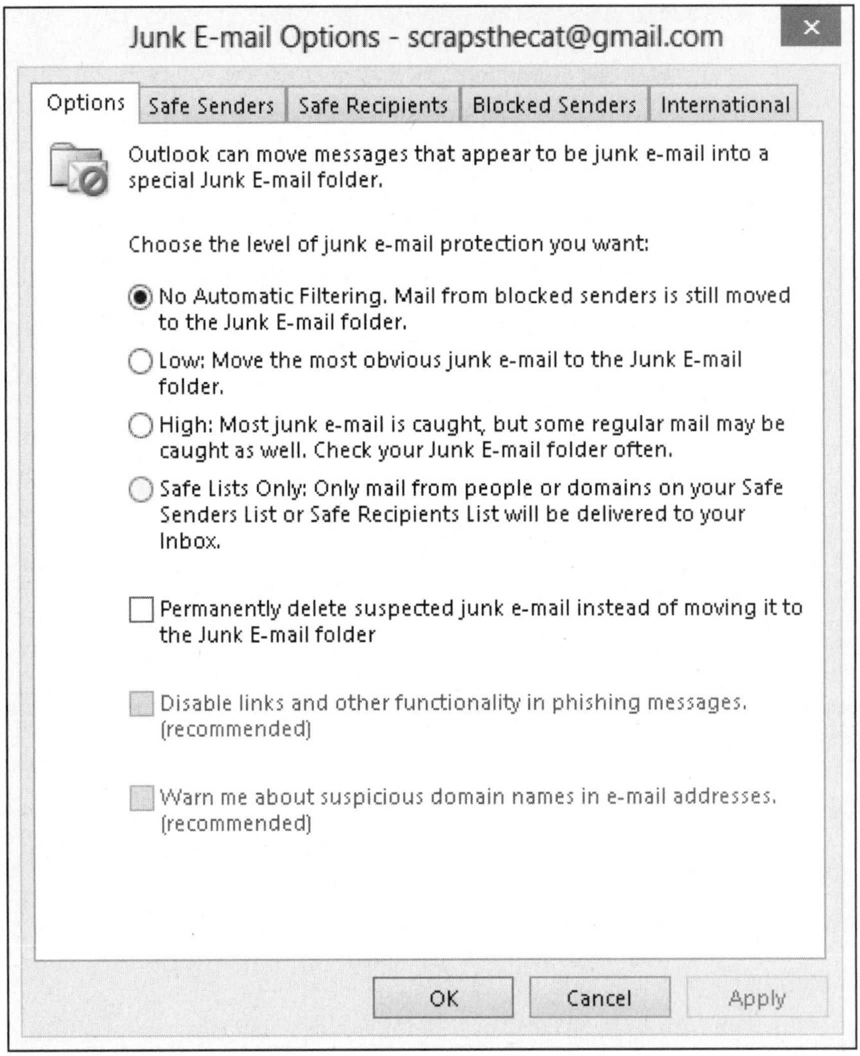

Junk E-mail Options - scrapsthecat@gmail.com ☒

| Options | Safe Senders | Safe Recipients | Blocked Senders | International |

Outlook can move messages that appear to be junk e-mail into a special Junk E-mail folder.

Choose the level of junk e-mail protection you want:

◉ No Automatic Filtering. Mail from blocked senders is still moved to the Junk E-mail folder.

◯ Low: Move the most obvious junk e-mail to the Junk E-mail folder.

◯ High: Most junk e-mail is caught, but some regular mail may be caught as well. Check your Junk E-mail folder often.

◯ Safe Lists Only: Only mail from people or domains on your Safe Senders List or Safe Recipients List will be delivered to your Inbox.

☐ Permanently delete suspected junk e-mail instead of moving it to the Junk E-mail folder

☐ Disable links and other functionality in phishing messages. (recommended)

☐ Warn me about suspicious domain names in e-mail addresses. (recommended)

[OK] [Cancel] [Apply]

Figure 19-6:
The Junk
E-mail
Options
dialog box
lets you
define how
aggressively
you want
Outlook's
spam filter
to work.

5. **Click OK.**

The Options dialog box appears again.

6. **Click OK.**

Creating a Safe Senders list

A Safe Senders list lets you define all the e-mail addresses you want to accept messages from, and Outlook routes all e-mail from other e-mail addresses directly to your Junk E-mail folder.

The advantage of a Safe Senders list is that it guarantees you will never receive spam. On the downside, though, it also guarantees that if someone tries to contact you whose e-mail address doesn't appear on your Safe Senders list, you will never get that valid message, either.

To create a Safe Senders list, follow Steps 1 through 4 in the preceding section, "Setting up Outlook's junk e-mail filter," to display the Junk E-mail Options dialog box. Then follow these steps:

1. **In the Junk E-mail Options dialog box (refer to Figure 19-6), click the Safe Senders tab.**

   The Safe Senders tab of the Junk E-mail Options dialog box appears.

2. **(Optional) Select (or clear) the Also Trust E-mail from My Contacts check box.**

   Selecting this check box tells Outlook that if you store someone's e-mail address in your Contacts list, you will also accept e-mail from that person, too.

3. **(Optional) Select (or clear) the Automatically Add People I E-mail to the Safe Senders List check box.**

   This tells Outlook that if you send e-mail to someone, you'll accept his or her messages in return.

4. **(Optional) Click the Add button.**

   The Add Address or Domain dialog box appears.

5. **Type a complete e-mail address. (Or type a domain name — for example, if you trust everyone from Microsoft.com to send you valid e-mail, type @microsoft.com in this dialog box.)**

6. **Click OK.**

7. **Repeat Steps 4 through 6 for each additional e-mail address or domain you want to add.**

8. **Click OK until all the dialog boxes disappear.**

If you click the Safe Recipients tab, you can repeat these steps to define another list of e-mail addresses that you'll accept as valid.

Creating a Blocked Senders list

If a particular e-mail address persists in sending you spam, you can choose to selectively block that single e-mail address or domain. To create a Blocked Senders list, follow Steps 1 through 4 in the earlier section, "Setting up Outlook's junk e-mail filter," to display the Junk E-mail Options dialog box. Then follow these steps.

1. **In the Junk E-mail Options dialog box (refer to Figure 19-6), click the Blocked Senders tab.**

   The Blocked Senders tab of the Junk E-mail Options dialog box appears.

2. **Click the Add button.**

   The Add Address or Domain dialog box appears.

3. **Type an e-mail address or domain name and then click OK.**

   The Options dialog box appears again.

4. **Click OK until all the dialog boxes disappear.**

Using Office Web and Windows RT

Office 2013 gobbles up a huge chunk of hard-drive space and bombards you with waves of features that you'll probably never need (or use) in a million years. In case you want to use Microsoft Office but find it too complicated, try the free Office Web (http://office.microsoft.com/en-us/web-apps/) version instead.

Office Web provides simplified versions of Word, Excel, and PowerPoint that you use over the Internet. As long as you have an Internet connection, a browser, and a free Windows Live ID, you can use Office Web to create, edit, and share files with others.

Perhaps the greatest advantage of Office Web is that multiple people can collaborate on a single document from anywhere in the world. Instead of swapping files back and forth (and risk losing track which file may be the latest one), Office Web lets you store a single copy of your document online for everyone to access.

Of course, the biggest drawback of Office Web is that you need an Internet connection to use it. However, as Internet access becomes cheaper and more accessible, this disadvantage shouldn't be a problem for most people.

Even better, anyone with a browser can use Office Web, including Windows, Mac OS X, and Linux users. Office Web is basically Microsoft's answer to Google Docs, so if the idea of using a word processor, spreadsheet, or presentation program over the Internet appeals to you, then give Office Web a try.

In case you don't like the idea of accessing Office 2013 through the Internet, grab a tablet running Windows RT, which comes with a bundled version of

Office 2013. By using Office 2013 on your Windows RT tablet, you can take your programs and files with you and save them in either of these ways:

✔ Save your files to a USB flash drive so you can transfer them to your computer at a later time.

✔ Save your files to SkyDrive.

By using the version of Office 2013 that comes bundled with Windows RT, you can still be productive with your favorite Microsoft Office programs without lugging around a heavy and bulky laptop computer running the full version of Windows 8.

Chapter 20

Almost Ten Ways to Make Office 2013 Easier to Use

· ·

*I*f you haven't noticed by now, there are plenty of features buried in Office 2013 that you probably don't need most of the time. However, if you're a die-hard Office 2013 power user, you may want to peek at some of the more advanced features buried inside the operating system.

Although these advanced features may take time to learn and master, you may find the effort worth it to make Office 2013 behave exactly the way you want it to. Best of all, you can learn these new features by playing with them at work — so that way, you can learn something new and get paid for doing it at the same time.

Build Your Own Apps for Office

If you're like most people, you probably just want to use a program, make it do what you need it to do, and then go home afterwards. However, if you find yourself wishing Office 2013 could do something more, then you may want to take some time to develop your own apps for Office 2013.

To create apps for Office 2013, you just need to use industry-standard programming languages like HTML5, JavaScript, CSS3 (Cascading Style Sheets), and XML. By creating your own Office 2013 apps, you can extend Office 2013's capabilities. If you create a particularly useful app, you can even sell or give it away to others. To learn more about creating your own Office 2013 apps, visit the Microsoft site (`http://msdn.microsoft.com/en-us/office/apps`) that provides a brief tutorial on how to create your first Office 2013 app.

Collaborating with the Review Tab

If you're the only person who needs to edit, view, and use your Office 2013 documents, you can safely skip over this section. However, if you're like many people, you need to collaborate with others.

The old-fashioned way of collaborating meant printing paper copies, sending them to others, and writing directly on them, but with Office, you can highlight, mark up, and edit documents electronically so that you can distribute files by e-mail or through a network. Each time someone makes a change to a document, Office 2013 tracks these changes with a different color and even identifies the contributor by name. Now you can see who wrote what, and you can selectively keep those comments that are most valuable and ignore the ones you don't like.

Some of the more useful commands hidden on the Review tab include

- **New Comment:** Lets you insert a comment directly into a document without affecting the existing text.
- **Track Changes:** Highlights any new text or data that someone adds to or deletes from an existing document.
- **Compare:** Examines two files and highlights the differences between the two. This tool also gives you the option of selectively merging the changes into a single document.

By using the features stored on the Review tab, you can send multiple copies of a file to others, let everyone make comments, mark up the text, move data around, and then merge everyone's comments and changes into a single, final version.

Using Word's References Tab

Most people use Word just to write letters or short reports. If you need to create longer documents, then you may be interested in using the features buried on Word's References tab, such as

- **Table of Contents:** Creates a table of contents based on the header styles used in a document.
- **Insert Footnote:** Creates a footnote at the bottom of the page.
- **Insert Endnote:** Creates a list of notes at the end of a document.

✔ **Insert Caption:** Automatically numbers figures, tables, or equations.

✔ **Insert Table of Figures:** Creates a list of figures, tables, or equations that you created using the Insert Caption command.

✔ **Mark Entry:** Tags words or phrases to appear in an index.

✔ **Insert Index:** Creates an index based on words or phrases tagged with the Mark Entry command.

Using Excel's Data Tab

Most people type data directly into an Excel worksheet and then manipulate that data through formulas or other commands. However, you can also design a worksheet and then import data from another location (such as stock quotes that you retrieve from a website), from a text file, from an Access database, or even from a database file created by another program (such as an ancient dBASE database).

Some of the features available on Excel's Data tab include:

✔ **From Access:** Retrieves data from an Access database.

✔ **From Web:** Retrieves data stored in a table on a web page.

✔ **From Text:** Retrieves data stored as an ASCII text file.

✔ **From Other Sources:** Retrieves data stored in other sources, such as an SQL Server or XML file.

Saving and Sending Files

The traditional way to send a file to someone is to save your file, load your e-mail program (such as Outlook), create a new message, attach your file (if you can remember where you stored it), and send it over the Internet.

Here's a faster way to send a file:

1. **In the file that you want to send, click the File tab.**

2. **Click Share.**

   The Share window appears.

3. **Click E-mail and click one of the following:**

- *Send as Attachment:* Attaches the Office 2013 file. Recipients will be able to view and edit this file only if they also have Office 2013.

- *Send a Link:* Sends a link to a file when you're collaborating over a local area network.

- *Send as PDF:* Converts the file to PDF (Portable Document Format) before attaching it to the message. Recipients who don't have special PDF-editing software will be able to view the file only, but not edit it.

- *Send as XPS:* Converts the file to XPS (Open XML Paper Specification) format before attaching it to the message. Recipients will need a program that can open and display an XPS file, which preserves formatting and works similar to a PDF file.

Encrypting a File

After creating a file, you may want to show it to others, but not let anyone else modify it. You could trust that nobody will mess up your file, but a better option is to password-protect it so nobody can modify it without your permission.

To password-protect a file, follow these steps:

1. **Click the File tab.**

2. **Click Info and then click the Protect button (such as Protect Document or Protect Presentation).**

   A menu appears.

3. **Click Encrypt with Password.**

   An Encrypt Document dialog box appears.

4. **Type a password and click OK.**

If you forget your password, you won't be able to access your own file, so make sure you remember your password. Many third-party companies sell password-cracking tools for retrieving the password to Office 2013 files. These tools can be useful if you forget your own password, but they can also be used by malicious people to peek at documents that you may not want them to see, so don't think that passwords alone can protect your Office 2013 documents from prying eyes.

Checking File Compatibility

Not everyone may be using Office 2013, so if you need to share files with people stuck with older versions of Microsoft Office, you need to make sure your files can be opened by others. Otherwise you risk creating a great document that goes unnoticed because nobody else can see what you did.

To check your file's compatibility with previous versions of Office, follow these steps:

1. **Click the File tab.**
2. **Click Info and then click the Check for Issues button.**

   A menu appears.
3. **Click Check Compatibility.**

   A Compatibility Checker dialog box appears, listing any parts of your file that may not be compatible with older versions of Office.

Ignoring the Silly Office Ribbon

Although the Office Ribbon represents a more visual way to use Microsoft Office, some people still prefer the classic pull-down menu interface of previous versions of Microsoft Office. For those who don't want to give up their familiarity with pull-down menus, you can buy an add-on program dubbed Classic Menu for Office (which is available at `www.addintools.com`).

This program essentially gives back your pull-down menus so you can choose between the Office Ribbon and the traditional pull-down menus. Now you can have the best of both worlds without giving up either one.

The main drawback with this add-on program is that if you have to use someone else's copy of Office 2013 that doesn't have this add-on installed, you may feel lost trying to use the Ribbon alone. For this reason, it's a good idea to become familiar with the Office Ribbon and use this Classic Menu for Office add-on program to help you make the transition from an older version of Office to Office 2013.

Index

• *Q* •

• *S* •

• T •

x-axis, 193–194
XML programming language, 383

y-axis, 193–194

• Z •

zip file, 292

Apple & Mac

iPad 2 For Dummies,
3rd Edition
978-1-118-17679-5

iPhone 4S For Dummies,
5th Edition
978-1-118-03671-6

iPod touch For Dummies,
3rd Edition
978-1-118-12960-9

Mac OS X Lion
For Dummies
978-1-118-02205-4

Blogging & Social Media

CityVille For Dummies
978-1-118-08337-6

Facebook For Dummies,
4th Edition
978-1-118-09562-1

Mom Blogging
For Dummies
978-1-118-03843-7

Twitter For Dummies,
2nd Edition
978-0-470-76879-2

WordPress For Dummies,
4th Edition
978-1-118-07342-1

Business

Cash Flow For Dummies
978-1-118-01850-7

Investing For Dummies,
6th Edition
978-0-470-90545-6

Job Searching with Social
Media For Dummies
978-0-470-93072-4

QuickBooks 2012
For Dummies
978-1-118-09120-3

Resumes For Dummies,
6th Edition
978-0-470-87361-8

Starting an Etsy Business
For Dummies
978-0-470-93067-0

Cooking & Entertaining

Cooking Basics
For Dummies, 4th Edition
978-0-470-91388-8

Wine For Dummies,
4th Edition
978-0-470-04579-4

Diet & Nutrition

Kettlebells For Dummies
978-0-470-59929-7

Nutrition For Dummies,
5th Edition
978-0-470-93231-5

Restaurant Calorie Counter
For Dummies,
2nd Edition
978-0-470-64405-8

Digital Photography

Digital SLR Cameras &
Photography For Dummies,
4th Edition
978-1-118-14489-3

Digital SLR Settings
& Shortcuts
For Dummies
978-0-470-91763-3

Photoshop Elements 10
For Dummies
978-1-118-10742-3

Gardening

Gardening Basics
For Dummies
978-0-470-03749-2

Vegetable Gardening
For Dummies,
2nd Edition
978-0-470-49870-5

Green/Sustainable

Raising Chickens
For Dummies
978-0-470-46544-8

Green Cleaning
For Dummies
978-0-470-39106-8

Health

Diabetes For Dummies,
3rd Edition
978-0-470-27086-8

Food Allergies
For Dummies
978-0-470-09584-3

Living Gluten-Free
For Dummies,
2nd Edition
978-0-470-58589-4

Hobbies

Beekeeping
For Dummies,
2nd Edition
978-0-470-43065-1

Chess For Dummies,
3rd Edition
978-1-118-01695-4

Drawing For Dummies,
2nd Edition
978-0-470-61842-4

eBay For Dummies,
7th Edition
978-1-118-09806-6

Knitting For Dummies,
2nd Edition
978-0-470-28747-7

Language &
Foreign Language

English Grammar
For Dummies,
2nd Edition
978-0-470-54664-2

French For Dummies,
2nd Edition
978-1-118-00464-7

German For Dummies,
2nd Edition
978-0-470-90101-4

Spanish Essentials
For Dummies
978-0-470-63751-7

Spanish For Dummies,
2nd Edition
978-0-470-87855-2

Available wherever books are sold. For more information or to order direct: U.S. customers visit www.dummies.com or call 1-877-762-2974.
U.K. customers visit www.wileyeurope.com or call (0) 1243 843291. Canadian customers visit www.wiley.ca or call 1-800-567-4797.

Connect with us online at www.facebook.com/fordummies or @fordummies

Math & Science

Algebra I For Dummies,
2nd Edition
978-0-470-55964-2

Biology For Dummies,
2nd Edition
978-0-470-59875-7

Chemistry For Dummies,
2nd Edition
978-1-1180-0730-3

Geometry For Dummies,
2nd Edition
978-0-470-08946-0

Pre-Algebra Essentials
For Dummies
978-0-470-61838-7

Microsoft Office

Excel 2010 For Dummies
978-0-470-48953-6

Office 2010 All-in-One
For Dummies
978-0-470-49748-7

Office 2011 for Mac
For Dummies
978-0-470-87869-9

Word 2010
For Dummies
978-0-470-48772-3

Music

Guitar For Dummies,
2nd Edition
978-0-7645-9904-0

Clarinet For Dummies
978-0-470-58477-4

iPod & iTunes
For Dummies,
9th Edition
978-1-118-13060-5

Pets

Cats For Dummies,
2nd Edition
978-0-7645-5275-5

Dogs All-in One
For Dummies
978-0470-52978-2

Saltwater Aquariums
For Dummies
978-0-470-06805-2

Religion & Inspiration

The Bible For Dummies
978-0-7645-5296-0

Catholicism For Dummies,
2nd Edition
978-1-118-07778-8

Spirituality For Dummies,
2nd Edition
978-0-470-19142-2

Self-Help & Relationships

Happiness For Dummies
978-0-470-28171-0

Overcoming Anxiety
For Dummies,
2nd Edition
978-0-470-57441-6

Seniors

Crosswords For Seniors
For Dummies
978-0-470-49157-7

iPad 2 For Seniors
For Dummies, 3rd Edition
978-1-118-17678-8

Laptops & Tablets
For Seniors For Dummies,
2nd Edition
978-1-118-09596-6

Smartphones & Tablets

BlackBerry For Dummies,
5th Edition
978-1-118-10035-6

Droid X2 For Dummies
978-1-118-14864-8

HTC ThunderBolt
For Dummies
978-1-118-07601-9

MOTOROLA XOOM
For Dummies
978-1-118-08835-7

Sports

Basketball For Dummies,
3rd Edition
978-1-118-07374-2

Football For Dummies,
2nd Edition
978-1-118-01261-1

Golf For Dummies,
4th Edition
978-0-470-88279-5

Test Prep

ACT For Dummies,
5th Edition
978-1-118-01259-8

ASVAB For Dummies,
3rd Edition
978-0-470-63760-9

The GRE Test For
Dummies, 7th Edition
978-0-470-00919-2

Police Officer Exam
For Dummies
978-0-470-88724-0

Series 7 Exam
For Dummies
978-0-470-09932-2

Web Development

HTML, CSS, & XHTML
For Dummies, 7th Edition
978-0-470-91659-9

Drupal For Dummies,
2nd Edition
978-1-118-08348-2

Windows 7

Windows 7
For Dummies
978-0-470-49743-2

Windows 7
For Dummies,
Book + DVD Bundle
978-0-470-52398-8

Windows 7 All-in-One
For Dummies
978-0-470-48763-1

Available wherever books are sold. For more information or to order direct: U.S. customers visit www.dummies.com or call 1-877-762-2974
U.K. customers visit www.wileyeurope.com or call (0) 1243 843291. Canadian customers visit www.wiley.ca or call 1-800-567-4797.

Connect with us online at www.facebook.com/fordummies or @fordummies

DUMMIES.COM®

Wherever you are in life, Dummies makes it easier.

From fashion to Facebook®, wine to Windows®, and everything in between, Dummies makes it easier.